# THE FOOD FOR THOUGHT COOKBOOK

London's most famous vegetarian restaurant
shares at last its recipes for success.

'A joy to possess.'

*Health Now*

'Its witty presentation and highly
imaginative use of ingredients will soon
have you reaching for the chopping board
and cookpot.'

*Home and Freezer Digest*

'An interestingly different book . . . might
well tempt a cannibal to become
vegetarian.'

*Health Guardian*

# THE FOOD FOR THOUGHT COOKBOOK

by

Guy Garrett and Kit Norman

THORSONS PUBLISHING GROUP

First published 1987

Full page illustrations by Rachel Mendes
Other illustrations by Rachel and
Christopher Mendes

British Library Cataloguing in Publication Data

Garrett, Guy
The Food For Thought cookbook
1. Vegetarian cookery
I. Title      II. Norman, Kit
641.5'636          TX837

ISBN 0-7225-1435-2

Published by Thorsons Publishers
Limited,
Wellingborough, Northamptonshire, NN8 2RQ
England

Printed in Great Britain by
BL&U Printing Ltd

7 9 10 8 6

# Contents

# Introduction

'When is your cookery book coming out?' is a question frequently asked at Food For Thought by our customers. The reply, until recently, has been somewhat evasive and accompanied by a rather sheepish look. In truth, several attempts have been made to compile such a book, but these have been thwarted at various stages in their development by the genuine difficulties in gathering the material in the time available. Running a business and writing about it are sometimes mutually exclusive!

So how do you collect three-hundred-odd recipes from seven or eight different people using their own quantities, weights, measures and techniques, and assemble this diverse and sometimes complex information into an easily comprehended form?

The answer, I decided, was to let each cook write their own recipes, complete with insights and comments where they thought appropriate. Some chapters contain almost exclusively the work of one chef, whereas others contain the work of several. In each case I have allowed their original style to filter through in order, I hope, to communicate the variety that characterizes Food For Thought cooking. It can be seen clearly that each cook has his or her own particular way of approaching their profession.

My task has been to link the various chapters together, to make sure that weights and measures match up and to provide a necessary degree of continuity. The recipes themselves range from simple and easy to prepare dishes through to the more advanced and time consuming dishes contained for example, in chapter nine. The

recipes reflect the simplicity of approach which is very much dictated by Food For Thought itself; the nature of our business requires cuisine which is unpretentious and varied, utilizing the best quality ingredients available. You will look in vain in this book for specialist aspects of vegetarian cooking or vegetarianism and its associated politics, cures, religions and diets. You will find instead, I hope, no-nonsense advice and insights into cooking in general, with extra information which has been gleaned as a result of running Food For Thought.

The main aim of this book is to 'normalize' vegetarian cooking and to get away from the 'alternative' label with which it has so often been stigmatized. The principles involved are no different from those which should be applied to all cookery: if food does not taste interesting, then it is simply not good cookery.

The recipes contained in this book are not, of course, guarantees of a perfect end result each time. No cookery book could hope to do that, for such recipes depend on considerable input from the user. However, there are sections which are intended to guide you when things do go wrong, as they are bound to from time to time.

It remains for me to thank all those who have contributed to this book; Steve Wilcox, David Biddulph, Angela Gamble, Katie Garrett, Douglas Huggins, Josephine Miller and Clarice Ashdown, who have taken the time and trouble to write their recipes down. Siriporn Duncan, whose recipes also appear here, virtually invented the format of Food For Thought cooking and over the best part of a decade, has tirelessly trained, advised and inspired so many cooks at the restaurant. Things might have been very different had she not arrived early on the scene.

I would also like to thank Kit Norman, my co-author and one time cook at Food For Thought, for his recipes and for casting his expert eye over all the technical aspects of this book.

Finally, I would like to thank my mother for the previous work she did in collecting recipes, and Romy Johnson, who took pity on my pathetic efforts with a typewriter and rewrote the book in the process!

# About Food For Thought

Food For Thought is not, as many have assumed, a co-operative. Neither is it one of a national franchise chain so beloved of the modern catering industry. We do not claim to be the original users of the name, though in 1971 there weren't many others.

Food For Thought is entirely family run and owned—the autonomy bestowed on the business, we think, benefits it.

It was in the early seventies that a remarkable Australian named Margot Boyce-White had the foresight to convert an old banana ripening warehouse into a small basement restaurant. Situated bang in the middle of what used to be London's thriving vegetable market, Covent Garden, the area by then was in ignominious decline. Covent Garden was suffering an air of neglect due to the recent departure of the fruit and vegetable market to larger premises across the river. Margot must have possessed extraordinary powers of imagination for it was difficult to see the area as much more than yet another once-glamorous inner city scene of urban dereliction.

Once open, Margot's Food For Thought developed an excellent reputation and was instrumental, along with Nick Carr-Saunder's Neal's Yard complex around the corner, in establishing Covent Garden as an area of alternative interests. The area's handsome and largely unmodernized building facades were an attraction in their own right.

Margot was, however, perhaps a little ahead of her time, for by the mid-seventies she had grown tired of the many petty regulations and the problems that are the corollary of a depressed area; vandalism, drug abuse and general squalor. It was at this point that she met John and Jane Damant, my mother and stepfather, while on holiday in France. John and Jane were, at that time, living in France attempting to survive off the earnings of their paintings and the odd bit of building work. They were only too eager to take up the opportunity offered to them by Margot: she wanted to sell up.

Frantic phone calls were made, deals were struck, money was wrung from reluctant bank managers and finally in January 1977, on a cold Monday, after much heart searching and preparation, John and Jane found themselves in the tiny basement restaurant contemplating the imminent arrival of their first customers.

Their original idea had seemed simple enough; the aim was to provide cheap but substantial meals using the best quality fresh ingredients, with a simple menu format. In 1977, a full, balanced meal at Food For Thought was to cost no more than £1. In keeping with the restaurant's unpretentious image there would be little in the way of luxuries in the surrounding environment. White-washed walls, wooden tables and earthenware crockery were enlivened with their own colourful oil paintings, not to mention John's exuberant serving style!

Although John had owned and run an hotel in Guernsey, and Jane had coped with cooking for a large and discerning family, the demands of starting and running such a business were very different from anything either had previously experienced. However, as has so often been the case, Food For Thought itself seemed to dictate the way things were to develop, as though possessing a will of its own.

On that first morning their number was three, their ranks having been swollen by 50 per cent by the timely arrival of Siriporn, a girl from Thailand, who had previously worked as a waitress at Food For Thought in Margot's days. She was now to demonstrate her formidable skills as a cook, as she prepared soup, casserole and a delicious bean bake. Jane, as if in a dream, baked her first-ever bread, made quiches, crumbles and a few salads. John cleaned and laid tables downstairs and tore about London on his hapless bicycle, buying in last-minute goods and getting lost.

It was dark when they had started and it was dark when they finished their day's work; nobody's feet had touched the ground but they had survived without a major disaster and it seemed that the demand was there. Indeed, by the end of the week, the workforce had increased to five and the menu had settled into the format which has persisted to this day.

Our menu is still simple vegetarian fare, freshly cooked and reasonably priced. We always have a choice of soup, casserole or stew, baked dish, stir-fried vegetables, quiches and salads. The desserts usually comprise fruit crumbles, trifles or tarts and fresh fruit salad. We bake bread daily. The main difference, these days, is that we may have upwards of twenty staff frantically chopping, washing, frying, stirring, cleaning or serving at any one time—evidence indeed of the correctness of the original idea. In short we are very, very busy!

Things may be slightly less anarchic nowadays, but the principles remain the same. After building the restaurant into a major success, John and Jane decided to leave it in the hands of my sister, Vanessa, and her Polish husband, Jurek. For four years John and Jane had sweated away in what they regarded as the somewhat alien environment of London. Now they wanted once again to try and fulfil an old ambition—to paint. One year later I joined Vanessa and Jurek to complete the new team, fresh from miserable prospects in Devon, and it is this team which persists today. A day in the life of Food For Thought would go something like this:

At 3.00 a.m. Jurek rises when most of us don't know we exist and drives to New Covent Garden market in Vauxhall—the bicycle of yore has now thankfully given way to a van. At the market he will buy enough vegetables and fresh fruit for two days. The quantities are staggering; 10 sacks of potatoes, 32 boxes of mushrooms, 4 crates of cauliflowers, 16 boxes of leeks to mention but a few. At 6.00 a.m. the van arrives back at Food For Thought, splay-wheeled under the weight of produce and just in time to witness the arrival of the first bleary-eyed staff.

There then begins a frantic cacophony of chopping, buzzing of machinery and the strains of snatched, surreal conversation, the content of which must cause early passers-by great concern. Soon, enticing smells miraculously emerge from the steam filled kitchen and, as the rest of London arrives for work—a leisurely 10.30 a.m. or so it seems—the lunchtime menu is being prepared.

Meanwhile, Vanessa will have been doing the bookwork, counting money, organizing staff (who's sick today?) and wrestling with Britain's monumentally inefficient service system. Indeed, such are the problems and time wasted attempting to get basic equipment repaired on time that Jurek often has to double as a maintenance man.

My role is to be present at the restaurant servicing, recruiting, pacifying, advising, and generally talking to people (the latter being a favourite occupation of mine!). In the afternoons I compile the evening menu with the chef and it is through such discussions that much of the material for this book has been gleaned. Having opened at 12 noon, we would expect to serve flat-out until 3 or 3.30 p.m., both the take-away and restaurant queues stretching out into the street.

The nature of Food For Thought makes big demands on both the staff and its management. The working environment is cramped, uncomfortable and often nerve-racking. It can be similarly so for customers, so small are the premises, but humour plays a vital role in diffusing the situation. Tempers can (and sometimes do) fray, but generally it is a place of relaxed informality where creativity amongst the staff is encouraged and tolerance is the by-word.

Over the years the most important thing to have emerged is the need to communicate—between staff and management, between restaurant and customers—and I believe it is this fundamental point which is overlooked in so many aspects of modern catering, not to mention life! In a world where things are increasingly impersonal, people relish the opportunity to become involved. This shows in our customers, many of whom eat at Food For Thought every day of the week, whose comments, both favourable and adverse, provide a vital pointer to our consistency—or lack of it.

Similarly, amongst our staff, there is enormous involvement. They are given freedom to experiment with new recipes and encouraged to use their own ideas—in response they work hard and often with great originality. It is my hope that some of these sentiments are apparent in this book.

Our staff are as diverse as ever, the only things they have in common are youth and individuality. Many have no formal catering qualification and most use Food For Thought as a 'stepping stone' to other walks of life. At any one time there are at least six different nations represented and this is reflected in the variety of the cuisine and in the generally international atmosphere of the restaurant.

With all the stresses and strains inherent in catering, there can, on the other hand, be few businesses as rewarding. To complete the cycle of buying, preparing, cooking, serving and selling in one day and to receive compliments from satisfied customers is to be involved in one's work in a way few people can in the modern world.

# How to Use This Book

The recipes in this book have evolved under the influences and requirements peculiar to Food For Thought: quality, variety and value. Our prices are low and, because of this, many of our customers eat every day of the week at Food For Thought. We, therefore, have to ensure that the menu is varied but consistent and, of course, well-balanced if we are to continue to satisfy such people.

The very same qualities are required of home cooking and that is why I hope these recipes will be particularly useable. They are intended to complement and broaden the weekly menu of the reader and, hopefully, suggest a few novel ideas as well. For special occasions there is a chapter containing recipes developed from our Gourmet Evenings, an idea itself derived from the general desire to introduce a little more sophistication into our repertoire.

There are chapters on fresh fruit and vegetables—what is available and when, how to choose the best quality and what they are best suited to. There are chapters on herbs and their uses, dried produce, pasta and flavourings. This information is provided more as a reference than an exhaustive guide and is designed to give those relative newcomers to vegetarian cooking a little insight into the planning of their meals. There is a lot of nonsense talked about the relative pros and cons of one foodstuff or another; the main point to remember is that variety in flavour, texture and colour almost automatically guarantees a balanced diet.

The format of the recipes themselves is designed to be easy to follow with logical, numbered step-by-step instructions with a minimum of cross-references so that gener-ally all the information required for one recipe is contained on one page. Where there are exceptions, for example in sponge and sauce-making, we have devoted an entire section to these subjects, illuminating the variations and possible pitfalls.

There are also chapters on stock and savoury sauce making as we consider this to be the single most important aspect of vegetarian cookery. If you can get your sauce to taste of something interesting, the chances are that you will avoid the danger of the sweet, bland and soggy vegetarian cookery that is the hallmark of the sloppy sauce maker! In these sections we hope to provide the information necessary to lay at rest fears of sauce making and the apparent air of mystery that, for some, surrounds this topic.

The reader will find little or no information on freezing or pre-preparing vegetarian food. There are two reasons for this; the first is that we do not possess a deep-freeze or a microwave at Food For Thought because we expect to make and sell all our food on one day. Waste is kept to a minimum by cooking to order (as far as this is possible). Consequently, we are not in the best position to recommend freezing procedures.

The second and more compelling reason is that most vegetarian food does not like being frozen. The colours are lost, the textures often become mushy and the subtle flavours vegetables possess are often swamped. Having said that, it is understood that many people do not have the time to mess about with vegetable stocks and sauces. The answer then is that it is possible to pre-prepare stocks and sauces and to freeze them in bulk. This can be quite an effective method if you are organized enough.

The one point you cannot escape, however, is that food—all food—takes time to prepare if you want to do it properly. In order to eat well-balanced and nutritious food, the vegetarian in particular has to be organized and have a well-stocked kitchen. Soaking beans over night, buying what looks best at the green grocer and adapting the recipe accordingly, saving stale bread for toppings and roasts, reserving juices and cooking water for future dishes—all these should be second nature. In most cases by-products will keep a day or so in the fridge and used correctly will save time and add flavour to your cooking.

There is also very little on kitchen utensils in this book. Our feeling is that kitchens are a rather private affair and where one piece of equipment may be the panacea for all ills to one person, another might consider it to be worthless junk. There are a few notable exceptions, however:

● A large hard-wood chopping board of the solid (rather than glued) variety. They are expensive but essential.
● A selection of good quality knives. Avoid cheap plastic handled affairs; they are often awkward to use and reluctant to take an edge. Wooden handled knives are best; keep them very sharp with a steel or composite sharpening stone. Always store knives on a magnetic rack—not in the kitchen drawer where they are a danger to the unwary and tend to get blunted.
● Wooden spoons and spatulas for all your sauce making.
● A good heavy saucepan is useful for sauce making and sautéing vegetables. A pan which is too light (and therefore thin) will tend to burn food.
● A pressure cooker. This is perhaps the single greatest time saver in the kitchen and is particularly useful when cooking pulses. One point; always make sure that the vent is not obstructed before using— if the pressure cooker is used for pulses, the froth produced in their cooking can often block it.
● Electrical aids. Without doubt the most useful is a blender. For making soups, mayonnaise and toppings, both savoury and sweet, a blender will save you a lot of elbow grease. It is not essential, however, to the vast majority of these recipes.
● Your oven. If your baked dishes are unpredictable it is worth checking that it is correctly calibrated; with use and age thermostats in particular can become faulty. The relevant Board will be able to offer a service to check and rectify this.

It remains simply to wish you all the best in your cooking.

GUY GARRETT

**Note:** All the recipes are designed to be generous so, according to your appetite, you will have sufficient for 4 to 6 ample portions.

Chapter 1

# The Vegetables

In England, and especially in the South-east, we are blessed with an ever-improving choice of both domestically-produced and imported vegetables of good quality. With the upsurge of public awareness has also come a great interest in organically farmed vegetables, which until recently were virtually unobtainable. The problem these days is not so much whether or not a particular vegetable is available, but rather what is its origin and how has it been grown. Can we expect it to have good flavour as well as a good appearance?

Such questions we attempt to answer in the following chapter, which covers most of the commonly available vegetables throughout the year. If you have your own garden this information will probably be of no interest to you; it is primarily intended for those who have to rely on their green grocer for fresh vegetables.

## The Brassicas

This family of vegetables is generally considered to be at their best during the winter months, although many varieties are grown all the year round. The general rule for Brassicas is that they should always be absolutely fresh or they will tend to develop a powerful and offensive taste in cooking. They should always be cooked lightly to best appreciate their flavour and texture.

## Sprouting Broccoli

These delicate and decorative sprouts may be either purple or white in colour and when cooked have an excellent flavour. Delicious in stir-fried dishes and attractive as a decoration, sprouting broccoli is a versatile vegetable.

## Calabrese

Not to be confused with sprouting broccoli, this altogether stouter and more massive vegetable is now far more widely available than broccoli. Grown both domestically and abroad, it has a sweeter flavour than broccoli and is available most of the year.

## Cauliflower

Also, confusingly, sometimes called broccoli in certain parts of England, this vegetable can be superb in vegetarian cookery. The head should be tight and be the palest yellow or green in colour.

Extremely versatile by virtue of its colour and texture, cauliflower can be used both raw in salads or lightly cooked in casseroles. Its flavour, when young, should be delicate and it is at its best in winter. Later, summer vegetables are sweeter and more powerful in flavour.

## Spring Greens/ Greens

Dark green with fleshy, crinkled leaves this vegetable can be difficult to use. Often coarse and bitter in flavour, they can be acceptable well shredded and served with a powerful sauce.

## Cabbage

There are many different varieties, all with their own flavour. White or Dutch cabbage and red cabbage are usually available year-round and are particularly useful raw, shredded in salads, where their mild flavour and robust texture provide useful contrast. More seasonal cabbages are 'prima' in spring and Savoy in autumn—both of these posess a fine flavour making them excellent choices for stir-fried vegetables or for stuffing. You could use the stuffing recipe on page 103.

## Brussels Sprouts

Sprouts should be used carefully, for their flavour can be over-powerful. Always best after 'the first frost', they should be tight and shiny, avoid very large examples. Sprouts are suitable for inclusion in baked dishes with strong sauces, as a bulking agent.

# Onions and Related Vegetables

## Spanish Onions

These are large, usually available all the year round and are useful if you are cooking large quantities of food. Their flavour is rather sweet and mild, which should be borne in mind when using them, and they can also be rather watery.

## English Onions

Smaller and stronger in flavour, the quality varies depending on the time of year. They should be hard to the touch and in such condition are probably the best all-round cooking onion. If they are sprouting, or if there is the slightest hint of soapiness about their flavour, they should be discarded or your cooking will be tainted. Onions are normally well-sweated or fried before being used in stews or bakes as they take a long time to cook.

## Shallots

Although not easily available, shallots should be used, where possible, for sauce making or for really peppy salads and dressings. Hotter, less sweet and drier than onions, they are sadly under-used in English cookery, as any Frenchman will tell you.

## Spring Onions

These are now available year-round, but the smaller, domestically-produced ones have the best flavour. Delicious in salads, particularly potato salad, they also make a sharp garnish when finely sliced for soups. Use with care—many people find onions in general and spring onions in particular hard to digest.

## Garlic

This is a marvellous vegetable—or do you call it a herb? It can be tricky to use and downright unsociable afterwards, but that is a small price to pay. Buy garlic which is very white or purple-white in colour. The cloves should be of a good size and rock hard. Avoid any garlic that yields to firm thumb pressure or has sprouts. Similarly, avoid any grocer who does not allow you to test for these qualities.

Garlic can be chopped, crushed or blended with oil for salads and in dressings, gently fried for sauces or added whole for a milder flavour in baked dishes. Its flavour depends on how it is cooked and cut; used whole its flavour is milder; it is at its fiercest crushed and used raw in salads. Garlic should always be carefully cooked—NEVER allow it to brown or burn in a pan or it will become bitter and taint any subsequent sauce.

Do not be afraid to use plenty when the recipe calls for it. You will soon find out who your friends are in any case!

## Leeks

This most subtle and versatile of winter vegetables is now also available for much of the year. Ideally leeks should not be too large or they may have a woody centre. They are used in cooking either baked, braised or simmered. Their flavour is delicate and sweet with undertones of onion. They may be used in soups, bakes and hot pots or raw in salads where they add a depth and roundness to the flavour. A word of warning however; leeks are invariably gritty unless washed really thoroughly. The best way is to split them lengthwise and then cut them across and rinse them well in a colander under running water.

# Squashes

These comprise a wide variety of vegetables and ones which have, in general, been badly treated by traditional English cuisine. They also are available most of the year, being imported from one part of Europe or another. But where possible, it is always best to buy locally-produced squashes as these delicately flavoured vegetables are not suited to travelling.

## Courgettes and Butter Squash

All too often these are served roughly diced and over cooked; the unappetizing and tasteless mush which results has been the courgette's downfall. In fact this is not necessary—buy courgettes that are firm, shiny green or green and yellow speckled and which are not more than 4-5 inches (10-12 cm) long. The locally grown ones are available from July to September and imports are available all year round. Courgettes are very versatile and may be used raw in salads or lightly cooked in hot savouries. Try them cooked gently in butter, a tablespoon of water, salt and pepper in a tightly-lidded saucepan as a side-dish in their own right. Otherwise they are essential as bulking agents to set off strong Mediterranean dishes, such as Ratatouille.

## Marrows

Far more seasonal, these are available only in early- and mid-summer. Lacking much flavour on their own they are surprisingly good stuffed with a savoury rice and served, for example, with mushroom sauce. Split them lengthways and scoop out the pithy centre before filling them with stuffing and baking in the oven covered with foil. Marrows are also good chopped in wheatberry and cheese dishes.

## Cucumbers

A more familiar variety of squash, available all year round. New crop varieties are available in mid-summer and are the crispest and the least bitter. Indispensable in salad making, they also have their uses in cold summer soups, Gazpacho on page 69 and Cucumber and Yogurt Soup on page 69 for example.

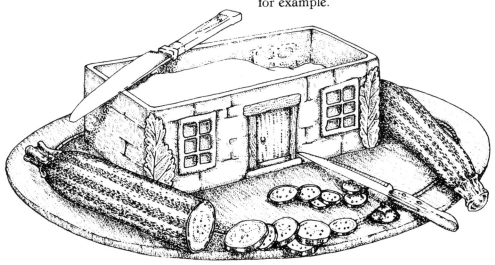

# Root Vegetables and Tubers

This general class of vegetables forms the basis of much vegetarian cookery and at Food For Thought this is no exception. These vegetables tend to be starchy and sweet, so their use must be balanced with sharp or rich sauces and relieved with crunchy, lighter vegetables—such as those in the previous two groups.

Their food value is high and they may be used at all stages of the cooking and preparation of vegetarian food: baked, simmered, roasted, liquidized and grated raw. They may be used to thicken soups and their discarded tops and tails are basic to stock making. They are relatively cheap and, with a few seasonal variations, many are available all the year round, with 'new' and 'main' crop harvests providing variation in quality.

In most cases peeling root vegetables is quite unnecessary. A good scrub with a nail brush under running water is often adequate.

## Parsnips

Sweet and nutty in flavour, parsnips make an excellent homely ingredient to many dishes. Try them roasted with rosemary in, for example, the recipe for Savoury Stout Crumble on page 106, or in a delicious Nutty Parsnip Soup on page 74. Remember that their flavour can be quite dominating and should be enhanced with peanuts or cashew nuts or contrasted with, for example, piquant mustard sauces. Avoid, if possible, very large parsnips which tend to have a woody centre.

# Carrots

Unlike parsnips, carrots vary in flavour enormously. From the bland and woody main crop to the sweet and fragrant new crop available in early summer. Unfortunately it seems that the only types generally grown in England are the rather large and tasteless varieties. If you can get them, buy the small new crop varieties grown in Norfolk. Avoid those wrapped in polythene—they are imported and often taste of nothing.

Main crop carrots are essential as colour and bulking agents in hotpots and bakes. The new carrots are delicious sliced diagonally and used in stir-fries. They may also be cubed, diced or shredded raw for incorporation in salad dishes.

# Beetroot

This underrated vegetable has a delicious sweet, earthy flavour and luscious colour which make it indispensable as a salad ingredient. It is generally bought ready cooked so that all you need to do is to peel away the soft skin and slice or cube it ready for use in salads, e.g. Beetroot and Red Cabbage Salad on page 54. Beetroot also makes a distinctive soup (see page 76 for Borsch) but is not recommended for stews or baked dishes as its colour will tend to dominate everything.

# Jerusalem Artichokes

Their knobbly appearance puts off many people, which is sad because Jerusalem artichokes have a unique smoky, nutty flavour and agreeable texture. There is no need to peel them if they are small. They are delicious in soups with nuts or used with a cheesy or cream sauce in casseroles or bakes in place of parsnips.

# Turnips

Disregard any turnips over 2 inches (5 cm) in diameter as they tend to be fibrous and over powerful in flavour. The smaller ones, however, are superb cooked as a side dish in the following manner; Simmer in 2 tablespoons of water, a little butter or margarine, salt and pepper and cover tightly, cook until tender. Serve as they are or in a bechamel sauce made from the juice they were cooked in and flavoured with nutmeg. The best turnips are available in spring.

# Celeriac

This ugly looking vegetable is, in fact, delicious. Available from late summer to autumn its flavour, as its name suggests, is not unlike celery. Used grated raw in salads (see page 48), it is also used sparingly in soups, stews and stock making. As an ingredient in nut roasts it adds a certain lightness to the flavour.

# Fennel

This is a vegetable whose flavour you either love or loathe. It has overtones of aniseed though not as strong. It can be used raw in salads where it is particularly good with orange and French dressing or in soups. Unless you particularly like its flavour its use in baked dishes is not recommended as it tends to dominate.

# Potatoes

There are literally scores of varieties available, all of which have their particular adherents. Potatoes are highly versatile—they may be mashed, creamed, sautéed, roasted or boiled/steamed whole. They may also be baked in their jackets. They are used to thicken soups and they make an excellent topping for bakes when used with **cheese and onions—see Lentil and Aubergine Moussaka on page 98.** Generally they are scrubbed or scraped rather than peeled to preserve their full nutritional value and flavour.

Avoid potatoes that are withered, sprouting or have a green tinge. 'Reds' or Desirée varieties hold their form better for boiling, whites (King Edwards, Maris Piper, for example) are good mashers and fry nicely.

New crop potatoes grown domestically are incomparably better than those imported from abroad which can often taste of nothing so much as mould. Better to wait until April…

**21**

## Radishes

Alongside the more commonly available domestic radish there are also Chinese radishes, which are large and white, and Spanish radishes which are black. Their uses in salads are manifold, but it should be remembered that their flavour and hotness varies considerably.

# 'Pod' Vegetables

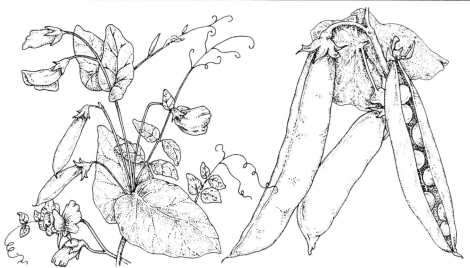

Depressingly familiar in many English greengrocers are the gross, swollen forms of over-mature broad beans or mammoth stringy runners. Peas are usually the size of the proverbial cannon ball and imported French beans are often expensive and tired. The infuriating fact behind all this is that we possess a superb climate for growing this produce, so what has gone wrong? Quite simply the best produce is spirited away from the enormous company-owned farms by the large frozen food processors, leaving that which has been rejected as out-sized. This is then sold fresh via the retailer. What a ludicrous state of affairs, where the best vegetables are frozen and the worst sold fresh.

Should you be lucky enough to find these vegetables fresh and young, snap them up, for they are like gold dust!

## Green Beans, French Beans, Bobby Beans

These are best when firm and not too large—3 inches/8 cm for French beans, a little longer for bobbies. The flavour is excellent and most suitable for salads or lightly cooked as a delicious side dish, when the texture should be 'squeaky' or crunchy.

## Runner Beans, Stick Beans

A bean with a beautiful flavour, but which should be avoided if the seeds are 'bulbous' in the pod or the skin is coarse and scaly. Properly sold they should be slender, straight and firm. To prepare, simply run a sharp knife along the edge of the bean just below the surface to remove any stringiness. They are best in the summer months; when included in casseroles and soups they impart an excellent flavour.

## Broad Beans

These beans, when young, have a distinctive and sophisticated flavour all their own.

Again, too often, they are sold when far too mature. It is best to avoid pods where the beans inside them are easily visible. The beans themselves should be not larger than 1/2 inch/1.5 cm in size. The young ones are delicious as a side dish simmered in a little water for 1 or 2 minutes only and served with butter, parsley and salt and pepper. The larger ones are good in baked dishes, but remember to use enough liquid as they tend to be dry.

## Peas

Very much the same applies to fresh peas as to broad beans—the best are usually frozen. Avoid the large, over mature examples unless you have plenty of time for cooking them and lots of imagination for flavouring. Otherwise peas are very colourful and versatile—raw in salads and cooked in, for example, cracked wheat or nut roast dishes.

Try also Fresh Pea Soup (page 67).

# Leafy Vegetables

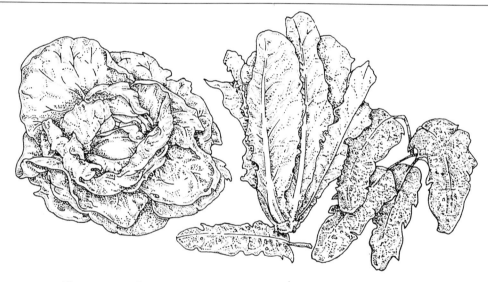

## Spinach

There are two types of spinach available in England. The coarser, greener, smooth-leaved variety available year round and sometimes known as perpetual spinach; or the finer, crinkle-leaved 'beet' spinach with its distinctive reddish stem marking. The former has an assertive earthy and metallic flavour which goes well with cheese sauces, pasta, eggs and piquant dishes.

The finer 'beet' spinach is excellent for soups and may even be eaten raw in salads. All spinach should be thoroughly washed three or more times in running water. When cooking spinach use very little water—a tablespoon or so—cover tightly

and boil. When cooked, drain and squeeze out excess water. A little grated nutmeg to flavour is recommended. It is worth noting that spinach cooks down considerably—a very full saucepan of spinach will reduce to a quarter of its original volume when cooked.

## Lettuce

The range of lettuces has expanded considerably in recent years. The most common varieties are:

● Round lettuce—floppy, green leaves with good flavour. Available year-round.

● Webb's—attractive crinkle leaf with crisp

23

texture and fine flavour. Available year-round.

- Cos lettuce—Tall leaf, pale and crunchy with sharp flavour.

- Iceberg—pale, dense, almost cabbage-like, with very crisp succulent leaves but little flavour.

## Chinese Leaf or Cabbage

A beautiful looking pale green vegetable with tall, crisp leaves. Use raw instead of lettuce in salads and garnish. Roughly chopped, it makes a good addition to stir-fried vegetables.

# Lentil Sprouts, Alfalfa, Bamboo Shoots, Bean Sprouts, Mustard Cress

These freshly-sprouted vegetables are becoming more and more widely available. Their use is limited to salads and garnish due to their high water content, but they add a pleasant variety and sharpness to any recipe.

They must always be used absolutely fresh or they become bitter and lose their nutritional value. For real freshness, many of these can be sprouted and grown at home. In most cases this presents no problems.

# Vegetable 'Fruits'

## Aubergines or Eggplants

This vegetable has a magnificent glossy brown-purple skin which, disappointingly, becomes a dull brown when cooked. Aubergines have a subtle, almost intangible flavour, both slightly bitter and earthy. This makes them ideal for use as a 'base' vegetable in moussaka, for example. Before using, cut in half and sprinkle with salt and leave for 2 hours. This draws any excessive bitterness from the aubergine, but make sure that you rinse it well before use.

## Sweet Peppers, Capsicum or Pimentos

This vegetable, now available year-round, comes in four colours: red, which is the sweetest, green, which is the sharpest, and white and yellow which fall somewhere between the first two in flavour.

Used raw in salads they are valuable for their strong colours and add pep, particularly to pasta and rice based salads. Their flavour can be overpowering so they should be used with caution.

When used in cooking, the same care is needed. The flavour, so distinctive and appetizing in some dishes, can spoil other more delicate ones with its sweetness. Stuffed Peppers (see page 104) are excellent and this recipe demonstrates their use best of all.

Avoid any vegetable that is wrinkled or soft. Peppers should be firm and glossy. It is also worth noting that many find this vegetable indigestible.

## Tomatoes

The best flavoured tomatoes are undoubtedly those large, misshapen ones you see in France and Italy. Unfortunately, the Tomato Marketing Board has ensured conformity amongst domestic growers—the usual Guernsey, Jersey or English tomato is a variety that is perfectly round, red and firm, pleasing to the eye but flat and wet on the palate! Don't be fooled by the Dutch Beefsteak tomatoes—they are even worse. However, things are not all grim and in summer the domestic tomatoes become cheap and relatively tasty.

Their uses in salads are obvious—both for decoration and colour. When using fresh tomatoes as opposed to tinned ones in cooking, remember that the relative sweetness of the fresh ones will require an adjustment in the seasoning. Similarly you may need to reduce tomatoes when you cook them for a sauce to intensify their flavour.

# Avocados

These beautiful vegetables are available in two different varieties: the smooth, glossy-skinned types and those with darker, more knobbly surfaces. Unfortunately, avocados are fast becoming yet another casualty of the 'cash crop syndrome' more commonly associated with fruits than vegetables. As a result, they are grown year round in various parts of the world in order to capitalize on demand in the market place. The rub is that they are often sold hopelessly under-ripe and lacking flavour even when ready to eat.

The quality is best in mid- to late-summer, when they can be tested for ripeness under slight thumb pressures—they should yield. On certain varieties the skin will darken as the vegetable ripens; you can often buy them cheaper in this state and they are perfectly edible.

Avocados at their best are a genuine luxury: rich, creamy and smooth. They may be eaten as a starter, halved lengthways, de-stoned and dressed with a little Vinaigrette; sliced in salads to add colour and richness; used as a delicious dip (see page 58), or used as a soup.

It is worth making two points about avocados. First, it is usually possible to ripen very hard examples to perfection on a window sill. Secondly, avocados are very rich and can result in an upset stomach if eaten in quantity.

# The Pulses: Beans, Peas and Lentils

If fresh vegetables play the role of producing variety in colour and texture to vegetarian cookery, then pulses are often cast as the poor relation: relatively colourless, of similar textures, difficult to digest and stodgy. Indeed, to avoid these problems it is necessary to understand a little about the composition of pulses.

First, in a vegetarian diet they are a valuable source of protein, vitamin B and iron provided that they are properly cooked.

Their close, starchy texture means that they have to be cooked for considerable periods of time if they are to be palatable or digestible. In this sense, pressure cooking is preferable to boiling, not simply because of the time saved, but also because more of their vitamin B content is retained that way.

Second, from the culinary point of view, the flavour of most pulses is extremely subtle, some would say bland. It is, therefore, important to use them properly in your cooking. Too high a proportion of pulses to sauce and fresh vegetables will result in a dry, uninteresting and indigestible meal. This is especially true of lentils. Too few pulses and your cooking will lack body and nutrition.

So what is the true role of the pulse? Put simply, pulses are to be used in conjunction with bold, spicy or cheesy sauces as an anchor of flavour and texture. Root vegetables in particular make good contrasting partners.

It is wise to form the habit of planning a day in advance which beans you want to use, so that you can soak them overnight. The general rules to follow are that pulses are best soaked, overnight if possible, or for at least a few hours before cooking. They should be soaked in plenty of water—at least twice their own volume. This has the effect of breaking down the starches that can cause indigestion. Soaking also ensures more rapid and even cooking.

Once soaked, the beans should be drained and rinsed very thoroughly in cold running water. It is not recommended that you cook the beans in the water in which they have been soaked. After being rinsed, pulses may be boiled, steamed or pressure cooked. The last method finds the most favour at Food For Thought for the reasons already given. When pressure-cooking pulses always make sure that you use plenty of water—covering the beans by at least 2 inches/5 cm.

The final flavour of the pulse is enhanced by the addition, at this stage, of garlic, sliced onion or herbs appropriate to the recipe you have chosen. The final colour of, for example, haricot beans will be changed by the addition of a little turmeric in their cooking. This results in an attractive vivid

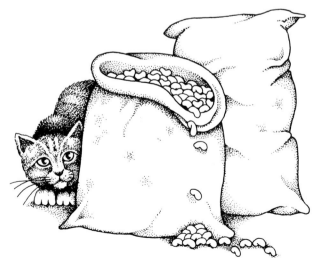

yellow bean more appropriate to salad making. It is best not to add salt at this stage as this can harden the bean. Seasoning, in any case, can be adjusted at a later stage in the recipe.

What follows is a table showing cooking times for the various pulses most commonly available in this country. I have also included a little information on the various beans themselves and while such comment is always rather subjective, I hope it will be useful nonetheless.

Always start the cooking process with a 10 minute boiling period, as some beans contain toxins that must be destroyed in this way to avoid poisoning.

One final point: once cooked, it is important to rinse pulses in plenty of water. The cooking liquor may be reserved for use in other cooking.

Approximate Cooking Times for Pulses, Pre-Soaked

| Pulse Type | Cooking Time — Minutes under pressure | Cooking Time— Hours simmering |
|---|---|---|
| Blackeye beans | 10 | 1/2 |
| Pinto beans | 10 | 11/2 |
| Kidney beans | 10 | 11/2 |
| Aduki beans | 10 | 11/2 |
| Haricot beans | 10 | 1 |
| Flageolet beans | 10 | 11/2 |
| Butter beans | 10 | 11/2 |
| Chickpeas | 25 | 21/2 |
| Red lentils | 6 | 1/2 |
| Other lentil types | 10 | 3/4 |
| Split peas | 12 | 1 |

## Blackeye Beans

Firm in texture and attractive to look at, these beans are particularly good in strong, creamy sauces. Their relative lack of flavour means that they are not effective in salads.

## Pinto Beans

These beans possess a smooth texture and beautiful flavour—possibly the best of all dried pulses. Their rather drab beige colour when cooked precludes their use in salads but, as a base in rich savoury bakes, they are excellent. See Pinto Bean Carbonnade on page 101.

## Kidney Beans

An extremely versatile and popular bean, useful in Chillied Hot Pots (page 114), and salads. This is due to their ability to retain their colour when cooked. The flavour is robust, the texture can be coarse with a thick skin.

## Aduki Beans

A sweet and distinctly peppery flavour characterizes this vegetable. Aduki beans are one of the few pulses with enough flavour to dominate a dish; try Shepherdess Pie on page 96, in which this flavour is counterbalanced with sage, mushrooms and leeks. It is worth noting that aduki beans, like all pulses, absorb plenty of water even after they have been cooked—allow for this in your sauce making.

## Haricot Beans

This is the one everybody knows as a result of the ubiquitous 'baked bean'. Although its flavour is inherently bland and nonedescript, haricots have the advantage that they will readily absorb the flavour of the sauce in which they are cooked. Cooked with a little turmeric, they attain a luscious yellow colour and may then be used in salads where their tough skin is useful in preventing the bean breaking up.

## Flageolet Beans

Pale green in colour, these beans are similar in flavour to haricots. They break up easily, however, and are not terribly attractive when cooked. However, they do go well with a parsley sauce.

## Butter Beans

Large, flat beans of good flavour and firm texture. Slightly sweet and 'powdery' if over cooked, they are nonetheless excellent in rustic hot pots (try West Country Casserole on page 123) where their relatively tough skins prevent them from breaking up. Use with plenty of colour from fresh vegetables as their own is bland.

## Chickpeas

This all-purpose pulse has a very distinctive flavour and unique firm texture. Use it in salads, curries and for making Hummus —see page 57. Ensure that chickpeas are well cooked—they take a long time.

## Red Lentils

Smaller than their green and brown cousins, red lentils are very good in soups where their short cooking time allows one to make a nourishing dish relatively quickly. All lentils have the property of thickening soups and sauces, so they are useful in wheat- or gluten-free diets.

## Green and Brown Lentils

Lentils have the advantage that they need not always be pre-soaked. It is important, if this is the case, that you allow enough water in the cooking process, for they will absorb proportionally more water than if pre-soaked. Lentils have an earthy flavour and floury texture so they must have plenty of sauce. Try Cauliflower and Mushroom Dahl on page 114.

## Split Peas

These, like lentils, possess a distinctive flavour. They are best used in soup making—try Split Pea and Garlic soup on page 77. It is almost always advisable to liquidize split peas for soup making—this has the effect of creating a smooth soup with plenty of body.

# Chapter 2
# Grains, Spices, Herbs and Flavourings

In this chapter I have compiled advice on the cooking and usage of the 'non' vegetable ingredients most commonly used in vegetarian cuisine. These include the various cereals whose role is fundamentally in providing carbohydrate, roughage and an essential 'body' to many dishes.

Herbs and spices, covered quite extensively, are given the prominence they should deserve. Understanding the way in which different herbs work, fresh or dried, is of vital importance.

Also discussed are some of the more useful flavourings that go to make a more interesting dish. The list is not exhaustive, but the most important products are there. They range from seed pastes of peanut and sesame through extracts and concentrates to products of fermentation: wines, beers and ciders. All may be used with imagination to enhance your cookery.

# Cereals

## Rice

There are scores of different varieties of rice now available. Wild rice has the best flavour, but is very expensive. Brown unpolished rice has good flavour, too. Rice also varies enormously in its absorbency; fine, long grain rices cook more rapidly and absorb less water than short grain rice. At Food For Thought we use Italian short grain brown rice which has a nutty flavour that makes it a particularly good base for stir-fried vegetables.

How to Cook Rice:
There are two basic methods; the 'boiling method' is to rinse the rice in cold water, to shake off loose starch, then to boil in a large quantity of water, strain and rinse in hot water, adding a little oil afterwards to prevent the grains from sticking. This method is more suited to long grain, low absorbency rice.

The absorption method is perhaps more suited to brown short grain rice; here is our recipe, which is sufficient for 4-6 people.

Pour two cupfuls of rice into a metal sieve and run cold water through the rice, agitating it gently with the fingers, to remove the surface starch which can cause the rice to stick later. Then place the rice in a heavy saucepan and cover with 4-5 cupfuls of cold water. Add 1 teaspoon of soya sauce, a bay leaf and a clove of garlic and, without covering, bring to the boil. Continue to boil for 5 minutes then lower the heat until the rice is 'poppling'—somewhere between a simmer and boiling—and cover with a tight-fitting lid. Gradually all the cooking water should be absorbed over a period of up to one hour. It is important not to raise the lid during this time as vital water will be lost. Should more water be required before the rice is cooked, it may be added, preferably hot and by the cup. The rice should not be stirred while cooking as this breaks up the grains, causing the rice to release starch and resulting in stickiness.

The end result should be firm, fluffy rice, free of lumps and mushiness. This method may not be the quickest, but it ensures

maximum flavour. If speed is of the essence, the boiling method is recommended.

# Whole Grain Wheat or Wheat 'Berries'

This is unmilled wheat seed and may be cooked in exactly the same way as rice. It will take a little less time to cook, however. When cooked, it adds a delicious flavour and very different texture to salads. It also goes well with cheesy baked dishes.

Other cereals worth experimenting with include buckwheat, barley and cracked wheat in its various forms.

# Cracked Wheat or 'Bulghur'

This is a delicious product of wheat which is very rapidly prepared and may be used in baked dishes and salads. Simply pour boiling water or stock over the cracked wheat and leave to stand and cool for 20 minutes. It is then ready for use.

# Pasta

Pasta is now far more widely available than before. Alongside the usual varieties available: dried spaghetti, macaroni, vermicelli, spiral and shell pastas there are also freshly prepared varieties, for example, lasagne, tagliatelle and ravioli. We shall not go into pasta types in detail here—far better to visit an Italian delicatessen and see for yourself. The fresh pasta tends to have better flavour and to take a shorter time to cook, but it cannot be kept more than two days. Dried pasta, on the other hand, is more widely available and convenient.

All pasta is based on wheat, usually the 'Durum' variety, sometimes mixed with eggs or vegetables—often spinach. Pasta forms an excellent vehicle for rich sauces and vegetables and provides useful energy. The image pastas have of being highly fattening is actually a myth; the sauces they are habitually served with are often the real culprit. That said, however, pasta almost begs for such sauces. Without bold, interesting or rather rich accompaniments, pasta is bland. Similarly, when used in salads, strong colours and rich dressings of Parmesan, chives, oil and fresh basil will transform the flavour of the pasta.

How to Cook Pasta:
Pre-packed pastas usually come with full cooking instructions and it is best to follow these—always using plenty of boiling water with a little oil added to it to prevent boiling

over. When cooked, pasta should have an opaque appearance and be 'al dente'—that is, tender but offering a slight springy resistance between the teeth.

Fresh pasta needs less cooking; tagliatelle, for example, can be dropped into boiling water and cooked for just a few minutes prior to use. Stirring the pasta while it is cooking helps to prevent sticking and, once cooked, rinse the pasta quickly in plenty of cold water. After draining, a little oil, salt and pepper will prevent sticking.

Fresh pasta is especially good in baked dishes, Lasagne (page 89) for example. In this case no pre-cooking is required—the lasagne sheets are layered in the sauce and baked, using the sauce itself to cook in. Remember to allow for the fact that the pasta will asborb liquid from the sauce in order to avoid a sticky result.

# Herbs and Spices

In the past herbs were used far more freely and in a great many more applications than is now the case. The food available in pre-industrial times was certainly less varied and probably of poorer quality; herbs were used to introduce more interesting flavours. Herbs were also used with varying degrees of success in the treatment of certain illnesses and, as such, were an intrinsic part of everyday life.

In more recent times, particularly in this century, with the advent of modern food additives, flavour 'enhancers' and processed food, we seem to have lost our understanding of how and when to use herbs. Modern drugs have further distanced most people from what were once very familiar plants. It is only in the last decade that the use of herbs in both cooking and healing has become more widespread, again. The great chefs of our time always had a full knowledge and range of herbs, but what of the average home cook or even average restaurant? All too often we were seduced by delicious sounding recipes using this or that herb only to be let down by the soapy, musty flavour that resulted.

Herbs should always enhance and enrich a dish and never be so dominant as to be instantly recognizable. They should be noticeable by their absence rather than their presence, and herein lies the key; experience will tell you what your palate prefers. In my opinion, fresh herbs are so vastly superior to those that are dried that they are to be used in preference whenever possible.

To this end, it is worth cultivating a small herb garden or even just a window box with a few of the more useful types. Those that I

would recommend are thyme, chives, tarragon, rosemary, bay (remember this is a tree!), basil and marjoram.

Used fresh, herbs can be introduced at a later stage in the cooking and used more generously than their dried counterparts. Dried herbs should be used more sparingly and at an earlier stage in the cooking as their flavour takes longer to develop. This is because the drying process concentrates certain flavours and eliminates others—particularly the volatile oils which give many fresh herbs their lovely bouquet.

If you have access to a greengrocer who sells fresh herbs, take advantage of this! The choice is improving all the time, although it is still fairly bleak in some regions with parsley and chives being the only herbs normally available. Supermarkets stock an enormous range of dried herbs but, as we shall see, some of these are to be treated with great caution.

## Basil

Basil must be used fresh or not at all. At its best, its light, sharp and lemony flavour transforms all tomato and pasta dishes, especially salads. The dried variety is different altogether and its musty flavour means that it is to be used only in an emergency. Better to opt for a different recipe altogether.

## Bay

One of the most useful all-rounders, bay imparts a richness to brown sauces, tomato sauces and pasta dishes. Fresh bay leaves are far preferable to dried ones. Cultivate your own, or perhaps you may be lucky enough to live near a bay tree—they are popular as decorative shrubs. I would not, however, recommend taking the leaves from bay trees found in pots outside smart restaurants!

## Chervil

Not unlike parsley in appearance, the flavour is more delicate. Used in soups and salads.

## Coriander

The fresh leaves give an exotic fragrancy to both cakes and savoury dishes while the seeds, stronger in flavour, are used in curries. One point worth noting is that coriander leaves can 'turn' a soup, for example, overnight. The process itself is obscure, but the result can be very unpleasant. It is always best to consume dishes flavoured with this herb immediately.

## Dill

Dill weed, easier to use than the seed, has a delicate piquancy that goes well with cucumber and yogurt, salad dishes containing potatoes, cashewnuts or green vegetables.

## Marjoram

This herb has a spicy flavour, not unlike nutmeg. It is good in nutty dishes, lentils, with mushrooms and in savoury stuffings. Wild marjoram or oregano is stronger and less sweet in flavour. The dried varieties of marjoram should be used with caution or an unpleasant, bitter taste will result.

## Mint

Mint has a strong, cool, sweet smell that goes beautifully with salads, particularly potato, and cold soups such as Gazpacho or Cucumber and Yogurt. Dried mint is simply not worth using; musty and bitter. Mint is easy to grow—grow your own!

## Parsley

Whether using the delicately flavoured broad-leafed 'Hamburg' variety or the stronger coarse-leafed English variety, parsley is indispensable. Used not only for decoration, as is so often the case, parsley possesses a fine, clean flavour almost reminiscent of apples. The stalks are excellent for stock making and the leaves, finely chopped, make an attractive garnish for all hot savouries. The dried variety is best left alone, especially as parsley is available fresh all the year round.

# Rosemary

This herb has a pungent aromatic smell—a little goes a long way. An important ingredient in nut roasts, rosemary goes well with roast parsnips and pumpkins. The dried variety is perfectly acceptable.

# Sage

Powerful and aromatic, sage is good with onions and leeks where its slightly camphor taste lightens the dish. Although it dries relatively well, injudicious use will result in a soapy, musty flavour.

# Tarragon

Tarragon is another herb whose delicate flavour is all but squandered in the drying process. When fresh its light, appetizing and aromatic flavour is used to complement white wine sauces and many salads. It may also be bottled in wine vinegar where it imparts a delicious flavour.

# Thyme

Its strong, aromatic and slightly sharp taste makes this herb an excellent addition to stews, soups, stuffing and nut savouries. It should be used sparingly, however, for it can easily overpower more delicate flavoured dishes. It is easy to grow and dries acceptably.

Mixtures:

# Bouquet Garni

There are many versions of this classic French herbal combination, but generally bay leaves, marjoram, parsley and thyme are the main constituents. These herbs are either tied together or placed in a muslin bag and used to flavour hot pots and soups.

# Fines Herbes

This consists of chives, tarragon and parsley chopped finely and used in salads, quiches and tomato dishes.

# Mixed Herbs

Something of a hotch-potch, usually containing dried herbs such as oregano, sage and thyme which can be used to aromatize the flavour of stuffings and sweet root vegetables. Overuse will result in a musty, 'disinfectant' flavour.

# Spices

Spices, like herbs, contain aromatic oils which are released into the food during the cooking process. Just as drying herbs drives off many of these aromatic oils, spices often suffer the same fate. For purposes of convenience, spices are often bought pre-ground and although perfectly useable in this state, they are never as flavoursome as when they are freshly ground.

For this reason, if you like spicy food, it is worth investing in a general purpose mill or at least a pestle and mortar, so that you can grind your own.

To the uninitiated, to taste a curry made with freshly ground spices comes as a revelation. The flavours are far more varied, subtle and complex while the presence of the aromatic oils takes much of the 'heat' away from the curry.

Here is a list of the more useful spices available.

## Caraway Seeds

Caraway is characterized by a very pungent flavour reminiscent of aniseed—one either loves or loathes it. It tends to dominate whatever it is combined with so treat it with caution. Used in cake- and bread-baking, caraway also goes well with cucumber and beetroot.

## Cardamom

With its lemon-eucalyptus flavour, carda-mom seeds are another essential in curry making. The seeds may be left whole or crushed for more instant flavour.

## Cumin Seeds

These seeds have an aroma of lemon and 'freshly mown grass'. Before use, crush them in a pestle and mortar and add to curries and other hot dishes early in the cooking. The flavour that cumin seeds produce is an important mediating factor in such dishes—it adds interest and depth to the simple heat of, say, chilli.

## Cinnamon

This spice is generally used to flavour sweets: fruit crumbles, compotes and egg custard. It is available either as a powder or as whole 'sticks' (bark). Used in hot mulled wine and punches it adds an agreeable winter warmth.

## Cloves

Cloves are to be used with great respect. Their flavour is extremely pervasive and often one clove is enough to flavour an entire dish for six people. They go especially well with apple- and pear-based desserts and are useful for flavouring winter drinks. In bechamel sauce making, an onion stuck with 2-3 cloves will impart a delicious flavour when cooked in milk with a bay leaf. The milk is then used to make the sauce. See page 86.

## Ginger

This versatile and widely used spice is derived from a wierdly shaped root. When dried and ground, the powder forms the base for most curry powders, in which its unique aroma plays a large part. Used by itself, ground ginger improves the flavour of stir-fried vegetables imbueing the dish with an agreeable astringency. Used fresh, the root has a sweeter, milder flavour and is particularly good in Sweet-and-Sour Hot Pot (page 122), for example.

The stem is also used, preserved in syrup. In this form ginger is used in baking cakes and as an accompaniment to sweets and fruit compotes.

## Mustards

Mustards may be divided broadly into two groups: those that are the result of grinding the seed into a fine powder which may then be used when mixed into a paste with oil or water, or used as a thickening agent; and those which are preserved whole in oil and vinegar and often flavoured with herbs and spices.

Of the former variety, English mustard is probably the best known and is distinguished by its powerful flavour. This characteristic makes it an intrinsic part of salad dressings—used in conjunction with oil, vinegar and garlic, mustard gives bite to green salads, counteracting any bitterness. English mustard can also transform white sauces, which can be bland without a little astringency.

'Whole' mustards or 'grain' mustards are quite different in flavour. They tend to be milder and nuttier in character and, when prepared and conserved with herbs, as, for example, are those from Dijon in France, take on subtle flavours of the added ingredients. Such mustards tend to be better suited to dressings for bean and rice based salads, or when cooking savoury dishes based on root vegetables. In this application an excellent rich, piquant flavour will result, nicely balancing the inherent sweetness of root vegetables.

# Nutmeg and Mace

These two very similar flavours are derived from the same plant. The flavour of 'sweet-vanilla-pepper' goes very well with bechamel sauces, mashed potatoes, spinach and egg savouries and sweets. It is always best to grate nutmeg freshly for maximum flavour.

# Paprika, Cayenne Pepper and Chilli Powder

The similarity in the appearance of these spices can lead to confusion; indeed their flavours are not unalike—the difference lies in their relative heat. Paprika is made from ground sweet peppers or pimentos and is consequently mild. Cayenne or chilli powder is made from ground chillis and is consequently very hot. In general, these spices should be added early in the cooking to allow their flavour to develop and disperse into the vegetables. When using fresh chillis, the relative heat of this spice can vary enormously—the green ones are milder than the red—use with caution!

Remember to cut out and discard any seeds as these are bitter. It is also a wise idea to wear protective rubber gloves when fine chopping fresh chillis as the juice can get under your nails and burn away painfully for days!

# Pepper

There is, quite simply, no substitute for freshly ground black or white pepper. The black variety is commonly used whole, crushed or coarsely ground so that its oils are less dispersed. The white variety has a lighter flavour and is used in pale sauces, finely milled. The robust flavour of black pepper is one of the best stimulants of appetite and is indispensable to all savouries.

It is worth noting that a good pepper mill is important. There is a lot of junk on the market and it is always best to opt for those with a stainless steel grinding mechanism, as this is less prone to wear and corrosion. The best quality mills are made in England, France or Germany. Those from the Far East can be infuriatingly inefficient.

# Turmeric

Turmeric is used not only for its savoury, peppery flavour, but also for its colouring properties. Haricot beans, for example, when pressure-cooked with turmeric, become a beautiful yellow colour. Turmeric can also be used to colour rice when saffron is unavailable, or too expensive.

# Curry Powder or Paste

The paste is generally better than the powder as it tends to have more flavour. Both powder and paste are mixtures of ground curry leaves, coriander, cardamom, chilli, cloves, ginger and other spices. In the case of paste these are suspended in oil. The 'heat' of the preparation will depend on the relative proportion of its ingredients— 'vindaloo' is one of the hottest. Always ensure that the curry powder you are using is fresh, for if stored for too long the flavour becomes dulled. Pastes tend to keep rather better.

## Garam Masala

Like curry powder there is no precise, definitive recipe for garam masala. It will be found to contain many of the same spices as curry powder, but the end result is a milder, more aromatic flavouring often better suited to vegetables, whose subtle flavour is not always enhanced by very spicy sauces. It is best used near the end of the cooking.

A general point to make about curries is that it is often useful to have a range of spices available, in ground, combined and whole form. In this way it is easier to alter the flavour of any sauce to produce the desired effect. For example, when used in conjunction with a commercially prepared paste or powder, a few freshly ground cardamon, coriander and cumin seeds will add a distinctive and pleasant aromatic dimension to the end result. The addition of Garam Masala later in the cooking will have a similar effect.

Equally, if you wish to create a hotter curry, add a few fresh or dried chillis rather than extra curry paste, which can adversely affect the flavour.

# Flavourings

Herbs and spices add interest, variety, subtlety and heat to a dish. One of the problems remaining to the vegetarian is how to achieve that essential 'savouriness' that is normally the hallmark of a dish containing meat. In fact, to the meat-eater, vegetarian food is often disappointing or unsatisfying for this reason alone; vegetables, in themselves, tend to be sweet and lacking in substantial flavour.

This need not be the case, for the correct use of some of the following flavourings will add that essential savoury 'anchor' flavour. This is not to be misunderstood; we are not trying to mimic the flavour of meat dishes as this is self-defeating. Rather, we are trying to achieve a more satisfying dish. There are good reasons why this is so: the savoury flavour peculiar to meat arises partly from the glutamic acid it contains. This is also present in wheat and soya from which soya sauce is made. Yeast extracts have similar properties and, correctly used, can transform a sauce.

Using these extracts and preparations it is perfectly possible to give vegetarian dishes the same appetizingly savoury qualities. Such preparations should be used with great care, however. Too little and the sauce will lack substance and provide no base for the more delicate vegetable flavours. You will have created the vegetarian's bug-bear: the Bland Meal. Over-use of flavourings will result in murky and often bitter dishes, all tasting alike.

Here are some of the more important preparations.

## Soy, Soya, Soye Sauce

The purest soya sauces are made from fermented soya beans, roasted wheat and salt. The Japanese 'Tamari' is an exceptionally natural product, but generally it is best to buy the best quality available. Cheaper brands often have a fairly horrific list of additives: anything from the relatively innocuous caramel colouring and 'nature identical' monosodium glutamate to the rather more sinister enhancers, preservatives and colourants. The message is simple: soya sauce is vital in vegetarian cookery, so buy the best.

Soya sauce can be used at any stage in the preparation of vegetarian food. Beforehand as a marinade, for sautéing or frying vegetables in, such as stir-fried vegetables, or as an addition to water when cooking rice or beans. It can be used to darken and thicken sauces during their cooking or added to the finished dish as an accompaniment. Toasted nuts, if brushed beforehand with a little soya, are transformed and make an excellent addition to salads.

Soya sauce is, therefore, versatile in the true sense of the word. It is not, however, the panacea to all evils. It should not be used in white sauces where it will darken

and dominate. Be careful not to burn it when using as part of a sauté or an unpleasant, bitter flavour will result. Finally, resist the temptation simply to add soya sauce if all else fails. You will emerge with a dish that tastes of soya sauce and be none the wiser yourself as to what went wrong!

## Miso

This paste, also prepared from soya beans and salt, has a harder, saltier flavour. It may be used as a stock flavourer and is particularly good in soups.

## Yeast Extract

This can be seen as the Western version of soya sauce for it contains similar chemical constituents, even though it is made from different ingredients. Its flavour is also similar, but it may be used only in a far more restricted way. Stirred into soups and stews in moderation, yeast extract will provide the essential savoury base to the flavour of the dish. Do not over-use or burn it, as a bitter flavour will result. Malt extract may be used in a similar manner.

## Tahini

Tahini comes in two varieties; light and dark. They are both made from sesame seeds and oil, but vary in flavour and strength. We tend to use the former, whose creamy rich flavour is more suited to sauce making than the rather more dominant nutty flavour of the darker variety. The addition of tahini to a sauce will create a smoother, richer flavour. It is particularly good in root vegetable- or pulse-based dishes, but it can mask the colour of other vegetables.

## Peanut Butter

Made from crushed peanuts, this paste may be used in a similar fashion to tahini, but it has a stronger, sweeter flavour that is better suited to spicy sauces and, for example, egg noodles.

## Mustards

(See spices, page 36-7).

## Creamed Coconut

This, as its name suggests, is derived from coconut and is sold in 'bar' form rather like soap. Used in curry sauces, it dissolves more completely than desiccated coconut and gives a delicious flavour to all spicy dishes: curries, tagines and noodles.

## Stock Cubes

Although we do not use these at all at Food For Thought, it is understood that they do have their uses in domestic situations. They contain a combination of yeast and vegetable extracts, colourants and spices and as such are very much a matter of personal preference; there are plenty of brands on the market. Where possible it is always best to make your own stock, though as time-savers stock cubes are useful. Choose additive-free, unsalted varieties wherever possible.

39

# Alcohol in Cooking

The inclusion of wine or other alcohols in savoury dishes does not, as is commonly supposed, render the dish alcoholic. The vast majority of the alcohol is, in fact, evaporated off during the cooking process, leaving the flavour of the wine, ale or cider itself to add interest to the sauce.

Another common supposition is that it doesn't really matter what quality of wine or beer is to be used in cooking. This is wrong. It is important to buy good quality alcohol of the right variety. Match its flavour to the ingredients; in this respect trial and error is often the mechanism involved!

## Red Wine

Red wine is an essential ingredient in many of the more hearty, dark 'ragouts', such as Kidney Bean Bordelaise (page 119). It lends a dry and rich flavour to the sauce and improves the colour of the final result. Like all alcoholic additives it is used early in the cooking and initially simmered rapidly to drive off the alcohol. Prolonged cooking then allows the flavour of the wine to permeate the vegetables. The most appropriate cooking wines are Bordeaux reds for hot pots and Italian Chiantis for the richer pasta sauces.

## White Wines

White wines impart a delicate fruitiness or dryness to sauces and work well with fresh herbs—in particular tarragon. The classic white wine sauce, or 'chasseur', appears in the recipe on page 125.

Best are the fruitier white wines from southern France and Italy. The drier northern French wines are too acid, while the sweet German and Yugoslav wines are inappropriate.

## Sherry

The drier sherries are best in savoury dishes—cheap varieties are perfectly adequate in this respect. Mushroom Consommé is particularly good finished with sherry. Sweeter sherries are, of course, excellent in fruit trifles and sponges.

## Cider

Cider gives a strong rustic flavour to dishes and combines well with mustard. With West Country Casserole, for example, the apple flavour may be enhanced by the addition of a little apple juice or concentrate.

'Medium dry' rather than dry or sweet varieties is the best compromise.

## Beer

The additon of pale ale to sauces will produce a sharp slightly bitter flavour. More useful perhaps are the milk stouts or brown ales for rich, dark sauces where the high roast of the barley in the beer gives a delicious mellow flavour to the sauce. Very bitter beers, such as Guinness, are to be used with great care. More versatile are beers such as Newcastle Brown Ale or Mackeson whose higher sugar content tends to prevent them from dominating the flavour with bitterness.

## Brandy, Rum and Whisky

These alcohols are particularly good in sweets and are, of course, a traditional ingredient at Christmas time. They are less appropriate to sauce making in vegetarian cookery than they are to that of meat, because of the relative strength of their flavours.

Other important additions to sauces are dealt with in more detail in the chapter on stock and sauce making.

# Pickles and Sharpeners

As will have become apparent by now one of the recurring themes in this book is an emphasis on the need for contrasting flavours, textures and colours. These are the keys to any cookery, but especially for vegetarian cookery.

In order to counteract the sweetness of vegetables, oiliness of cheese and nuts and the savoury richness of your sauces, pickled vegetables are particularly good. In addition the sharpness of such vegetables, which is derived from the preservative vinegar, helps one digest oily food.

It is always useful to keep a stock of the following.

## Olives

Two basic varieties: black or green. The black olives have a strong flavour and tend to be more oily. They are very good added to hot pots with a tomato-based sauce or mustard-based baked dishes. In salads, their sumptuous black colour adds interest. Kalamata olives from Greece are perhaps the best, and it is from these that a member of our staff has made his own 'olive pâté' which is a delicious spread and sauce flavourer. His own brand, named **Chalice** Foods, is available in many health food shops.

Green olives have a sour taste and tend to be harder in texture. Sadly many imported green olives are unpleasant; hard, small and preserved in too much brine, they have earned themselves a bad reputation. If you can, buy the larger, plump tinned varieties as these are often superior.

## Gherkins and Pickled Cucumbers

These are available in a wide variety of forms and add a delicious piquancy to savouries and salads. The French style gherkins or 'cornichons' are very sharp and crisp—ideal for baked savouries.

The larger Polish type, preserved in vinegar and flavoured with herbs, are more mellow and thus better suited to salads.

Also useful are capers. Fiercly hot, they are the pickled flower buds of the bush **Caparis Spinosa** grown in Sicily. Use these in salads, sauces and in baked dishes.

Check the ingredient list of the label of all preserved foods—many have daunting additives.

41

# Chapter 3
# Salads, Dips and Dressings
## Salad Making

There are three main points to remember when making salads. The first is that the vegetables should be absolutely fresh and of the best quality. Damaged or slightly tired vegetables may be used in cooking but never in salads. This will ensure that colours are as lush as possible and textures interesting and varied. This is particularly important where herbs are concerned for when dried, herbs lose their flavour and are a poor substitute for the real thing.

The second point is that when cooking salad ingredients such as pulses, French beans, pasta or rice, care should be taken to avoid overcooking, otherwise the resulting salad will be mushy and nondescript.

Third, keep colour combinations in your salads simple, as salads look far more appetizing when they contain only three or four ingredients. Throwing in every vegetable in an attempt to improve the salad simply results in a disappointing mess. Remember, there are certain vegetables which just lend themselves to decoration—red peppers, radishes, carrots and parsley, for example. Fruit also adds a wonderful splash of colour and an interesting tang to the flavour.

Basic prerequisites are a small sharp knife, a hardwood chopping board and a pepper mill. A blender is a very great help and, indeed, is essential for certain dips. However, in the absence of such equipment a large jam jar with a lid is perfectly adequate for mixing all the dressings that follow.

When using nuts, it is a good idea to toast them before they are incorporated into the salad as this improves their flavour and gives them an attractive golden colour. A little tamari may be brushed over them before toasting to add to their flavour.

Avoid over-dressing a salad or it will become oily and limp looking. Don't be afraid of creating powerful and full-flavoured dressings; the effect of the vegetables is to dilute the flavour of the dressing. Also try to balance and contrast flavours. For example, pasta-based salads need bold dressings, fresh herbs and crunchy, strong-flavoured vegetables to contrast the relative blandness of the pasta. Bean salads benefit from spicy dressings and colourful vegetables.

## Light Salads

Such salads are made purely from the best fresh produce. Remember not to dress them until the last possible moment or the more delicate ingredients will go soggy.

Keep colour combinations simple; herbs should be fresh where possible.

You will find a wide variety of dressings here, ranging from the basic vinaigrette to the more exotic dill and yogurt or mint and cottage cheese dressings. Remember that when you use cottage cheese, yogurt, cream or Feta cheese your dressings will tend to mask the more vivid colours of the vegetables. You can get around this problem either by garnishing the salad with fresh herbs, such as parsley or chives, or by serving a colourful heavy salad alongside.

43

# Basic Vinaigrette

This is the basis to most salad dressings to which any herb or flavouring may be added.

1/2 teaspoon sea salt
1/2 teaspoon English mustard powder
1/4 teaspoon freshly ground black pepper
1-2 cloves garlic
1 tablespoon red wine vinegar
3 tablespoons sunflower oil

###### 1
Place all the dry ingredients in a jam jar.

###### 2
Crush the cloves of garlic and add.

###### 3
Add the vinegar and shake well until the mustard has dissolved.

###### 4
Add the oil, and again shake well.

Note:
The vinaigrette may be kept in the fridge in a screw-top jam jar for up to 2 weeks. Remember to shake the vinaigrette well before use in order to ensure that it is well emulsified. The quantity given above is the smallest amount you can make. For a salad to serve a large number of people, double up the quantities.

# Salad Chinois

Serves 4

3 medium heads of chicory
Juice of half a lemon
1 teaspoon molasses
1 teaspoon clear honey
1/4 teaspoon ground ginger
1 teaspoon sea salt
2 tablespoons oil
2 medium carrots (finely sliced)
4oz/125g bean shoots
3 spring onions (finely chopped)

###### 1
Cut the chicory lengthwise into halves. Remove the root and any bad leaves and slice finely.

###### 2
Whisk together the lemon juice, molasses, honey, ginger, salt and oil.

###### 3
Mix the vegetables together and just before serving toss the dressing through.

# Salad Noisette

### Serves 4

1/2 small white cabbage
1/2 cup hazelnuts
2 dessert apples
Juice of half a lemon
2 tablespoons oil
2 teaspoons clear honey
1 teaspoon sea salt
1 heaped tablespoon chopped parsley
1/2 cup plain yogurt

_____ 1 _____

Wash the cabbage and remove the heart and any blemished leaves then shred it finely.

_____ 2 _____

Toast the hazelnuts under the grill on a medium heat for 5 minutes.

_____ 3 _____

Wash the apples then quarter them. Remove the core then slice thinly across the width of the segments.

_____ 4 _____

Whisk together the lemon juice, oil, honey and salt. Combine all of the ingredients mixing well.

# Celery and Chicory Salad with Minty Cottage Cheese Dressing

### Serves 4

FOR THE SALAD:
12 sticks celery (sliced)
5 heads chicory (sliced on the diagonal)
1 head fennel (cored and finely chopped)
3 oranges (peeled and cut into segments)
Juice of half a lemon

FOR THE DRESSING:
1 tablespoon cottage cheese
1 tablespoon natural yogurt
2 tablespoons finely chopped mint
Sea salt and freshly ground pepper

_____ 1 _____

Combine the salad ingredients in a bowl and squeeze the lemon over them.

_____ 2 _____

To prepare the dressing, blend the cottage cheese and yogurt until smooth. Add the mint and salt and pepper to taste.

_____ 3 _____

Pour the dressing over the salad and toss gently. Serve chilled.

# Chicory and Pepper Salad With Lemon and Fresh Coriander

### Serves 6-8

This salad is very simple to make and is perfect for a hot summer day.

FOR THE SALAD:
6 heads chicory (finely chopped)
2 red peppers (finely chopped)
2 small green peppers (finely chopped)
8oz/250g cooked peas (fresh or frozen)
2 tablespoons chopped fresh coriander
Juice of a lemon

_____ 1 _____

Prepare the vegetables and mix together with the coriander.

_____ 2 _____

Squeeze the lemon over the salad and serve chilled.

# Red Cabbage and Watercress Salad

Serves 4

FOR THE SALAD:
1/4 medium red cabbage
1 bunch of watercress
Juice of 1 lemon
3 tablespoons oil

FOR THE DRESSING:
1 tablespoon honey
2oz/50g sesame seeds (lightly toasted)
1/2 teaspoon sea salt
Pinch of freshly ground pepper

———————— 1 ————————
Wash the cabbage and then remove the root and any limp or brown leaves. Shred finely.

———————— 2 ————————
Cut away the roots of the watercress, wash the leaves and then combine with the cabbage.

———————— 3 ————————
Whisk the lemon juice, honey, oil, salt and pepper to a smooth dressing.

———————— 4 ————————
Add the dressing and the sesame seeds to the cabbage and watercress. Toss the salad just before serving.

# Beansprout and Watercress Salad with Lemon and Walnut Oil Dressing

Serves 4

FOR THE SALAD:
1lb/500g beansprouts
3 bunches watercress (with the stalks removed)
3 oranges (peeled and cut into bite-sized pieces)
1/2 cup of walnuts and a little tamari

FOR THE DRESSING:
1/4 teaspoon sea salt
1/4 teaspoon freshly ground black pepper
1/2 teaspoon tamari
Juice of 1 lemon
2 tablespoons walnut oil

———————— 1 ————————
Preheat the oven to 400°F/200°C/Gas Mark 6. Place the walnuts on a baking tray and brush lightly with tamari. Roast in the oven until golden brown. When the walnuts are cool chop them roughly.

———————— 2 ————————
Mix the beansprouts, watercress, oranges and walnuts in a bowl.

———————— 3 ————————
Combine all the dressing ingredients together in a separate bowl.

———————— 4 ————————
Pour the dressing over the salad, toss gently and serve immediately.

46

# Chicory and Watercress Salad With Lemon and Olive Oil Dressing

Serves 4

FOR THE SALAD:
4 heads chicory (sliced on the diagonal)
Juice of 1 lemon
1/2 cup almonds and a little tamari
3 bunches watercress (with the stalks removed)
6 large oranges (peeled and cut into bite-sized pieces)
1 head fennel (cored and finely sliced)
—optional

FOR THE DRESSING:
2 tablespoons fresh coriander leaves (chopped)
1/2 teaspoon freshly ground black pepper
Juice of half an orange
2 tablespoons olive oil

——————— 1 ———————
Place the sliced chicory in a bowl and squeeze over the lemon juice to prevent the chicory browning.

——————— 2 ———————
Preheat the oven to 400°F/200°C/Gas Mark 6. Place the almonds on a baking tray and brush lightly with tamari. Roast in the oven, turning occasionally, for 10-15 minutes until golden brown. Leave to cool.

——————— 3 ———————
Mix all the salad ingredients together in a bowl.

——————— 4 ———————
To dress the salad simply sprinkle the coriander and pepper over the salad vegetables, add the orange juice and the olive oil and toss lightly. Serve chilled.

# Coleslaw with Lemon Yogurt Mayonnaise

Serves 6

FOR THE SALAD:
10 large carrots (grated)
1 large white cabbage (thinly sliced)
4 green apples (coarsely chopped)
3 sticks celery (coarsely chopped)
1 small onion (finely chopped)
1/2 cup walnuts (coarsely chopped)

FOR THE DRESSING:
1/4pt/150ml basic mayonnaise (see recipe on page 53)
2½fl oz/75ml soured cream
2½fl oz/75ml natural yogurt
1/2 tablespoon French grain mustard
Sea salt and black pepper to taste
Juice of half a lemon

——————— 1 ———————
Combine the salad vegetables in a bowl.

——————— 2 ———————
Blend the mayonnaise, sour cream and yogurt in a bowl.

——————— 3 ———————
Mix the mustard, salt and pepper with the lemon juice and add to the yogurt mixture, blending well.

——————— 4 ———————
Pour the dressing over the salad and toss well. Serve decorated with half walnuts.

# Grated Celeriac with Lemon and Sour Cream Dressing

Serves 4

FOR THE SALAD:
1 large head of celeriac (coarsely grated)
Juice of 1 lemon
1/4 cup sunflower seeds
1 small carton mustard and cress
1/2 small onion (finely chopped)
2 tablespoons chopped parsley

FOR THE DRESSING:
1/4pt/150ml natural yogurt
1/4pt/150ml soured cream
1/4 teaspoon sea salt
1/4 teaspoon freshly ground black pepper
1 teaspoon French grain mustard
Juice of half a lemon
2 cloves garlic (crushed)—optional

_____ 1 _____
Place the grated celeriac in a bowl and pour over the lemon juice. This prevents the celeriac from turning brown.

_____ 2 _____
Preheat the oven to 400°F/200°C/Gas Mark 6. Dust the sunflower seeds in a little salt and roast in the oven until a golden brown. Leave to cool. Cut the mustard and cress from its growing container leaving half an inch of stem beneath the leaves.

_____ 4 _____
Combine all the salad ingredients together in a bowl.

_____ 5 _____
To prepare the dressing, first blend the yogurt and soured cream together in a bowl until smooth. In a separate bowl mix the salt, pepper, mustard and lemon juice (and the crushed garlic if desired), then add to the yogurt and cream mixture and blend well.

_____ 6 _____
Pour the dressing over the salad and chill. Serve garnished with finely chopped parsley.

# Cucumber and White Cabbage Salad with Dill and Yogurt Dressing

Serves 8

FOR THE SALAD:
2 cucumbers (cubed)
1 large white cabbage (thinly sliced)
8oz/250g radishes (quartered)
12 gherkins (finely chopped)
6 capers
4 spring onions for garnish

FOR THE DRESSING:
1/2pt/300ml natural yogurt
Juice of half a lemon
1 tablespoon chopped dill
Sea salt and freshly ground pepper

_____ 1 _____
Prepare the salad vegetables and mix in a bowl.

_____ 2 _____
To make the dressing, combine the yogurt, lemon juice and dill adding salt and pepper to taste.

_____ 3 _____
Pour the dressing over the salad and serve garnished with finely chopped spring onions.

48

# Tomato and French Bean Salad with Tarragon Dressing

Serves 4

FOR THE SALAD:
1lb/500g French beans
2lb/1kg salad tomatoes (quartered)
2 shallots (finely chopped)
2 sprigs fresh tarragon (chopped)
1/4 cup black olives

FOR THE DRESSING:
1/4 teaspoon sea salt
1/4 teaspoon freshly ground black pepper
1 clove of garlic (crushed)
3oz/90g blue cheese
Juice of 1 lemon
2 tablespoons olive oil

―――――――― 1 ――――――――
Top and tail the beans, cook in lightly salted boiling water until tender. Do not overcook the beans as they will then lose their colour. Drain the beans and cool in cold water.

―――――――― 2 ――――――――
Place the salad vegetables and the olives in a bowl.

―――――――― 3 ――――――――
To prepare the dressing, mix the salt, pepper, garlic and crumbled cheese in a bowl with the lemon juice. Add the olive oil and mix thoroughly.

―――――――― 4 ――――――――
Pour the dressing over the salad and toss gently. Serve chilled.

# Greek Salad with Oregano and Olive Oil Dressing

Serves 6

FOR THE SALAD:
8-10 salad tomatoes (quartered)
1 cucumber (cubed)
1 small onion (finely chopped)
1/2 cup black olives
1 tablespoon parsley (finely chopped)
4oz/125g Feta cheese

FOR THE DRESSING:
1/2 teaspoon sea salt
1/2 teaspoon English mustard powder
1/2 teaspoon freshly ground black pepper
2 cloves garlic (crushed)
1 tablespoon wine vinegar
3 tablespoons olive oil
1 tablespoon chopped fresh oregano or
1/2 tablespoon dried oregano

―――――――― 1 ――――――――
Combine the tomatoes, cucumber, onion, olives and parsley in a salad bowl.

―――――――― 2 ――――――――
To prepare the dressing, briskly whisk or blend the remaining ingredients, except for the cheese.

―――――――― 3 ――――――――
Pour the dressing over the salad and toss well with wooden spoons. Then crumble the Feta cheese over the salad.

# Heavy Salads

These salads are thus termed because they contain a relatively high proportion of cooked vegetables, such as pulses or cereals, rice, bulghur or pasta. They are generally more sustaining than their lighter counterparts, but the two complement each other very well. When using pasta in the salad, ensure that the pasta is not over-cooked otherwise it will become gluey and dull to look at. Use a strong dressing with good olive oil, basil and perhaps olives for maximum effect. Such salads should look luscious and glossy.

Where rice is being used, be sure that it is not overcooked as it will become lumpy. The flavour of rice is improved by the use of spicy dressings or the addition of nuts.

Cracked wheat and wheat 'berries' also make excellent salad bases. The former produces a beautifully light 'heavy' salad whose creamy colour contrasts well with vivid greens and reds. Wheat berries are good with sprouted seeds of all sorts.

The golden rule is to always allow any cooked food to cool thoroughly before inclusion in any salad. Warm food will have the effect of cooking the fresh ingredients— the result? Quite horrible! In order to avoid this it is always possible to cook rice, pasta or beans in advance, making sure that they are covered and chilled if they are to be left overnight.

# Kidney Bean and Mushroom Salad with Spicy Tomato Dressing

Serves 6

FOR THE SALAD:
2 cups kidney beans (soaked overnight in cold water)
4oz/125g button mushrooms (quartered)
6 spring onions (finely sliced)
2 green peppers (finely chopped)
1/2 medium onion (finely chopped)
2 tablespoons chopped parsley

FOR THE DRESSING:
1 tablespoon tomato purée
Juice of 1 lemon
1 tablespoon fresh basil (finely chopped)
2 cloves of garlic (crushed)
1/4 teaspoon paprika
2 drops Tabasco
Sea salt and freshly ground pepper

———————— 1 ————————
Drain and rinse the beans. Cook in plenty of water until soft, but not mushy. Drain and rinse in cold water and leave to cool.

———————— 2 ————————
Prepare the vegetables and when the beans have cooled combine all the salad ingredients together.

———————— 3 ————————
To prepare the dressing, mix the tomato purée and lemon juice in a small bowl. Add the herbs and flavourings and mix well.

———————— 4 ————————
Add the dressing to the salad and combine thoroughly. Serve the salad garnished with chopped parsley.

# Potato and Chicory Salad with Garlic Vinaigrette

Serves 4-6

FOR THE SALAD:
2lb/1kg new potatoes
2 heads chicory (coarsely chopped)
2 shallots (finely chopped)
6 chives (finely chopped)

FOR THE VINAIGRETTE:
1/2 teaspoon sea salt
1/2 teaspoon English mustard powder
2 cloves of garlic (crushed)
1/2 teaspoon freshly ground black pepper
1 tablespoon wine vinegar
3 tablespoons sunflower oil

———————— 1 ————————
Boil the potatoes until cooked through testing with a sharp knife. Do not over-cook as this will result in a mushy salad. Drain and leave to cool.

———————— 2 ————————
When the potatoes are cool cut into bite-sized pieces and add the other prepared vegetables.

———————— 3 ————————
Whisk or blend the ingredients for the vinaigrette.

———————— 4 ————————
Pour the vinaigrette over the vegetables and mix well with a wooden spoon. Check the seasoning and add salt and pepper if necessary.

Note: When I make potato salad I leave the skins on for extra flavour and for the vitamins they contain. If you prefer, however, simply peel the potatoes before or after cooking.

# Chickpea and Rice Salad with Curried Mayonnaise

Serves 4-6

FOR THE SALAD:
2 cups chickpeas (soaked overnight in cold water)
2 cups brown rice
Dash of tamari
6 carrots (diced)
2 green peppers (sliced)
1/2 cup raisins
2-3 tablespoons chopped parsley
1 small handful chopped chives for garnish

FOR THE DRESSING:
1/4pt/150ml basic mayonnaise (see recipe on page 53)
Juice of half a lemon
1/4 teaspoon curry powder
1 clove of garlic (crushed)
Sea salt and freshly ground pepper

———————— 1 ————————
Drain and rinse the chickpeas. Cook in plenty of salted water until tender but not mushy. Drain and rinse in cold water and allow to cool.

———————— 2 ————————
Cook the rice in plenty of water with a dash of tamari to add extra flavour, until the rice is firm to the bite. Drain and rinse in cold water and leave to cool.

———————— 3 ————————
When the rice and chickpeas are cool, combine with the prepared vegetables, raisins and parsley.

———————— 4 ————————
To prepare the dressing, mix the mayonnaise with the lemon juice, curry powder, garlic and salt and pepper to taste.

———————— 5 ————————
Pour the dressing over the salad and mix well. Serve garnished with chopped chives.

# Rice Salad with Curried Peanut Butter Dressing

Serves 4

FOR THE SALAD:
3 cups Italian short-grain brown rice
Tamari
1/2 cup hazelnuts
1 red pepper (seeded and finely chopped)
1 green pepper (seeded and finely chopped)
6oz/150g button mushrooms (quartered)
4 spring onions (finely chopped)
2 tablespoons parsley (finely chopped)
Finely chopped chives for garnish

FOR THE DRESSING:
2 tablespoons crunchy peanut butter
1 tablespoon natural yogurt
1/2 teaspoon sea salt or tamari
1/2 teaspoon freshly ground black pepper
1/2 teaspoon curry powder

———————— 1 ————————
Boil the rice in plenty of cold water to which has been added a dash of tamari. Do not over cook the rice—it should be firm to the bite. Drain and allow to cool thoroughly.

———————— 2 ————————
Pre-heat the oven to 400°F/200°C/Gas Mark 6. Place the hazelnuts on a baking tray and brush them lightly with tamari. Toast the nuts in the oven for 10 minutes, turning occasionally. Allow to cool.

———————— 3 ————————
Wash and prepare the vegetables.

## 4

When the rice and hazelnuts have cooled combine with the vegetables.

## 5

To prepare the dressing, place the peanut butter and yogurt in a mixing bowl and whisk with a fork until smooth.

## 6

Add the salt, pepper and curry powder to the mixture and whisk for a few more seconds.

## 7

Pour dressing over the salad and toss well with wooden spoons. Garnish with chopped chives and serve.

# Potato Salad with Garlic Mayonnaise

Serves 4-6

FOR THE SALAD:
2lb/1kg new potatoes
4 sticks celery (finely chopped)
1/2 medium onion (thinly sliced)
1 dessertspoon chopped parsley
4 spring onions for garnish (finely chopped)

FOR THE MAYONNAISE:
(Makes approx. 1pt or 600ml)
2 egg yolks
1/2 teaspoon sea salt
1/2 teaspoon freshly ground black pepper
1 tablespoon French grain mustard
1/4pt/150ml white wine vinegar
4 cloves garlic (crushed)—optional
Approx. 3/4pt/450ml sunflower oil
2 tablespoons natural yogurt

## 1

Boil the potatoes until cooked through, testing with a sharp knife. Do not over cook as this will result in a mushy salad. Drain and set aside to cool.

## 2

Prepare the other vegetables and cut the potatoes into bite-sized pieces, combining them all together in a large bowl.

## 3

To prepare the garlic mayonnaise, separate the egg yolks from the whites. If using a blender the yolks can be dropped straight into the blender bowl; if whisking by hand drop the yolks into a large mixing bowl.

## 4

Add the salt, pepper, mustard and vinegar and blend or whisk until the ingredients are well mixed. The garlic may also be added at this point, if desired.

## 5

If using a blender whisk on a slow speed pouring in the oil very slowly at first and then increasing the rate as the mayonnaise becomes smooth and creamy. If using a hand whisk use a similar technique adding the oil little by little in very small amounts initially and whisking vigorously to ensure the emulsification of oil and vinegar. The mayonnaise should become creamy and smooth.

## 6

Blend in the yogurt and whisk for a few more seconds.

## 7

Pour the mayonnaise over the salad vegetables and serve garnished with finely chopped spring onions.

Note: Should the mayonnaise curdle, a fresh yolk can be used placed in a separate mixing bowl. Add the curdled mayonnaise to the yolk incorporating it gradually, whisking all the time.

# Beetroot and Red Cabbage Salad with French Grain Mustard Dressing

Serves 8

FOR THE SALAD:
8 small beetroots (cooked and cut into
bite-sized pieces)
1 large red cabbage (finely sliced)
8oz/250g radishes (chopped into cubes)
2 tablespoons parsley (finely chopped)
6 spring onions (finely chopped)

FOR THE DRESSING:
1/4 teaspoon sea salt
1/2 teaspoon freshly ground black pepper
1 tablespoon finely chopped coriander
1 tablespoon French grain mustard
Juice of half a lemon
2 tablespoons red wine vinegar
2 tablespoons sunflower oil

----------- 1 -----------
Place all the prepared salad vegetables
together in a bowl.

----------- 2 -----------
To prepare the dressing, combine the dry
ingredients and the mustard and then add
the lemon juice and the vinegar and mix
thoroughly. Then add the oil, again mixing
well.

----------- 3 -----------
Pour the dressing over the salad vegetables
and toss well. Serve chilled and garnished
with chopped parsley.

Note: If you find the dressing a little too
sharp you can add a few drops of clear honey
or more oil.

# Butterbeans Cooked in Turmeric with Basil and Garlic Dressing

Serves 6-8

FOR THE SALAD:
4 cups butter beans (soaked overnight in
cold water)
1 teaspoon turmeric
4oz/125g peas (fresh or frozen)
10 spring onions (finely chopped)
2 red peppers (finely chopped)
1 green pepper (finely chopped)
2 tablespoons chopped parsley
1 tablespoon chopped basil

FOR THE DRESSING:
1/2 teaspoon sea salt
1/2 teaspoon freshly ground black pepper
1/2 teaspoon English mustard powder
2 cloves of garlic (crushed)
2 drops Tabasco
1 pinch chilli powder
1 tablespoon white wine vinegar
3 tablespoons olive oil

----------- 1 -----------
Drain and rinse the butterbeans thoroughly and cook in plenty of salted water
until tender but not mushy, adding the
turmeric just before they are ready. Drain
and rinse the beans in cold water and leave
to cool.

----------- 2 -----------
Lightly cook the peas in boiling water, drain
and leave to cool.

----------- 3 -----------
When the beans and peas are cold combine
with the prepared vegetables and herbs in a
bowl.

## 4

To prepare the dressing, combine the dry ingredients, the garlic, the Tabasco and the vinegar together in a bowl. Mix thoroughly and then add the oil, again mixing well.

## 5

Pour the dressing over the salad and toss well. Leave the salad to stand for half an hour before serving to allow the beans to soak up the flavour of the dressing.

# Cracked Wheat, Tomato and Walnut Salad

Serves 4

4oz/125g cracked wheat
6 fl oz/175ml boiling water
3 medium tomatoes
1 small bunch parsley (finely chopped)
3oz/90g broken walnuts
2 tablespoons olive oil
1 tablespoon malt vinegar
2 teaspoons sea salt
Pinch of freshly ground pepper

## 1

Pour the boiling water over the cracked wheat and stir well until all of the water has been absorbed. Cover with a lid or tin foil and leave to cool.

## 2

Meanwhile cut the tomatoes into quarters and with a knife remove the seeds and inner flesh and discard them.

## 3

Whisk the olive oil, vinegar, salt and pepper together to make a smooth dressing.

## 4

When the wheat is cool, combine all the ingredients mixing well.

# Butterbean and Sweetcorn Salad

Serves 4

1 cup butter beans (soaked overnight)
1 green pepper (diced)
1 small onion (diced)
8oz/250g sweetcorn (tinned, without juice)
1 dessertspoon vinegar
1 teaspoon Dijon mustard
1 dessertspoon paprika
1 dessertspoon tamari
Pinch of sea salt and freshly ground pepper
2 tablespoons oil
1 dessertspoon chives (finely chopped)

## 1

Drain the beans, rinse and cover with water, bring to the boil and simmer for 1 hour or until tender. Drain and rinse well.

## 2

Combine the beans, pepper, onion and sweetcorn. Whisk together the vinegar, mustard, paprika, tamari, salt, pepper and oil to make a smooth dressing and toss this through the salad. Serve garnished with the chives.

# Pasta Salad with Basil and Parmesan Dressing

Serves 4

FOR THE SALAD:
3 cups uncooked spiral green pasta
1 red pepper (finely chopped)
1 green pepper (finely chopped)
1/2 cup stuffed green olives
3 spring onions (finely chopped)
2 tablespoons parsley (finely chopped)

FOR THE DRESSING:
1/4 teaspoon sea salt
1/2 teaspoon freshly ground black pepper
2 cloves of garlic (crushed)
1/2 tablespoon Parmesan cheese (grated)
1 tablespoon finely chopped fresh basil leaves
Juice of a lemon
3 tablespoons olive oil

### 1
Cook the pasta in plenty of lightly salted boiling water to which also has been added a little olive oil. Drain and refresh in plenty of cold water.

### 2
Combine the prepared vegetables with the cold pasta.

### 3
To prepare the dressing, place the cheese, salt, pepper, garlic and basil in a bowl and squeeze the lemon over.

### 4
Add the olive oil and mix until smooth.

### 5
Combine with the pasta and toss with a wooden spoon.

56

# Dips

Here are a few ideas for some dips which are ideal for parties or which can be served as an hors d'oeuvre. Strips of celery, carrot and cucumber or florets of cauliflower act as excellent 'dippers', as do crisps, twiglets or corn chips, and add an attractive splash of colour.

If using a blender, take care not to overblend as this will result in the dip becoming too runny. The dip should be a thick, creamy consistency. If you are not using a blender ensure that the ingredients are chopped as finely as possible.

All these dips can be kept, covered, in a refrigerator for 2 days.

## Hummus

2 cups chickpeas (soaked overnight in cold water)
1/2pt/300ml stock reserved from cooking the chickpeas
1 tablespoon tahini
Juice of half a lemon
1 tablespoon olive oil
1/2 teaspoon sea salt
1/2 teaspoon freshly ground black pepper
2 cloves garlic (crushed)
1/2 teaspoon ground cumin
3 black olives, a pinch of paprika and 2 sprigs of parsley for garnish

_____ 1 _____
Drain the chickpeas and cook them in lightly salted water until very soft. When cooked, drain and reserve 1/2pt/300ml of the stock.

_____ 2 _____
Purée the chickpeas with the stock using either a blender or a potato masher or a fork. (This is the only time a blender should be used; the rest of the ingredients should be blended by hand.)

_____ 3 _____
Blend in the tahini, lemon juice, olive oil, garlic, salt and pepper and cumin. Mix well.

_____ 4 _____
Serve chilled with a sprinkling of paprika, halved and stoned black olives and the sprigs of parsley.

## Minty Cottage Cheese and Yogurt Dip

3 tablespoons cottage cheese
1 tablespoon natural yogurt
2 sprigs of fresh mint and a few leaves for garnish
1 clove garlic (crushed)
Small handful chopped chives
Juice of half a lemon
Sea salt and freshly ground black pepper to taste

_____ 1 _____
Blend together the cottage cheese and the yogurt.

_____ 2 _____
Add the very finely chopped mint, the garlic, chives, lemon juice and salt and pepper and blend well.

_____ 3 _____
Serve chilled, garnished with mint leaves.

# Blue Cheese Dip

8oz/250g Roquefort cheese
4oz/125g cottage cheese
1/4pt/150ml natural yogurt
Bunch of chives (finely chopped)
1 clove of garlic (finely chopped)
—optional
Squeeze of lemon
Sea salt and freshly ground black pepper
to taste

———————— 1 ————————
Mash the blue cheese in a mixing bowl.

———————— 2 ————————
Sieve the cottage cheese into the bowl, add the yogurt and mix together until well blended.

———————— 3 ————————
Add the chives, garlic, lemon juice and salt and pepper to the dip and mix in.

———————— 4 ————————
Serve garnished with a sprinkle of chives.

# Piquant Party Dip

8oz/250g cottage cheese
1/2pt/300ml natural yogurt
1 small onion (finely chopped)
1 tablespoon chopped gherkin
1 tablespoon chopped celery
4 spring onions
1 tablespoon chopped parsley
1 tablespoon French grain mustard
Juice of half a lemon
1/2 teaspoon ground paprika
Sea salt and freshly ground black pepper
Pinch of paprika for garnish

———————— 1 ————————
Place the cottage cheese and yogurt in a mixing bowl.

———————— 2 ————————
Chop the spring onions very finely.

———————— 3 ————————
Add the vegetables to the cottage cheese and yogurt with the mustard, lemon juice, paprika, salt and pepper and mix thoroughly.

———————— 4 ————————
Serve chilled garnished with a sprinkle of paprika.

# Rich Avocado Cream Dip

4 very ripe avocado pears
1 clove garlic (crushed)
Squeeze of lemon
Sea salt and freshly ground pepper to taste
3 spring onions (very finely chopped)
2 tablespoons sour cream
2 tablespoons natural yogurt
Chopped chives for garnish

———————— 1 ————————
Halve and stone the avocados, scoop out the flesh into a mixing bowl. Mash the avocado with the garlic, lemon juice and salt and pepper. Add the finely chopped spring onions.

———————— 2 ————————
Blend the sour cream and yogurt in a separate bowl until smooth.

———————— 3 ————————
Gradually add the yoghurt mixture to the avocado stirring all the time until the dip is thoroughly blended.

———————— 4 ————————
Serve chilled and garnished with chopped chives.

# Spicy Chilli Dip

4 ripe tomatoes
1 dessertspoon oil for cooking
1 sprig of thyme
1 tablespoon tomato purée
1/4 cup warm water
Dash of Tabasco
Dash of tamari
Sea salt and freshly ground black pepper
to taste
2 cloves garlic (crushed)
1 red pepper
4 spring onions
2 chillies
1 sprig parsley
1 dessertspoon chopped coriander leaves
Chopped parsley for garnish

———————— 1 ————————
Skin the tomatoes by placing them in a bowl and pouring enough boiling water over them to cover. Leave for a moment only, then plunge into cold water; the skin should then be easy to remove. Chop the skinned tomatoes thoroughly.

———————— 2 ————————
Heat the oil in a saucepan and cook the tomatoes with the thyme until very soft. Add the tomato purée and the water.

———————— 3 ————————
Mince or grate the other vegetables finely and stir into the tomatoes.

———————— 4 ————————
Remove the sprig of thyme and add the Tabasco, Worcester sauce, salt and pepper to taste.

———————— 5 ————————
Serve chilled and garnished with chopped parsley.

Note: This is an excellent accompaniment to Mexican corn chips.

# Curried Walnut Mayonnaise

1/2pt/300ml basic mayonnaise
(see page 53)
Juice of half a lemon
1/2 teaspoon curry powder
1/2 small onion (finely chopped)
6oz/150g shelled walnuts (finely
chopped)
Sea salt and freshly ground black pepper
to taste
Chopped parsley for garnish

———————— 1 ————————
Place the mayonnaise in a mixing bowl, add the lemon juice and the curry powder and stir in well.

———————— 2 ————————
Add the onion and walnuts and blend well. Season to taste.

———————— 3 ————————
Chill and serve garnished with a pinch of curry powder and roughly chopped parsley.

# Chapter 4
# Soups

Our soups are very popular at Food For Thought, which is why we have included quite a wide range here. They are relatively quick to prepare and, eaten in conjunction with some wholewheat bread, form the ideal light lunch.

The emphasis is, as usual, on the use of quality ingredients: the use of fresh herbs, a little wine or some interesting spices will enliven the flavour of the end result enormously.

Basic also to successful soup making is the use of good stock. With this in mind it is always useful to reserve cooking liquor from certain beans, or juice from cooked mushrooms and other vegetables. The exception to this general rule is with 'brassica' cooking water, which tends to become over powerful unless used immediately.

# Stock Making for Soups and Sauces

## Basic Stock

1 teaspoon black peppercorns
1 bay leaf
1 small onion (roughly chopped)
1 celery end or 1 stick of celery (roughly chopped)
4-5 carrot tops or 1 carrot (roughly chopped)
1 1/2pts/900ml cold water

### 1

Place all the ingredients in a saucepan or pressure cooker, bring to the boil and simmer for up to one hour. (It is far preferable to use a pressure cooker for this in which case you need cook the stock at pressure for 20 minutes only. Even if you cannot spare this length of time, a few minutes cooking will produce a stock of acceptable flavour.)

### 2

When the stock has cooked for long enough, strain and set aside ready for use.

If you have time and space stocks are well worth making a little effort for. When a dish needs liquid adding to it in the process of cooking, water alone will always dilute any flavour you may have built. Stock has a more neutral effect and therefore will help the dish to develop a flavour. It is worth noting that when you add stock to a dish, the stock should be warm, otherwise the time spent cooking will be greatly lengthened.

The stock pot should be one of the first things to go on the stove when you start preparing food; at least put the water on with the bay leaf and pepper, adding the other vegetables as they are being prepared for your dishes.

In addition to the basic recipe above, you can add any suitable washed trimmings from the vegetables you are using: leek ends, parsley stalks and parsnip tops are particularly suitable.

The liquid left from cooking certain pulses can also be used as stock, particularly from light-coloured beans such as chickpeas, butter beans and haricots. Lentils, too, will give a good, strong-flavoured stock.

However, the stock from darker beans is usually too strong and bitter. In fact, kidney beans and aduki beans should be well rinsed when they are cooked to get rid of any residual bitterness there may be from the liquid in which they were cooked.

If using milk in a sauce it can be brought to the boil with the basic stock ingredients in place of the water. Remove from the heat when it has boiled and let it stand for 20 minutes or so before straining it off.

# Garnishing Soups

The use of an appropriate garnish on soups (and all dishes for that matter) will improve its final appearance and flavour. Fresh herbs, grated cheese or a swirl of cream help to make the final result attractive and offset the singular colour of blended soups in particular.

Use bright, contrasting colours for your garnish: parsley is especially popular because of its vivid green and versatile flavour. Spring onions and chives are also useful, particularly with light, creamy soups such as potato where their slight oniony sharpness prevents the dish from being bland.

Fresh basil is a marvellous accompaniment with tomato-based soups, especially minestrone. Effective use of fresh herbs on green soups, such as spinach or watercress, can be made by first adding a swirl of cream and then sprinkling the herbs over this.

Cheese works well as a final seasoning and garnish. A little grated Cheddar stirred in just before serving will give a thin tasting soup body and flavour. Use it in milky or creamy soups to get a chowder-like effect. Grated Parmesan looks good sprinkled over the top of brown soups and endows all tomato soups with an authentic Italian flavour. Be careful not to over use or the dish will become bitter and unpleasant-smelling.

Fresh or sour cream may be either stirred in or spooned on top of the soup. Sour cream has a distinctive and sharp flavour, enhancing the dish. Ordinary cream tends to moderate and enrich the flavour and smooth out the texture.

A light dusting of ground spices over the cream is an ideal finishing touch. Use paprika, cayenne, nutmeg or freshly milled pepper for the best effect.

Another excellent garnish for most soups is the addition of croûtons. These only take a little time to prepare and are delicious made with wholewheat bread. Cut a few thick slices of stale bread into neat cubes, toss them in about a dessert-spoonful of melted butter and season generously with salt and pepper and dried herbs such as oregano, basil and marjoram. Toast them lightly in a moderate oven for 10 minutes and serve alongside or in the soup.

# Light Soups

The following soups are intended as light starters. They should stimulate the appetite for the main course without filling the stomach too much. Suitable for all times of the year or day, these soups are delicately seasoned and are often clear and un-blended. This allows the shape and colour of the vegetables to come through.

# Carrot and Cashew Soup

1/2 cup broken cashews (raw)
1 teaspoon tamari
1 medium onion (chopped)
2 stalks celery (chopped)
1lb/500g carrots (grated)
1 1/2 pints/900ml vegetable stock or hot water
1 teaspoon ground coriander
1/2 teaspoon whole cumin
Sea salt and freshly ground pepper
Finely chopped spring onions for garnish

—————————— 1 ——————————
Splash a little oil in a small tray and roast the cashews in a moderate oven for 10-15 minutes until lightly browned. While hot sprinkle over the tamari.

—————————— 2 ——————————
Meanwhile fry the onion with a little oil in a large saucepan until well browned then add the celery and carrot and continue frying until very soft.

—————————— 3 ——————————
Add the stock and simmer for about 20 minutes.

—————————— 4 ——————————
Stir in the cashews and seasonings then purée in a blender.

—————————— 5 ——————————
Reheat, check for seasoning and consistency and serve garnished with spring onions.

# Cream of Spinach Soup

1 medium onion (chopped)
2 cloves garlic (crushed)
1 medium carrot (grated)
2 sticks celery (chopped)
1 1/2 pints/900ml vegetable stock
8oz/250g spinach (well washed)
Sea salt and freshly ground pepper
1 tablespoon parsley (finely chopped)
1/2 pint/300ml single cream
Pinch of nutmeg

—————————— 1 ——————————
Fry the onion and garlic in a little oil until soft.

—————————— 2 ——————————
Add the carrot and celery and continue frying until very soft.

—————————— 3 ——————————
Add the stock and bring to the boil.

—————————— 4 ——————————
Add the spinach, pushing it down into the liquid with a spoon and boil until it has completely reduced (3-4 minutes).

—————————— 5 ——————————
Blend the mixture well, add a little salt and pepper and taste for seasoning.

—————————— 6 ——————————
Return to heat and bring to the boil.

—————————— 7 ——————————
Just before serving stir in the parsley.

—————————— 8 ——————————
Ladle into bowls then finish with a swirl of cream and a dusting of nutmeg.

# Carrot and Almond Soup

1oz/25g butter or margarine
1 clove garlic (crushed)
4oz/125g onion (chopped)
8oz/250g carrots (grated)
2 sticks celery (chopped)
1 teaspoon thyme
1 teaspoon cumin
1 teaspoon tomato purée
1oz/25g flour
2pts/1200ml vegetable stock
1 tablespoon tamari
3oz/90g ground almonds
Sea salt and freshly ground pepper
1 tablespoon fresh chopped parsley

―――――――――― 1 ――――――――――
Melt the butter or margarine in a heavy bottomed saucepan and fry the garlic and onion in it until soft (7-10 minutes).

―――――――――― 2 ――――――――――
Add the carrot, celery, thyme and cumin to the pan and cook for a further 5 minutes.

―――――――――― 3 ――――――――――
Stir in the tomato purée and sprinkle over the flour and cook, stirring for a further 5 minutes.

―――――――――― 4 ――――――――――
Add the stock, tamari and almonds, bring to the boil and simmer for 20 minutes.

―――――――――― 5 ――――――――――
Add a pinch of salt and pepper and the parsley and blend in a food processor until smooth. Taste for seasoning and serve.

# Miso and Nori Soup

1 dessertspoon oil
1 clove garlic (crushed)
1 medium onion (finely sliced)
1/2 teaspoon ground coriander
1/2 teaspoon ground ginger
1 dessertspoon tomato purée
1 tablespoon brown miso
1 medium carrot (cut into strips)
2 sheets nori seaweed
2pts/1200ml vegetable stock
1 dessertspoon chopped chives

―――――――――― 1 ――――――――――
Heat the oil in a heavy bottomed saucepan and fry the garlic and onion until soft (7-10 minutes).

―――――――――― 2 ――――――――――
Add the spices, tomato purée and miso and mix well, then add the carrots.

―――――――――― 3 ――――――――――
Lightly toast the nori. Either wave the sheets through a gas flame 3 or 4 times or place them under a medium grill for 1 minute. Tear the nori into small pieces and add it to the pot with the stock and the chives.

―――――――――― 4 ――――――――――
Bring the soup to the boil and simmer for 10 minutes. Taste for seasoning, it may want a little black pepper.

# Tomato Soup

2oz/50g butter or margarine
1 clove garlic (crushed)
Pinch of thyme
1 bay leaf
4oz/125g onion (sliced)
4oz/125g leeks (white part only, finely sliced)
2oz/50g celery (finely chopped)
2oz/50g flour
2oz/50g tomato purée
2pts/1 litre stock
15oz/1 x 420g tin of tomatoes (roughly chopped)
Sea salt and freshly ground pepper
Chopped parsley for garnish

———————— 1 ————————

Melt the butter or margarine in a heavy saucepan.

———————— 2 ————————

Add the garlic, thyme, bay leaf, onions, leeks and celery and fry until lightly browned.

———————— 3 ————————

Sprinkle over the flour and cook, stirring for 5 minutes. Add the tomato purée and cook for 2 minutes.

———————— 4 ————————

Gradually whisk in the stock and add the tomatoes. Bring to the boil, stirring frequently and simmer for up to 1 hour. Season with a pinch of salt and pepper.

———————— 5 ————————

Blend the soup thoroughly (this is optional) and return to a clean pan. Taste for seasoning and adjust if necessary. Bring to the boil and serve garnished with a little parsley.

# Vegetable Vermicelli Soup

Oil for frying
2 or 3 carrots (finely diced)
4oz/125g mushrooms (finely sliced)
2oz/50g leeks (finely sliced)
1oz/25g celery (finely chopped)
Pinch of each of thyme and sage
1/2 teaspoon basil
2pts/1 litre vegetable stock
1 teaspoon yeast extract
1 dessertspoon tamari
1oz/25g vermicelli
Sea salt and freshly ground pepper

———————— 1 ————————

In a large saucepan heat a little oil, add the vegetables and lightly fry them for 5 minutes.

———————— 2 ————————

Sprinkle over the herbs, pour in the stock and stir in the yeast extract and tamari. Bring to the boil and simmer for 30 minutes.

———————— 3 ————————

Break the vermicelli into the soup and continue simmering until it is soft (10-15 minutes). Add a pinch of salt and pepper, taste for seasoning and serve.

# Siriporn's Lemony Soup

1 small onion (finely chopped)
2 tablespoons oil
2 sticks celery (finely chopped)
1 tablespoon toasted almonds (finely chopped)
1 dessertspoon sultanas (soaked in a little water for at least 1 hour)
1/3 cup cooked brown rice
1 1/2 pts/900ml vegetable stock
1 teaspoon grated lemon rind
2 egg yolks (well beaten)
Up to 1 teaspoon lemon juice (to taste)
Sea salt and freshly ground pepper
Sugar to taste (optional)
2 tablespoons spring onions or parsley (finely chopped)

—————————— 1 ——————————

Heat the oil in a heavy saucepan and cook the onion until soft. Add the celery, almonds, drained sultanas and rice and cook, stirring for 4 minutes.

—————————— 2 ——————————

Add the stock, bring to the boil and simmer until all the ingredients are quite soft.

—————————— 3 ——————————

Stir in the lemon rind, remove from the heat and allow to cool for 1 minute. Slowly add the beaten egg yolks, stirring briskly with a whisk all the time to prevent the eggs becoming lumpy.

—————————— 4 ——————————

Season with lemon juice, salt, pepper and a very little sugar (optional). Garnish with spring onions or parsley and serve very hot.

# Fresh Pea Soup

1lb/500g shelled fresh peas (or frozen, if peas are not in season)
1 small onion (finely chopped)
1pt/600ml potato stock
1pt/600ml milk
Sea salt and freshly ground pepper
1/4pt/150ml single cream

—————————— 1 ——————————

Cook the peas and onion in the stock. When the peas are well cooked, remove from the heat and blend with the stock.

—————————— 2 ——————————

Return to the heat, add the milk and bring to the boil. Season well with salt and pepper.

—————————— 3 ——————————

Serve very hot and stir in a tablespoon of single cream into each helping.

# Spring Vegetable Soup

(An alternative to Vegetable Vermicelli)

1 clove garlic (crushed)
2 tablespoons oil
1 small onion (finely chopped)
2 medium carrots (finely chopped)
1 cup fresh or frozen peas or any kind of
fresh beans, cut into pieces
3 or 4 leaves spring greens (cut in half
lengthwise and then chopped)
5 or 6 mushrooms (finely sliced)
1½pts/900ml vegetable stock or water
Handful of broken spaghetti or
vermicelli
Soy sauce, sea salt and freshly ground
pepper to taste

### 1

Heat the oil in a heavy saucepan and fry the onion and garlic gently until soft. Add the rest of the vegetables and cook, stirring, for a few more minutes.

### 2

Add the stock and bring to the boil, then throw in the pasta. Stir well, cover and bring back to the boil. Continue cooking until the vegetables and pasta are tender.

### 3

Season with salt, pepper and soy sauce and remove from the heat. If a thicker soup is preferred, the soup may be thickened by stirring in 1 tablespoon of cornflour mixed with a little cold water and bringing the soup back to the boil.

# Summer Coolers

The common distrust of cold soups should not put you off these two recipes. Served well chilled with fresh herbs, they are ideal for a light meal on those long, hot summer days that we don't get anymore!

# Gazpacho

## (Chilled Spanish Tomato Soup)

2 cloves garlic (peeled)
1 small onion (chopped)
2 tablespoons oil
1 tablespoon vinegar
9 fl oz/250ml tomato juice
1 green pepper (seeded and sliced)
1lb/500g tomatoes (roughly sliced)
1/2 cucumber (finely sliced—and save some for garnish)
2 eggs (well beaten)
1 1/2 tablespoons lemon juice
Pinch of cayenne
Pinch of paprika
1/2 teaspoon dill
1/2 teaspoon tarragon
Sea salt to taste
1 teaspoon raw cane sugar
2 1/2 cups fresh breadcrumbs (lightly fried in a little oil)
2 tablespoons mayonnaise (see page 53)
A few sprigs of watercress or finely chopped parsley for garnish

―――――― 1 ――――――
Liquidize the garlic and onion with the oil and the vinegar. Make sure that they are well puréed, and then add the tomato juice and the prepared vegetables, including the cucumbers.

―――――― 2 ――――――
Blend quickly so that the vegetables do not become over-puréed.

―――――― 3 ――――――
Add the beaten eggs, turn the mixture into a saucepan and heat slowly, but do not boil. Stir with a whisk from time to time while heating.

―――――― 4 ――――――
Remove from the heat, season with lemon juice, cayenne, paprika, dill, tarragon, salt and sugar. Add the breadcrumbs and mayonnaise and mix well.

―――――― 5 ――――――
Chill before serving garnished with finely sliced cucumber and watercress or parsley.

# Chilled Cucumber and Yogurt Soup

2pts/1200ml plain yogurt
1 teaspoon runny honey
2oz/50g onion (finely chopped)
Pinch of sea salt and freshly ground pepper
1 teaspoon fresh parsley (finely chopped)
1 teaspoon fresh mint (freshly chopped), plus a little extra for garnish
1 medium cucumber (finely diced)

―――――― 1 ――――――
Blend all the ingredients together, except the cucumber, and taste for seasoning.

―――――― 2 ――――――
Stir in the cucumber and chill in the refrigerator. Serve garnished with a sprig of fresh mint.

# Spicy Soups

Here are some recipes for spicy soups for those with jaded palates!

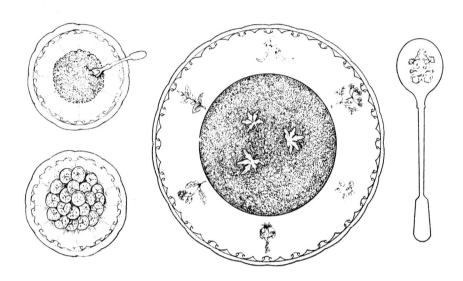

## Spicy Hot Gazpacho Soup

2 tablespoons olive oil
2 medium onions (finely chopped)
2 cloves garlic (crushed)
1-2 fresh chillies (finely chopped)
1/4 teaspoon paprika
2 medium carrots (grated)
1 stick celery (finely chopped)
1 teaspoon cumin
1 teaspoon coriander
1lb/500g fresh or tinned tomatoes
(blended)
1 small red pepper (finely chopped)
1 small green pepper (finely chopped)
3/4pt/450ml vegetable stock
Sea salt and freshly ground pepper
2 tablespoons fresh coriander
2 tablespoons fresh parsley
Lemon juice (to taste)

_____ 1 _____
Heat the oil in a large saucepan and sauté the onion, garlic and chillies very gently until soft.

_____ 2 _____
Add the paprika, carrots, celery, cumin, coriander, tomatoes and peppers. Barely cover with stock and simmer for 45 minutes.

_____ 3 _____
Blend the soup with the fresh coriander, parsley and lemon juice and enough stock to form a thickish, smooth soup. Leave a little of the fresh herbs for garnish.

_____ 4 _____
Re-heat the soup and check the seasoning. Garnish with a swirl of sour cream and the remaining coriander and parsley.

# Courgette and Coriander Soup

1 medium onion (chopped)
1 clove garlic (crushed)
2 medium carrots (grated)
4 medium courgettes (grated)
1½pts/900ml vegetable stock
½ teaspoon whole cumin seeds
2 teaspoons ground coriander
½ teaspoon garam masala
Dash of tamari
Sea salt and freshly ground pepper
Chopped chives or spring onions for garnish

_____ 1 _____

Fry the onion and garlic in a little oil until soft.

_____ 2 _____

Add the carrots and courgettes and continue frying until very soft.

_____ 3 _____

Add the stock, bring to the boil and simmer for 10 minutes.

_____ 4 _____

Add the cumin, coriander, garam masala, tamari and a pinch of salt and pepper and blend the mixture.

_____ 5 _____

Return to heat, taste for seasoning, check consistency and serve garnished with chives or spring onions.

# Curry Soup

1 small onion (finely chopped)
2 tablespoons oil
1 stick celery (finely chopped)
1 small carrot (diced)
1/4 cauliflower (broken into florets)
1/3 cup cooked aduki beans
1/4 cup cooked brown rice
1 tablespoon blackcurrant jam
2 bay leaves
1-2 tablespoons mild curry powder
2pts/1200ml vegetable stock
Sea salt and lemon juice, to taste
Sugar to taste
Chopped parsley for garnish

_____ 1 _____

Sauté the onion in the oil. When soft add the rest of the prepared vegetables, cooked beans, rice, the blackcurrant jam and bay leaves.

_____ 2 _____

Stir for a couple of minutes over a medium heat, then add the curry powder. Stir well and cook for a further minute.

_____ 3 _____

Add the stock, bring to the boil and simmer until the vegetables are well done.

_____ 4 _____

Season with salt, lemon juice and sugar. Serve very hot garnished with chopped parsley.

Note: If you prefer a richer curry soup, use only enough stock to cook the vegetables—1pt/600ml—and make the rest of the quantity up with milk.

# Mulligatawny

2 tablespoons oil
2 onions (chopped)
1 large clove garlic (crushed)
2 large cooking apples (peeled, cored and sliced)
1 small turnip (cubed)
2 carrots (diced)
1 tablespoon curry powder
1pt/600ml vegetable stock
Juice of half a lemon
1 teaspoon thyme
Sea salt and freshly ground pepper to taste
1 teaspoon raw cane sugar (optional)
1 tablespoon chopped parsley

_____ 1 _____

Heat the oil in a large saucepan and sauté the onion and garlic until soft. Add the rest of the prepared vegetables and fruit and continue cooking for a few minutes.

_____ 2 _____

Add the curry powder and enough stock to just cover the vegetables. Stir well, bring to the boil and simmer until all the ingredients are tender.

_____ 3 _____

Blend the soup and adjust the seasoning. Add the thyme and the lemon juice. Reheat and if you find it too sharp add a teaspoon of sugar.

_____ 4 _____

Sprinkle with fresh, chopped parsley.

Note: If you like a richer, thicker soup the quality of stock may be reduced. Sliced banana makes an excellent accompaniment to this spicy soup.

# Winter Warmers

The following soups are homely and substantial; ideal for thawing out during the winter months, they rely mainly on vegetables of that season.

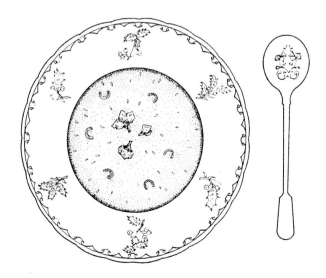

# Potato and Chive Soup

1 medium onion (chopped)
1lb/500g potatoes (roughly chopped)
4 cloves garlic
1 pint/600ml vegetable stock or water
1 dessertspoon grated Parmesan or 1 tablespoon grated Cheddar
Sea salt and freshly ground pepper
2 fl oz/70ml single cream (optional)
1 dessertspoon chopped fresh chives or spring onions for garnish

_____ 1 _____

In a large saucepan fry the onion in a little oil until very soft.

_____ 2 _____

Add the potatoes, garlic and stock, bring to the boil and simmer for at least an hour.

_____ 3 _____

Blend the mixture adding a little more stock if necessary and reheat.

_____ 4 _____

Sprinkle over the cheese and a little salt and pepper, stir in well and taste for seasoning.

_____ 5 _____

Remove from heat and stir in the cream if using it. Serve garnished with the chives or spring onions.

# Potato and Watercress Soup

1 tablespoon oil
1 medium onion (roughly chopped)
1 clove garlic (crushed)
1 1/2 teaspoons thyme
1 bay leaf
2 sticks celery (roughly chopped)
8oz/250g potatoes (sliced)
1 tablespoon tamari
1 1/2 teaspoons salt
Pinch of freshly ground pepper
1pt/600ml milk
1pt/600ml vegetable stock
1 bunch watercress
1/2 pint/300ml single cream
1 heaped tablespoon chopped parsley

_____ 1 _____

Heat the oil in a large saucepan and add the onion, garlic, thyme and bay leaf. Fry on a medium heat for 5 minutes.

_____ 2 _____

Add the celery and potatoes and continue cooking for 3 minutes.

_____ 3 _____

Add the tamari, salt, pepper, milk and stock. Bring to the boil and simmer for 15 minutes.

_____ 4 _____

Cut away the roots from the watercress and wash well. Roughly chop the cress and add it to the soup with the cream. Simmer for 5 minutes then add the parsley and blend until very smooth. Return to heat, taste for seasoning and serve.

# Nutty Parsnip Soup

Oil for frying
2oz/50g onion (sliced)
2oz/50g carrot (grated)
1oz/25g celery (chopped)
2oz/50g leeks (the white part finely sliced)
Pinch of thyme
1/2 teaspoon ground coriander
1/2 teaspoon mustard powder
1 dessertspoon tamari
1lb/500g parsnips (grated)
2pts/1200ml stock
1 tablespoon crunchy peanut butter
Sea salt and freshly ground pepper
Chopped parsley for garnish

———————— 1 ————————
Heat a little oil (1 dessertspoon, approx.) in a heavy-bottomed saucepan.

———————— 2 ————————
Add the onion, carrot, celery, leeks, thyme, coriander, mustard and tamari and cook with a lid on until very soft (about 10 minutes).

———————— 3 ————————
Add the parsnips and cook for a further 5 minutes before adding the stock. Bring to the boil and simmer for 30 minutes.

———————— 4 ————————
Add the peanut butter and a pinch of salt and pepper to the mixture and blend. It is not necessary to blend the soup to a very creamy consistency, keep it a little coarse to give it a nutty texture.

———————— 5 ————————
Return the mixture to a clean pan and bring to the boil. Taste for seasoning and adjust if necessary. Serve garnished with a little parsley.

# Mushroom Soup

3oz/75g butter or margarine
2oz/50g onion (sliced)
2oz/50g leeks (white part only finely sliced)
1oz/25g celery (chopped)
2oz/50g flour
2pts/1200ml vegetable stock
8oz/250g mushrooms (finely sliced)
1 dessertspoon tamari
1/2 teaspoon basil
Sea salt and freshly ground pepper
2 fl oz/70ml single cream (optional)
Parsley for garnish

———————— 1 ————————
Melt 2oz/50g of the butter or margarine in a heavy-bottomed saucepan and toss in the onions, leeks and celery and fry gently for 10 minutes or so until the vegetables are soft.

———————— 2 ————————
Sprinkle over the flour and cook, stirring for 5 minutes. Gradually whisk in the stock and stir until smooth.

———————— 3 ————————
Meanwhile, melt the remaining butter or margarine in a frying pan. Add the mushrooms, tamari and basil and fry them for 10 minutes before adding them to the rest of the vegetables.

———————— 4 ————————
Bring the mixture to the boil and simmer for 20 minutes. Add a pinch of salt and pepper and taste for seasoning. This soup can be blended for a creamy texture if you wish.

———————— 5 ————————
Stir in the cream if using it and serve garnished with a little chopped parsley.

# Brown Onion Soup

2oz/50g butter or margarine
8oz/250g onions (sliced)
2oz/50g leeks (white part only, finely sliced)
1oz/25g celery (finely chopped)
2oz/50g flour
1/4 teaspoon sage
2pts/1200ml vegetable stock
1 tablespoon sherry (optional)
1 teaspoon tamari
Sea salt and freshly ground pepper
Chopped spring onions or chives for garnish

_____ 1 _____

Melt the butter or margarine in a heavy bottomed saucepan, add the vegetables and fry until lightly browned (15-20 minutes).

_____ 2 _____

Sprinkle over the flour and sage and cook, stirring for a further 5 minutes. Gradually whisk in the stock and stir until smooth. Bring to the boil and simmer for 20 minutes.

_____ 3 _____

Mix in the sherry if using it, the tamari and a pinch of salt and pepper. Taste for seasoning and serve garnished with spring onions or chives.

# Red Lentil and Tomato Soup

1 large clove of garlic (crushed)
1 large onion (sliced)
2 tablespoons oil
1 bay leaf and a pinch of mixed herbs
1 x 15oz/420g tin of plum tomatoes (roughly chopped)
1 tablespoon finely chopped celery
3/4 cup red lentils (well rinsed but not previously soaked)
Sea salt, freshly ground pepper and soy sauce
Chopped parsley for garnish

_____ 1 _____

Sauté the garlic and onion in the oil until soft. Add the bay leaf, herbs and the tomatoes.

_____ 2 _____

Add the celery and lentils, cover with water or stock to double the depth of the vegetable mixture. Bring to the boil and continue cooking on a high heat for 15 minutes. Lower the heat and simmer until the lentils are tender (20-30 minutes).

_____ 3 _____

When cooked, the soup may be served as it is or put through a sieve. Check for seasoning and adjust with soy sauce and freshly ground black pepper. Serve garnished with chopped parsley.

# Borsch

1 medium onion (sliced)
2 tablespoons oil
1lb/500g cooked beetroot (skinned and
chopped)
Sea salt and freshly ground pepper
1 bay leaf
Juice and grated rind of half a lemon
1 or 2 tablespoons sour cream

_____ 1 _____

Heat the oil in a heavy saucepan and cook
the onion until soft.

_____ 2 _____

Add the cooked beetroot, salt and pepper,
the bay leaf and just enough cold water to
cover. Bring to the boil, reduce the heat and
continue to cook gently until tender—about
30 minutes.

_____ 3 _____

Blend and then add the grated rind and juice
of half a lemon.

_____ 4 _____

Adjust the seasoning and add sour cream
just before serving. If you like a slightly
sharper flavour, a dash of vinaigrette is
excellent. Or you can simply blend a
teaspoon of vinegar and a pinch of mustard
powder together and add to the soup.
Sprinkle chopped chives over as garnish.

# Cream of Artichoke Soup

1 medium onion (chopped)
1lb/500g Jerusalem artichokes (washed,
peeled, trimmed and thinly sliced)
1pt/600ml vegetable stock
1pt/600ml milk
Sea salt and freshly ground pepper
Pinch of grated nutmeg
1 teaspoon vinaigrette (optional, see
page 44)
1 bunch watercress or 2 tablespoons
chopped parsley

_____ 1 _____

Simmer the onion and artichokes in the
stock until quite tender.

_____ 2 _____

Blend to a smooth consistency, return to
the heat and add the milk. Bring slowly to
the boil.

_____ 3 _____

Season well with salt, pepper and grated
nutmeg and a dash of vinaigrette if liked.

_____ 4 _____

Add the chopped watercress at the last
minute or garnish with chopped parsley.

# Thanksgiving Soup

2 tablespoons butter
2 medium onions (finely chopped)
5 sticks celery (finely chopped)
1 medium carrot (grated)
5 medium cooking apples (grated)
1/4 teaspoon black pepper
1 teaspoon sage
1/2pt/300ml cider or apple juice
3/4pt/450ml stock
Juice of a lemon (to taste)
Sea salt and freshly ground pepper
8oz/250g strong, sharp Cheddar or
Stilton (grated or crumbled)
Handful of parsley

_____ 1 _____

Heat the butter in a large soup pot, sauté the
onions until soft but not brown. Add the
celery, carrots, apples and cook until soft
and tender.

_____ 2 _____

Stir in the pepper, sage, cider or juice and
stock. Simmer for 30 minutes.

_____ 3 _____

Blend the soup well.

_____ 4 _____

Add the grated cheese and blend again,

finally adjusting the consistency by adding enough stock to give a light creamy soup.

Season with lemon juice, parsley, salt and pepper.

# Meal-in-One Soups

These soups are substantial and nutritious enough to be eaten as a meal in themselves, accompanied by wholewheat bread, for example. They are ideal for a light lunch and are surprisingly sustaining. On cold days many shoppers wishing for a quick break and a bite come to Food For Thought for just such a meal. The following are the favourites.

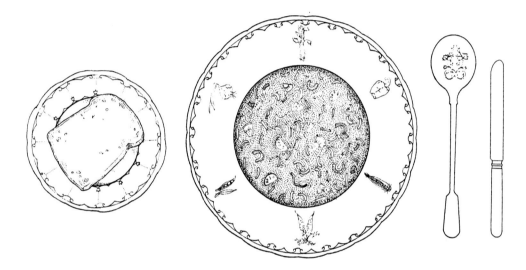

# Split Pea and Garlic Soup

1/2 cup finely chopped onion
1/2 cup finely chopped carrot
1/2 cup finely chopped celery
2 pints/1200ml vegetable stock or hot water
1/2 cup split peas (soaked in hot water 1 hour will give 1 cupful)
5 cloves garlic (chopped)
1 teaspoon ground coriander
1 teaspoon garam masala
1/2 teaspoon curry powder
Dash of tamari
Sea salt and freshly ground pepper

### 1
Fry the onion in a little oil until well browned.

### 2
Add the carrot and celery and fry for a further 5 minutes.

### 3
Add the split peas, garlic and stock and simmer for 1 hour.

### 4
Add the seasonings and simmer for a further 10 minutes. Check for flavour and serve.

**77**

# Minestrone Soup

1 tablespoon oil
1 medium onion (diced)
1 clove garlic (crushed)
1 small red or green pepper (seeds and pith removed and cut into strips)
1 medium carrot (quartered length-wise then chopped)
1 stick celery (chopped)
1 medium courgette (quartered length-wise then chopped)
1 small aubergine (cut into small cubes —1/2 inch/1cm approx.)
1/2 teaspoon oregano
1/2 teaspoon marjoram
1/2 teaspoon paprika
1 teaspoon cumin
1 dessertspoon tomato purée
1 tablespoon tamari
1 teaspoon sea salt
1 x 15oz/420g tin plum tomatoes
2pts/1200ml vegetable stock
1 tablespoon grated Parmesan
1/2 cup peas (fresh or frozen)
1oz/25g wholewheat spaghetti
Freshly ground pepper

## 1

Heat the oil in a large saucepan. Add the onion, garlic and pepper and fry until soft (about 10 minutes).

## 2

Add the carrot and celery and fry for 5 minutes.

## 3

Add the courgette, aubergine, herbs, spices, tomato purée, tamari and salt and cook, stirring for 5 minutes.

## 4

Tip the tomatoes into the sieve adding the juice to the pan. Break them open with your fingers and scoop the seeds and pulp into the sieve. Roughly chop the tomatoes and add to the soup along with any pulp that you can press through the sieve, discarding the seeds.

## 5

Add the stock, Parmesan cheese and peas. Break the spaghetti into the soup. Bring to the boil and simmer for 15 minutes or until the spaghetti is cooked. Taste for seasoning adding a little pepper.

# Potato and Buckwheat Soup

2oz/50g butter or margarine
8oz/250g onion (chopped)
2 sticks celery (chopped)
3oz/90g buckwheat
1 teaspoon marjoram
1/2 teaspoon cayenne
4oz/125g potatoes (sliced)
1 tablespoon tamari
2pts/1200ml vegetable stock
Sea salt and freshly ground pepper
1 tablespoon fresh chopped parsley

## 1

Melt the butter or margarine in a heavy-bottomed saucepan. Fry the onion and celery in it until soft (7-10 minutes).

## 2

Add the buckwheat, marjoram and cayenne and continue frying for a further 5 minutes.

## 3

Add the potatoes, tamari and stock, bring to the boil and simmer for 20 minutes making sure that the buckwheat is fully cooked.

## 4

Add a pinch of salt and pepper and the parsley and blend in a food processor until smooth. Taste for seasoning and serve.

# Leek and Potato Soup

1 dessertspoon oil
2oz/50g onions (chopped)
1lb/500g leeks (sliced)
1/2 teaspoon sage
2pts/1200ml vegetable stock
8oz/250g potatoes (sliced)
Sea salt and freshly ground pepper

––––––––– 1 –––––––––

Heat the oil in a heavy bottomed saucepan and toss in the onions and leeks. Sprinkle over the sage and cook slowly with a lid on until soft (10-15 minutes).

––––––––– 2 –––––––––

Add the stock and potatoes, bring to the boil and simmer until the potatoes are soft and start to break up (25-30 minutes).

––––––––– 3 –––––––––

Add a pinch of salt and pepper and blend well. Return to a clean pan, bring to the boil, taste for seasoning and serve.

Note: For a creamier consistency and colour, use 1pt/600ml warm milk and 1pt/600ml stock. Alternatively, stir in 2 fl oz/70ml cream before serving.

# Corn Chowder

1 tablespoon corn oil
1 small onion (finely chopped)
2 medium potatoes (peeled and cut into cubes)
1/4-1/2pt/150-300ml vegetable stock
1 x 9oz/270g tin sweetcorn kernels
1 bay leaf
1pt/600ml milk
Sea salt and freshly ground pepper
Juice of half a lemon or 1 teaspoon vinaigrette (see page 44)
2oz/50g grated cheese for garnish (optional)

––––––––– 1 –––––––––

Sauté the onion in the oil until soft, then add the potatoes and barely cover with stock. Bring to the boil and simmer for 10 minutes or until the potato is nearly cooked.

––––––––– 2 –––––––––

Empty the contents of the tin of sweetcorn into a liquidizer and blend very lightly, just until the corn is broken but not completely liquidized.

––––––––– 3 –––––––––

Add the sweetcorn, bay leaf and milk to the pan, season with salt and pepper and bring the soup to the boil.

––––––––– 4 –––––––––

When the potatoes are cooked, adjust the flavour with lemon juice or vinaigrette and garnish with grated cheese for a richer flavour if you wish.

# Siriporn's Corn Soup

## An alternative corn soup using fresh sweetcorn.

2pts/1 litre milk, or milk and vegetable stock in equal parts
3 corn cobs (fresh or frozen)
Sea salt, freshly ground pepper and soy sauce
2 eggs yolks
Juice of 1 lemon
Parsley to garnish

### 1
Heat the milk or milk and stock. Slice the corn from the cob with a sharp knife, so that it resembles flakes.

### 2
Add these to the milk and bring to the boil. Season well with salt, pepper and soy sauce.

### 3
Beat the egg yolks, add lemon juice and add this mixture into the boiling soup, stirring continuously so that the egg forms into threads. Garnish with plenty of fresh chopped parsley.

# Chapter 5
# The Savouries

The savoury dishes described in this chapter are various combinations of vegetables and pulses bound by a sauce. They are divided into hot pots and bakes—those that are cooked and finished on top of the oven and those that are finished by being baked off inside the oven. Many of these dishes are interchangeable, but some vegetables—leeks, cauliflower and spinach especially, deteriorate quickly when sitting on top of the oven. Where vegetables such as these are being used they should be added, after initial cooking, as near to the end of cooking as possible.

When initially cooking the vegetables, you should aim to just cook them so that they keep their shape and retain their crispness. Mushy vegetables do nothing for the appearance of a dish and neither are they pleasant to eat. Stir and turn the vegetables carefully, but not too often otherwise they will tend to break up.

The best way to tell whether or not a vegetable is cooked is to taste it. Take a piece out of the pan, allow it to cool a little and cut it with a cold knife before eating. This will give you a much more accurate idea. Bear in mind that the vegetables will continue to cook a little when you reheat them with the sauce, so softer vegetables can be slightly under done. Root vegetables and pulses, however, should always be cooked right through.

The sauce is very important in determining the flavour and appearance of a dish. After flavour, consistency is the most important aspect of a sauce; it should 'hold' the vegetables—just coat them. A thin sauce will run off the vegetables onto the plate and, apart from giving a watery appearance to the dish, will prevent the vegetables from having an attractive gloss. There are various ways to give a sauce 'body' and the making of sauces is fully described in the following recipes, but here are some basic methods.

# Roux and Onion-Based Sauces

If you read the recipes through before you start, so that you have a clear idea of what you are about to do, this will simplify the task of following the recipe. Assemble the ingredients before you start cooking and try to keep tidy as you work; this may seem obvious advice to give, but there are many who get themselves into a panic simply because their environment has become disorganized. Adhere to these basic guidelines and you will find these recipes enjoyable to prepare. Allow a little time at the end of your cooking for flavour adjustment, see page 87, and for garnishing and presentation. This should ensure that your meal reaches the table at its best.

# Roux

Roux sauces are based on equal parts of fat (margarine or butter) and flour, cooked together, seasoned, then made into a sauce with stock. The mixture of fat and flour—the roux—should change from being paste-like to crumbly while it is being cooked over a moderate heat. If the final sauce tastes gluey then the roux probably was not cooked for long enough before adding the stock.

Wholewheat flour is fine for all roux sauces; white sauces will not be the pure white that refined flour will give, however. Wholewheat roux sauces may be blended to produce a wonderfully smooth and creamy texture. The quantity of flour used will directly affect the thickness of the final dish. While initially you may rely on quantities given in our recipes for guidance, your own experience should eventually allow you to gauge more exact quantities and cooking times for the flour.

Onion, garlic and other finely chopped vegetables are often fried in the fat before being sprinkled over with flour. Adding a pinch of thyme with the flour will help a flavour develop. If the flour is lightly cooked before adding stock or milk you will get a light coloured sauce. A little Parmesan (1/2 - 1 teaspoonful) added to the roux before the stock or milk, makes a good base for light

sauces. Grated Cheddar, for example, may be added to a bechamel sauce for a cheese sauce.

At the other extreme, if the flour is well cooked and browned, you will get a brown sauce when you add the stock. At this stage tamari, miso, or yeast extract may be added to give a deeper colour and flavour. These ingredients will help to give you a rich brown sauce if used with discretion—they are strongly flavoured and should therefore be used by the teaspoonful. Tomato purée may be added to a roux with other spices or herbs, once the flour is cooked, but before adding the stock. Use tomato purée gener-ously (by the dessertspoonful), for a tomato sauce base and by the teaspoonful in other sauces. Used in this way a pleasant colour should result. Care should be taken, how-ever, when using tomato purée as it is a powerful seasoning and, while it can give character to a light brown sauce, too much will transform the sauce into a tomato one.

In general you should avoid overusing these condiments. For example, if you favour using tomato purée or yeast extract in all of your darker sauces, they will all tend to have a similar flavour. Varying the proportions and combinations will result in more diverse and distinctive sauces.

# Onion-Based Sauces

A good amount of finely chopped onion, well-cooked, will give a pulpy paste which, when mixed with stock can be used to give body to a sauce without resorting to flour. If necessary cornflour may be used to further thicken such sauces. Tomatoes, potatoes and other vegetables, when cooked to a pulp, can also help to give a thick sauce while ground nuts, such as almonds, walnuts and peanuts (especially in peanut butter form), make for interesting texture and flavour.

The method for cooking these sauces is to heat some oil in a pan, fry any whole spices being used for a few minutes, then to add a combination of onion, garlic, ginger, chillies, tomatoes and so forth, either blended as a paste or very finely chopped. This should simmer over a low heat for a while—20 minutes or so—then the other seasonings (powdered spices, tomato purée, tamari, nuts etc.) and stock are added. The sauce should then be simmered for as long as is practical—up to an hour, preferably.

When combined with other vegetables and pulses, dishes based on these sauces benefit greatly from standing on a low heat for some time. Many spices, chilli and curry powder especially, will initially have a shallow, very hot flavour which after an hour or two becomes infused into the dish and tastes much milder and fuller.

# Basic Tomato Sauce

Oil for frying
2 cloves garlic (crushed)
1 large onion (finely chopped)
2 sticks celery (finely chopped)
Pinch of thyme
1 dessertspoon tomato purée
1 x 15oz/420g tin tomatoes
1/2pt/300ml stock
1/2 teaspoon basil or oregano
Sea salt and freshly ground pepper
Cornflour

### 1

Heat a little oil in a saucepan and add the garlic, onion, celery and sprinkle over the thyme. Fry for 10 minutes until the onion is well cooked and starting to brown.

### 2

Stir in the tomato purée, roughly chop the tomatoes and add them with their juice and the stock. Simmer for 10 minutes then add the herbs and a pinch of salt and pepper. Simmer for a further 5 minutes then taste and adjust the seasoning if necessary.

### 3

Mix 1 dessertspoon of cornflour to a thin paste with a little cold water, remove the saucepan from the heat and whisk the cornflour paste in. If the sauce thickens enough before you have added all the paste don't add any more. Return the sauce to the heat and simmer for 2 minutes. If it is still too thin, repeat the process with the cornflour.

# Basic Bechamel (White Sauce)

1/2pt/300ml milk
1 bay leaf
1 teaspoon peppercorns
A few vegetable trimmings
1oz/25g butter or margarine
1 clove garlic (crushed)
1 small onion (finely chopped)
1 stick celery (finely chopped)
Pinch of thyme
1oz/25g flour
1 teaspoon mustard powder
Pinch of nutmeg
1/2pt/300ml stock
Sea salt and freshly ground pepper

———————— 1 ————————
Put the milk, bay leaf, and peppercorns with any vegetable trimmings (celery leaves, carrot tops etc.) in a saucepan, bring to the boil then remove from the heat and let it stand.

———————— 2 ————————
Melt the butter or margarine in a saucepan and add the garlic, onion, celery and sprinkle over the thyme. Lightly fry these for 5 minutes then sprinkle over the flour. Cook on a medium heat, stirring often for 5 minutes.

———————— 3 ————————
Stir in the mustard powder and nutmeg. Whisk in the stock, strain the milk and add that also. Bring the sauce to the boil and leave on a low simmer, whisking occasionally for as long as is practical, ideally 20 minutes or so. Add a pinch of salt and pepper and taste for seasoning.

# Cheese Sauce

For a cheese sauce add 2 teaspoons grated Parmesan cheese before adding the stock and stir in a good handful of grated Cheddar at the end of making the sauce, just before seasoning with salt and pepper.

# Basic Brown Sauce

1oz/25g butter or margarine
2 cloves garlic (crushed)
1 small onion (finely chopped)
1 stick celery (finely chopped)
1 small carrot (grated)
1 bay leaf
Pinch of thyme
1oz/25g flour
1 teaspoon mustard powder
1 teaspoon coriander
1pt/600ml stock
1 teaspoon yeast extract
1 dessertspoon tamari
Sea salt and freshly ground pepper

———————— 1 ————————
Melt the butter or margarine in a saucepan and add the garlic, onion, celery, carrot, bay leaf and thyme. Fry these for 10 minutes until well cooked then sprinkle over the flour. Cook on a medium heat, stirring often, for 10 minutes or until the flour browns.

———————— 2 ————————
Stir in the mustard powder and coriander and whisk in the stock. Add the yeast extract and tamari, bring to the boil and leave on a low simmer, whisking occasionally for 20-30 minutes. Add a pinch of salt and pepper and taste for seasoning.

# Final Adjustments to Consistency and Seasoning

## Consistency

With practice you will soon learn how to achieve the ideal consistency for a sauce. If it is too thick the dish will appear stodgy and mushy; too thin, and it will run off the vegetables. The sauce should just stick to the vegetables.

Too thick—gradually stir in some stock or water until the correct consistency is achieved. Check the seasoning and reheat. Too thin—If the sauce has not yet been combined with the vegetables, it may be thickened by being reduced. This process consists of rapidly boiling and stirring the sauce for 10-15 minutes to reduce the moisture content. In a roux-based sauce this process will also help the flour to work as a thickener.

If, however, the sauce and vegetables have already been combined, reduction is not appropriate as you run the risk of over cooking the vegetables. In this situation the best solution is to thicken with a little cornflour. The following method is recommended; mix one dessertspoonful of cornflour with a little cold water to form a thin, smooth paste. Turn the heat right down so that the dish is just simmering or take it right off the heat altogether and slowly add the paste stirring it right through the mixture. The consistency of the sauce will start to alter immediately, and it should be easy to tell when you have added enough. Simmer the sauce for a further 2 minutes to ensure that the flour is thoroughly cooked and that the sauce does not taste starchy.

## Seasoning

Adjustment of the seasoning is best left until the final stages of cooking. There are several good reason for this, but the most important is that the flavour of the dish continues to develop throughout cooking. Here are some hints to help you achieve the desired effect.

Bland—Salt and pepper will lift the basic flavour of a dish. They should be used sparingly throughout the preparation of the dish with the final adjustments made right at the end. If the dish still lacks flavour, add more of the spices and condiments that have been used in the recipe but avoid dried herbs for reasons given elsewhere in this book. Fresh herbs are at their best when added at this late stage—the heat of the dish lifts the aromatic oils present in these plants, providing a delicious, appetizing bouquet. Particularly effective are parsley, chives and spring onions.

Avoid at all costs the temptation simply to pour in soy sauce or other such flavourings as this will result in an unbalanced flavour.

Bitter—Sometimes a dish will contain a slightly bitter after-taste—for example when cooking with beer or cider. This can be rectified by the addition of a sweetener. This may vary according to the nature of the dish; West Country Casserole may be appropriately sweetened with apple juice concentrate. For other dishes the apple flavour of such concentrates may be too dominating, in which case you will have to resort to using a little sugar, honey or molasses.

Starchy—If too much flour has been used or it has not been cooked properly, the dish will be characterized by a gluey or starchy flavour. The addition of a little acid in the form of vinegar or lemon juice will help to cut through the stodgy flavour. Caution should be exercized, however; a little goes a long way.

Salty—Adding a balance of sweet and sour flavours will counteract the effects of too much salt. Try a teaspoon each of vinegar and sugar, adding a little more of each until their flavours can just be detected.

Hot—Often, just letting a dish stand for 15-20 minutes will alleviate the effect of too much chilli or other hot spices in a sauce.

The process of infusion is at work here, and it is as well to remember to take this into account when using such spices. It is also important to remember that when really hot dishes are served on a bed of rice, for example, the rice is a dilutant. Serving hot dishes with yogurt as a side dish, or stirring it into the final mixture will also have the effect of cooling the dish. Other useful 'coolants' include fruit, fruit juices such as orange juice, coconut milk, and raw vegetables.

# Bakes

In order to help you find your way around this chapter I have categorized our baked dishes as follows:

1. Those which are pasta based.
2. Those which have pulses as their main constituent.
3. Those which are characterized by their spicy or distinctive sauces.
4. Those recipes suitable for stuffing vegetables.
5. Those using fresh vegetables.
6. Summer bakes and stir fries.

The above categories are not intended as rigid boundaries; obviously a certain amount of overlap occurs between one type and another. However, if you alternate between one category and another a more balanced diet and combination of flavours should result.

The section is concluded with a few ideas on various toppings suitable for these recipes.

# Pasta-Based Bakes

These pasta dishes are far and away the most popular of all our creations. Both staff and customers ensure a complete sell-out every time and it is not difficult to see why; fresh pasta with a rich and tasty tomato or mushroom sauce, topped with herbs, olives and Parmesan cheese results in an immediately appealing, sustaining and easy-to-eat meal. Dried pasta may also be used in these recipes, but be sure to follow the manufacturer's cooking instructions. A glass of Chianti is an excellent accompaniment to all pasta dishes.

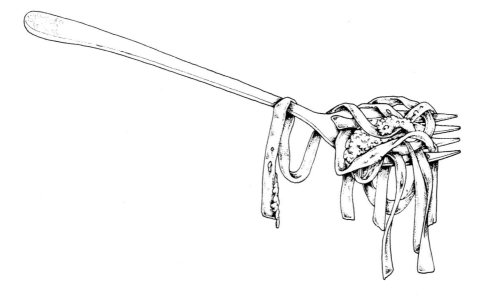

# Lasagne

1lb/500g fresh spinach lasagne
2 tablespoons olive oil
2 medium onions (chopped)
2 cloves garlic (crushed)
2 tablespoons tomato purée
1lb/500g tomatoes (liquidized)
4oz/125g carrots (grated)
1 stick celery (finely chopped)
2oz/50g mushrooms (finely chopped)
2 tablespoons fresh basil
1 bay leaf
1/2 teaspoon mustard powder
1 teaspoon coriander
1/2 teaspoon black pepper, sea salt, raw
cane sugar, lemon juice, tamari (to taste)
1lb/500g spinach (chopped)
4oz/125g cottage cheese
1 small onion (thinly sliced)
1 clove garlic (crushed)
8oz/250g mushrooms (sliced)
2 tablespoons Chianti
4oz/125g grated Cheddar cheese mixed
with 2oz/50g Parmesan
Chopped fresh parsley
Black olives

### 1

Heat the oil in a large saucepan, sauté the first amount of onions and garlic for 5 minutes. Stir in the tomato purée, tomatoes, carrots, celery, mushrooms, basil, bay leaf, mustard powder, coriander and pepper.

Bring to the boil and simmer for 45 minutes. Season with salt or tamari, sugar and lemon juice.

### 2

Cook the spinach in an inch/2.5cm of boiling water. Stir frequently and season with salt. Drain, cool and stir in the cottage cheese. Set aside.

### 3

Heat some more oil and sauté the remaining onions and garlic for 5 minutes. Add the mushrooms and wine and cook, covered, for 5 more minutes. Season with tamari, salt and pepper and then stir into the tomato sauce.

### 4

Grease a rectangular oven proof dish. Place a sheet of lasagne in the bottom and cover with a layer of spinach, then a layer of the tomato-mushroom sauce and one of the cheese mixture. Continue making layers in this way finishing off with a layer of sauce and a generous sprinkling of cheese. Additionally, chopped onion, peppers and/or mushrooms may be added to the final layer of cheese if you wish.

### 5

Cook in the oven at 375°F/190°C/Gas Mark 5 for 40 minutes. Cover with foil if the cheese begins to brown. Serve garnished with chopped parsley and black olives.

# Tagliatelle Pimentosa

1lb/500g fresh tagliatelle
(half white and half green)
1 medium red pepper (seeded and cut
into strips)
1oz/25g butter or margarine
1 small onion (diced)
1 clove garlic (crushed)
1oz/25g flour
1 glass dry white wine
3/4pt/400ml milk
1/4pt/150ml single cream
1 teaspoon mustard powder
Sea salt and freshly ground pepper
Small bunch of parsley (finely chopped)
2oz/50g grated Parmesan cheese
1 dessertspoon poppy seeds

———————1———————

Add a splash of oil to a potful of boiling
water and cook the pasta with the red
pepper in it for about 5 minutes until the
pasta is cooked but not mushy. Drain and
rinse well, then toss with a drop of oil and
set aside.

———————2———————

Heat the butter or margarine in a saucepan
and fry the onion and garlic for 3 minutes.
Sprinkle over the flour and cook for 1
minute. Gradually stir in the wine then
whisk in the milk, cream, mustard powder
and a pinch of salt and pepper. Bring to the
boil slowly and simmer for 15 minutes.

———————3———————

Add the parsley to the sauce then combine
with the pasta and pour into an oven proof
dish. Spread the Parmesan cheese over and
sprinkle with poppy seeds. Bake in the oven
at 400°F/200°C/Gas Mark 6 for 15-20
minutes until bubbling around the edges
and hot through.

# Tagliatelle Con Chianti

Serves 4-6
1lb/500g fresh spinach tagliatelle
A little salt
Olive oil
3 cloves garlic (crushed)
1lb/500g button mushrooms (thickly
sliced)
1/2 teaspoon fresh basil
Sea salt and freshly ground pepper
A little tamari
1 small onion (finely chopped)
1 rounded dessertspoon butter or
margarine
1 stick of celery (finely chopped)
1 small carrot (grated)
1 rounded dessertspoon of wholewheat
flour
A pinch of thyme
1 dessertspoon tomato purée
1 tin Italian peeled plum tomatoes
1pt/600ml vegetable stock or hot water
1pt/600ml good Chianti
1/2 teaspoon marjoram
1 heaped teaspoon oregano
1/2-3/4lb/250-340g fresh young spinach
1 handful of parsley (finely chopped)
1lb/500g Mozzarella cheese (thinly
sliced)
1 heaped teaspoon grated Parmesan
cheese

———————1———————

Cook pasta in plenty of water, (to which has
been added a little salt and olive oil), for 5
minutes. Drain, rinse and toss in a little
olive oil.

———————2———————

Fry the garlic gently in olive oil for 1 minute,
then add mushrooms and fry until just
cooked. Season with basil, salt and pepper
and a splash of tamari. Drain and reserve
any liquid.

###### 3

Fry onion in butter for a few minutes, then add celery and carrot and cook until soft.

###### 4

Stir in flour and thyme and cook over a low heat for a few minutes.

###### 5

Add tomato purée, reserved mushroom juices, and the juice from the tinned tomatoes. Add enough stock to make a sauce of medium consistency.

###### 6

Cook gently for a few minutes then add the wine and simmer for 5 minutes.

###### 7

Sprinkle over the herbs, salt and pepper and cook for a further 3 minutes. The sauce should be rather thin and strongly flavoured as the pasta will absorb both moisture and flavour.

###### 8

Wash spinach thoroughly and pack tightly into a saucepan, cover and cook for 5-10 minutes. Take care not to overcook. Drain and rinse well, pressing out excess moisture. Chop spinach and mix in parsley.

###### 9

Roughly chop tomatoes, then thoroughly combine all the ingredients except the cheeses. Check and adjust the seasoning.

###### 10

Place mixture into a greased oven proof baking dish. Cut the tagliatelle with a sharp knife if necessary, this will aid serving.

###### 11

Top with Mozzarella and Parmesan and bake in a medium to hot oven for 25-30 minutes.

# Pulse-Based Bakes

Lentils and beans by themselves, though excellent nutritionally, can be somewhat indigestible unless carefully cooked.

These recipes use distinctive sauces and toppings to enliven the flavour of the predominant pulses. Alongside nut roasts and loaves, these bakes are probably the most substantial vegetarian meals it is possible to produce.

Ideal winter sustenance!

## Brown Lentil Bake au Gratin

2 cups brown lentils (soaked in water for 2 hours)
2 tablespoons oil
2 large onions (sliced)
2 leeks (thinly sliced)
Sea salt and freshly ground pepper
1 teaspoon tamari
1pt/600ml Bechamel sauce (see page 86)
10oz/300g grated Cheddar cheese
4oz/125g button mushrooms (halved)

_____ 1 _____
Drain and rinse the lentils, place in a saucepan and cover with cold water. Bring to the boil and simmer for 20 minutes. When cooked drain and rinse.

_____ 2 _____
Heat the oil in a large skillet or cast iron casserole dish and sauté the onions and leeks until golden. Stir in the cooked lentils and remove from heat.

_____ 3 _____
Prepare the Bechamel sauce (see page 86) and add half the cheese and the tamari to it.

_____ 4 _____
Pour the sauce over the lentil mixture and mix well. Taste for seasoning and add salt and pepper as necessary.

_____ 5 _____
Stir in the mushrooms and turn the mixture into a 9 inch/23cm bread tin, sprinkle with the remaining cheese and bake in a moderate oven (350°F/180°C/ Gas Mark 4) for 20 minutes.

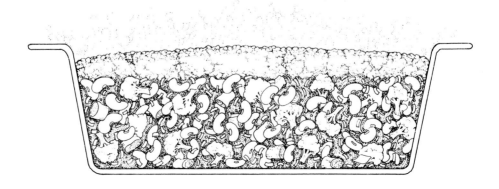

# Spicy Nut and Bean Loaf with Sweetcorn Sauce

8oz/250g pinto beans (soaked overnight)
2 tablespoons olive oil
2 medium onions (finely chopped)
2 cloves garlic (crushed)
1/2-2 chillies (finely chopped), to taste
2 tablespoons tomato purée
1 teaspoon coriander
1 teaspoon cumin
4oz/125g mushrooms (sliced)
2 medium carrots (grated)
2 sticks celery (finely chopped)
1 green pepper (seeded and chopped)
1 red pepper (seeded and chopped)
4oz/125g tin of sweetcorn
2oz/50g ground nuts, roasted cashews
or peanuts
4oz/125g breadcrumbs
2oz/50g grated Cheddar cheese
Handful fresh parsley (chopped)
Juice of half a lemon
Sea salt and freshly ground pepper, soy
sauce (to taste)
A little vegetable stock

FOR THE SAUCE:
2 tablespoons olive oil
1 large onion (finely chopped)
1 bunch fresh coriander
8oz/250g carrot (grated)
3/4pt/400ml stock
4oz/125g tin of sweetcorn
1 tablespoon lemon juice
4 tablespoons orange juice
1 bunch fresh parsley (finely chopped)

_____ 1 _____

Drain the beans, cover with fresh water and cook until they are very soft, about 45 minutes. The beans should mash easily.

_____ 2 _____

Heat the oil and sauté the onions and garlic until they are soft. Add the fresh chillies, tomato purée, coriander, cumin, mushrooms, carrots and celery. Stir well and simmer for 15 minutes until all the vegetables are tender.

_____ 3 _____

Stir in the peppers, sweetcorn, nuts and breadcrumbs, cheese and parsley. Season with lemon juice, soy sauce, salt and pepper. Combine with the mashed pinto beans and add stock as necessary to form a moist but firm loaf.

_____ 4 _____

Place the mixture in a greased 2lb/1 kilo loaf tin and press down well. Bake for 30 minutes at 350°F/180°C/Gas Mark 4.

_____ 5 _____

To make the sauce, heat the oil in a saucepan and sauté the onion for 5 minutes or until soft. Add the coriander and carrots. Cover the vegetables with stock and simmer for at least 15 minutes or until tender.

_____ 6 _____

Remove from the heat and blend with the drained sweetcorn and the lemon and orange juice until smooth. Return to the heat, add the chopped parsley and season to taste.

_____ 7 _____

To serve, turn out the loaf and cut into portions serving the sauce separately.

# Nut Roast with Tomato Sauce

4oz/125g walnuts
4oz/125g hazelnuts
2oz/50g margarine
1 large onion (diced)
2 medium carrots (grated)
3 cloves garlic (crushed)
2 stalks celery (finely chopped)
1 dessertspoon tomato purée
1 teaspoon cayenne pepper
1 teaspoon marjoram
1 teaspoon cumin
1/2 teaspoon coriander
1/2 cup chopped fresh parsley
4oz/125g breadcrumbs
4oz/125g mushrooms (finely sliced)
2 tablespoons tamari
Sea salt and freshly ground pepper
1pt/600ml vegetable stock
2 tablespoons sunflower seeds

FOR THE SAUCE:
1 dessertspoon oil
1 small onion (diced)
1 clove garlic (crushed)
1 x 15oz/420g tin plum tomatoes
1 dessertspoon tomato purée
2 tablespoons cornflour
Sea salt and freshly ground pepper

—————— 1 ——————
Grind the nuts in a food processor or wrap them in a teatowel and crush them with a rolling pin until they are broken down into coarse pieces.

—————— 2 ——————
Melt the margarine in a large saucepan and add the onion, carrots and garlic. Cover with a lid and cook on a medium heat for 5 minutes.

—————— 3 ——————
Add the celery and nuts and fry, stirring occasionally for 10 minutes.

—————— 4 ——————
Stir in the tomato purée and the herbs and spices. Then add the breadcrumbs, mushrooms, tamari and a good pinch of salt and pepper. Stir in enough stock to make a wet mixture so that it looks like a very thick sauce and simmer, stirring often for 5 minutes.

—————— 5 ——————
Add a little more stock if the mixture looks at all dry. Taste for seasoning, it may possibly need more salt. Tip the mixture into an ovenproof dish and scatter the sunflower seeds over the top. Bake at 325°C/170°F/Gas Mark 3 for 20-30 minutes until hot through.

—————— 6 ——————
To prepare the sauce, heat the oil in a saucepan and fry the onion and garlic for 5 minutes. Roughly break up the tomatoes and add them along with the tomato purée to the pan. Bring the mixutre to the boil and simmer for 5 minutes.

—————— 7 ——————
Mix the cornflour to a paste with 2 tablespoons of cold water. Whisk this into the sauce and simmer for 5 minutes before tasting for seasoning, adding salt and pepper as necessary. Serve with the nut roast.

# Fennel and Lentil Espagnole

1oz/25g butter or margarine
1 large onion (diced)
1 clove garlic (crushed)
1oz/25g flour
1 cup brown lentils (washed)
1 teaspoon thyme.
1 teaspoon marjoram
1 teaspoon coriander
1 x 15oz/420g tin plum tomatoes
1 tablespoon tamari
1pt/600ml vegetable stock
1 teaspoon yeast extract
3 medium carrots (cut into bite-sized pieces)
4 sticks celery (cut into bite-sized pieces)
1lb/500g fennel (cut into strips)
8oz/250g potatoes (thinly sliced)
2 tablespoons grated Parmesan cheese
Sea salt and freshly ground pepper
Chopped fresh parsley for garnish

### 1

Melt the butter or margarine in a large saucepan, add the onion and garlic and fry for 5 minutes. Sprinkle over the flour and cook for 2 minutes.

### 2

Add the lentils, herbs, coriander and roughly chop the tomatoes and add them with their juice. Stir in the tamari, stock and yeast extract. Bring to the boil and simmer, stirring occasionally for 15-20 minutes until the lentils are tender.

### 3

Heat a little oil in a frying pan and cook the carrots and celery for 7-10 minutes until the carrots are just cooked. Season with a pinch of salt and pepper and set aside.

### 4

Heat a little more oil in the pan and add the potatoes and fennel and fry them until cooked through and lightly browned. Add a pinch of salt and pepper and set aside.

### 5

Combine the carrots and celery with the lentil sauce and taste for seasoning and adjust as necessary. Pour into an ovenproof dish and spread the potato and fennel mixture on top. Sprinkle the Parmesan cheese over and bake in the oven at 400°F/200°C/Gas Mark 6 for 15-20 minutes until hot through. Garnish with fresh parsley.

# Shepherdess Pie

8oz/250g aduki beans (soaked
overnight)
1 bay leaf
1 dessertspoon tamari
1lb/500g potatoes
Oil for frying
1lb/500g leeks (sliced)
Pinch of sage
Sea salt and freshly ground pepper
1 large onion (diced)
8oz/250g mushrooms (sliced)
Pinch of fresh basil
2oz/50g butter or margarine
1 small onion (finely sliced)
1 small carrot (grated)
1/2 stick of celery (finely sliced)
2oz/50g flour
1 teaspoon tomato purée
1/2 teaspoon thyme
1/2 teaspoon rosemary
1 bay leaf
1/2 teaspoon mustard powder
1pt/600ml potato stock
1/2 teaspoon yeast extract
1 teaspoon tamari
2 tablespoons milk
1oz/25g butter or margarine
Pinch of nutmeg
4oz/125g grated Cheddar cheese

### 1

Drain and rinse the beans then cover with water, add a bay leaf, and boil for 1 hour or until tender. Just before the beans are cooked flavour with 1 dessertspoon of tamari. Drain, rinse and set aside.

### 2

Boil the potatoes in water until well cooked, then drain reserving the stock for the sauce.

### 3

Heat a little oil in a frying pan and fry the leeks and sage until just tender. Season with salt and pepper and set aside.

### 4

Heat a little more oil in the pan and fry the onions for 5 minutes then add the mushrooms and basil and continue cooking until the mushrooms are just tender. Season with salt and pepper and set aside.

### 5

Melt 2oz/50g butter or margarine in a saucepan and fry the onion, carrot and celery for 5 minutes. Sprinkle the flour over and cook, stirring for a further 5 minutes.

### 6

Stir in the tomato purée then add the thyme, rosemary, bay leaf and mustard powder. Whisk in the stock, bring the sauce to the boil and simmer for 10 minutes. Stir in the yeast extract and tamari and season to taste with salt and pepper.

### 7

Combine the beans, leeks, mushrooms and sauce and place in a casserole dish.

### 8

Mash the potatoes with the milk, butter or margarine, nutmeg and a pinch of salt and pepper. Carefully smooth this over the vegetables and spread the cheese on top. Bake at 350°F/180°C/Gas Mark 4 for 30 minutes until hot right through.

# Leek and Butterbean Dijonnaise

1 cup butterbeans (soaked overnight will
give 2 cups)
1 dessertspoon butter or margarine
1 small onion (finely chopped)
1 dessertspoon flour
2 teaspoons mustard powder
1 teaspoon coriander
Sea salt and freshly ground pepper
1 cup vegetable stock
1/4 pint/150ml white wine
1 dessertspoon whole grain mustard or
1 teaspoon prepared French (Dijon)
mustard
1 teaspoon honey
3 medium leeks (chopped)
1 teaspoon dill
1/4 medium head cauliflower (broken
into florets)
1 dessertspoon water
3 fl oz/100ml single cream (optional)
2oz/50g grated Cheddar cheese
1/2 cup breadcrumbs

—————————— 1 ——————————
Drain and rinse the butterbeans then cover
with water and simmer for 1 hour until
tender. Drain and reserve the stock.

—————————— 2 ——————————
Melt the butter in a saucepan over a
medium heat then add the onion and fry
until soft (5 minutes). Sprinkle over the
flour and cook stirring for another 5
minutes. Sprinkle over the mustard powder, coriander and a pinch of salt and
pepper. Whisk in the stock and wine and
simmer gently until it has reached a good
consistency. It should be rather thick as the
water from the vegetables will dilute it
further. Stir in the prepared mustard and
honey and leave on a low heat.

—————————— 3 ——————————
Heat a little oil in a frying pan and toss in
the leeks. Cook, stirring occasionally until
just tender (5-7 minutes) then sprinkle
over half the dill and a little salt and pepper.
Set aside.

—————————— 4 ——————————
Heat a little more oil in the pan then toss in
the cauliflower and cook, stirring over a
medium heat for a couple of minutes.
Sprinkle over a dessertspoonful of water,
cover tightly and turn heat to low. Check
after 5 minutes, it should be just tender.
Sprinkle over the remaining dill and a little
salt and pepper.

—————————— 5 ——————————
Combine the beans, vegetables, sauce and
cream and taste for flavour. Place in an
ovenproof dish. Mix the cheese and the
breadcrumbs together and spread over the
top. Bake in a moderate oven at 350°F/
180°C/Gas Mark 4 for 30 minutes or so
until bubbling around the edges and hot
through.

# Lentil and Aubergine Moussaka

1 cup brown lentils (soaked for 1 hour in
2 cups of hot water)
2 medium aubergines
2 teaspoons sea salt
3 medium potatoes
1 dessertspoon butter or margarine
1 small onion (finely chopped)
1 large onion (medium chopped)
Pinch of thyme
1 dessertspoon flour
1 dessertspoon tomato purée
1/2 pint/300ml potato stock
1 x 14oz/400g tin tomatoes
1/2 teaspoon yeast extract or Marmite
2 teaspoons tamari
Olive oil for frying
3 cloves garlic (crushed)
1 teaspoon oregano
A good pinch of marjoram
1lb/500g flat mushrooms (thickly sliced)
1 teaspoon basil
1/2 pint/300ml natural yogurt
8oz/250g cottage cheese
1 egg
4oz/125g grated strong Cheddar
1 dessertspoon grated Parmesan

---
### 1
Drain and rinse the lentils then cover with water and boil until just cooked (20-30 minutes).

---
### 2
Trim the stalks off the aubergines, quarter them lengthwise then cut into bite-sized pieces. Place them in a colander and sprinkle liberally with the salt mixing it well through. Leave to stand for 20-30 minutes.

---
### 3
Boil the potatoes until cooked and reserve the stock. When cool slice them.

---
### 4
Melt the butter in a saucepan and fry the finely chopped onion until soft (5 minutes or so). Sprinkle over the flour and thyme and cook, stirring occasionally over a moderate heat for 5 minutes. Mix in the tomato purée and cook for a further 3 minutes. Whisk in the stock and the juice from the tomatoes. Stir in the yeast extract and 1 teaspoon of tamari. Leave on a low simmer.

---
### 5
Heat some oil in a frying pan and add 2 of the crushed cloves of garlic. Fry for a minute or so then add the medium chopped onion and fry until very soft and starting to brown (10-15 minutes). Add the roughly chopped tomatoes, oregano, marjoram and a pinch of salt and pepper and cook for a further 5 minutes. Set aside.

---
### 6
Rinse the aubergines well under lots of cold running water. Drain and spread on kitchen paper to dry.

---
### 7
Heat some more oil in the pan, add the remaining garlic and the mushrooms, fry for 3 minutes then sprinkle over 1 teaspoon of tamari, the basil and a pinch of salt and pepper. Cook for 5 minutes until the mushrooms are barely cooked. Pour the juices into the sauce and reserve the mushrooms.

---
### 8
Heat some more oil in the pan and cover the bottom with aubergine pieces. Fry turning occasionally until lightly browned and soft. Cook all of the aubergines this way, it may take 2 or 3 batches.

---
### 9
Taste the sauce for seasoning. Mix half of the sauce with the lentils and spread over the bottom of a greased ovenproof dish. Next spread over the aubergines. Mix the rest of the sauce with the tomato and onion

mixture and spread that over the aubergines, then spread over the mushrooms.

_____ 10 _____

Beat the egg with a fork then whisk in the yogurt and cottage cheese. Carefully spread this mixture over the moussaka then arrange the sliced potatoes on top of this. Sprinkle over the Cheddar and Parmesan and finish with a good pinch of oregano scattered over the top. Bake in a moderate oven at 180°C/350°F/Gas Mark 4 for 1 hour—check after 45 minutes. When cooked the moussaka should be bubbling around the edges and hot through. The yogurt mixture should set to a custard-like consistency and should not be runny.

# Spicy Bakes

These dishes are for those who love sharp, contrasting flavours. They may be served with crudités such as fresh tomatoes, cucumber, spring onions, or fruit. Good accompaniments also are various chutneys, pickles and yoghurt-based dips.

# California Chilli Bake with Corn Bread Topping

8oz/250g pinto beans (soaked overnight)

FOR THE SAUCE:
2 tablespoons olive oil
2 large onions (finely chopped)
3 cloves garlic (crushed)
2 medium carrots (grated)
1 stick celery (finely chopped)
4 medium mushrooms (finely chopped)
2 dessertspoons tomato purée
2 x 15oz/420g tins plum tomatoes
(blended)
1/2 teaspoon black pepper
1/2-1 teaspoon chilli powder (to taste)
2 teaspoons cumin
2 teaspoons coriander
Juice of 1 lemon
Sea salt and freshly ground pepper
1 teaspoon sugar (to taste)
1 large carrot (cut into bite-sized pieces)
2 cloves garlic (crushed)
4oz/125g button mushrooms (halved)
1 small red pepper (diced)
1 small green pepper (diced)
3 medium courgettes (cut into bite-sized
pieces)

FOR THE CORN BREAD TOPPING:
6oz/150g maize meal
1 tablespoon wholewheat flour
1/2 teaspoon sea salt
11/2 teaspoons baking powder
1 egg
Scant 1/4pt/100ml milk
2 tablespoons sour cream
1 tablespoon oil
1 teaspoon honey
1/4 teaspoon cinnamon

_____ 1 _____

Drain and rinse the pinto beans and then cook them in fresh water for 11/2 hours. Drain and rinse with cold water and set aside.

_____ 2 _____

Heat the oil in a large saucepan and sauté the onions and garlic for 5 minutes. Add the grated carrots, celery and mushrooms and cook until tender. Stir in the tomato purée, tomatoes and spices. Cover the pan and simmer on a low heat for 1-2 hours. When cooked season with salt, pepper and lemon juice and set aside.

_____ 3 _____

Heat a little more oil in a large, heavy frying pan and sauté the carrot until tender. Season with salt, pepper and lemon juice and set aside. Next, sauté the mushrooms in a little oil and crushed garlic until tender. Season and set aside. Sauté the courgettes in a little oil and crushed garlic until slightly cooked but still crisp. Season with a pinch of coriander and salt and pepper.

_____ 4 _____

Combine the beans, sauce, vegetables and the drained sweetcorn and place in a large, greased casserole dish.

_____ 5 _____

Sift the dry ingredients for the corn bread topping together and add the egg and liquids. Mix lightly. Pour the topping over the Chilli Bake. The batter may disappear into the bake but will float once placed in a hot oven.

_____ 6 _____

Bake in a hot oven (425°F/220°C/Gas Mark 7) for 20-25 minutes. To check that the topping is cooked, insert a knife into the middle of the corn bread—it should be clean when it is withdrawn.
Serve immediately

# Pinto and Parsnip Carbonnade

1 cup pinto beans (soaked overnight will give 2 cups)
1 dessertspoon butter or margarine
1 small onion (finely chopped)
1 stalk celery (finely chopped)
1 small carrot (grated)
1 dessertspoon flour
Pinch of thyme
1 dessertspoon mustard powder
1 cup vegetable stock or water
1 teaspoon tamari
1 teaspoon yeast extract
1/3pt/200ml brown ale
2-3 carrots cut into bite-sized pieces
2-3 parsnips cut into bite-sized pieces
3 stalks celery (chopped)
1 teaspoon ground coriander
A good pinch of marjoram
Sea salt and freshly ground pepper
3-4 slices of lightly toasted wholemeal bread spread with French mustard

### 1

Drain and wash the beans then put in a pot, cover with water and simmer for 1 hour or until cooked. Drain and rinse.

### 2

Meanwhile, melt the butter in a saucepan, add the onion, finely chopped celery and grated carrot and fry until very soft.

### 3

Sprinkle over the flour and thyme and cook, stirring, for 5 minutes. Add the mustard, whisk in the stock and simmer for 5 minutes then stir in the tamari, yeast extract and beer and leave to simmer while you cook the other vegetables.

### 4

Heat some oil in a pan and fry the carrots and parsnips in it. When they have been sizzling for a few minutes add the celery and cook for 2-3 minutes then season with the coriander, marjoram and salt and pepper.

### 5

Combine the vegetables, beans and sauce in an ovenproof dish and cover with the bread, cut into triangles, mustard side down. Dot with a little oil or butter and bake at 350°F/180°C/Gas Mark 4 for 30 minutes or until bubbling around the edges and hot in the middle.

# Pinto Bean Hongrois

1 cup pinto beans (soaked overnight will
give 2 cups)
1 medium aubergine
1 dessertspoon sea salt
1oz/25g butter or margarine
1 medium onion (diced)
1 clove garlic (crushed)
1 red pepper (finely sliced)
1oz/25g flour
1 tablespoon paprika
1 teaspoon ground cumin
1/2pt/300ml milk
1/2pt/300ml stock
1 tablespoon tamari
Oil for frying
3 medium courgettes (cut into bite-sized
pieces)
4oz/125g button mushrooms
Sea salt and freshly ground pepper
1 tablespoon sesame seeds

_____ 1 _____

Drain and rinse the beans then cover them
with water and boil for 1 hour or until
cooked. Drain and rinse and set aside.

_____ 2 _____

Trim the stalk off the aubergine, quarter it
lengthwise and cut it into bite-sized pieces.
Sprinkle 1 dessertspoon of salt over the
pieces and leave to stand for 20 minutes.

_____ 3 _____

Heat the butter or margarine in a saucepan,
add the onion and garlic and fry for 5
minutes. Add the red pepper then sprinkle
over the flour, paprika and cumin and cook
for 1 minute. Whisk in the milk, stock and
tamari. Bring to the boil and simmer for 15
minutes.

_____ 4 _____

Rinse the aubergines in plenty of water and
drain well. Heat 1 tablespoon of oil in a
frying pan and toss the aubergine pieces in.
Fry for 5 minutes, adding a little more oil if
the pan becomes too dry.

_____ 5 _____

Add the courgettes and mushrooms and
continue frying until all the vegetables are
cooked (7-10 minutes). Season with a
pinch of salt and pepper.

_____ 6 _____

Combine the beans, sauce and vegetables
and pour into an ovenproof dish. Sprinkle
with sesame seeds and bake in the oven at
400°F/200°C/Gas Mark 6 for 20 minutes.

# Stuffed Vegetables

The stuffing and sauces used in the
following recipes are equally appropriate
with different vegetables of your own
choice. For example, large 'beefsteak' tomatoes may be stuffed, as may the outer
leaves of Savoy cabbage. Vine leaves and
aubergines may be used also.

# Stuffed Marrow with Mushroom Sauce

2-3 small marrows or 1 large marrow

FOR THE STUFFING:
8oz/250g bulghur
2 medium onions (chopped)
1 clove garlic (crushed)
2 tablespoons oil
4oz/125g mushrooms (finely sliced)
2 carrots (grated)
1 stick of celery (finely chopped)
2 leeks (finely chopped)
1 teaspoon sage
1 bay leaf
4oz/125g walnuts (coarsely chopped and roasted)
Handful of sunflower seeds
4oz/125g wholewheat breadcrumbs
1/4-1/2pt/150-300ml vegetable stock
Sea salt and freshly ground pepper
Juice of 1/2-1 lemon, to taste
Handful of fresh, chopped parsley

FOR THE SAUCE:
2 tablespoons olive oil
2 medium onions (finely chopped)
1 clove garlic (crushed)
1 stick celery (finely chopped)
8oz/250g mushrooms (finely sliced)
4oz/125g leeks (finely chopped)
1 teaspoon basil or 1 bunch fresh basil
1 bay leaf
1/4-1/2pt/150-300ml vegetable stock
Juice of half a lemon
Sea salt and freshly ground pepper
Grated Cheddar cheese

_____ 1 _____

Cut the marrows in half lengthwise, remove seeds and pulpy centre. Place in an oiled roasting tray with 1/2 inch/1cm of water and cover with foil. Steam for 45-60 minutes at 350°F/180°C/Gas Mark 4. The marrows should be tender and moist, but firm enough to support the stuffing. While the marrows are cooking, cook the bulghur by pouring 2pts/1 litre of boiling water over it and leave it to stand for 30 minutes.

_____ 2 _____

Sauté the onions and garlic in the oil until they are soft but not brown. Add the mushrooms, carrots, celery, leeks, sage and bay leaf and cook, covered, for 10 minutes.

_____ 3 _____

Stir in the cooked bulghur, roasted walnuts and sunflower seeds and breadcrumbs. Add enough stock to make a moist but not wet stuffing. Season with salt, pepper and lemon juice. Add the parsley and remove from the heat.

_____ 4 _____

To make the sauce, sauté the onion and garlic in the olive oil until soft but not brown. Add the celery, mushrooms, leeks, basil and bay leaf and cook under cover for 10 minutes. Add stock and simmer for 30 minutes. Remove from the heat and blend until smooth. Return the sauce to the heat and adjust to the desired consistency; reduce it by rapid boiling or thin it out by adding more stock. Season with salt, pepper and lemon juice.

_____ 5 _____

Stuff the cooked marrows with the filling and place on a greased baking tin. Sprinkle with Cheddar cheese and return it to the oven (400°F/200°C/Gas Mark 6) for 45 minutes.

Serve with the sauce poured over the stuffed marrows.

# Stuffed Peppers with Tomato Sauce

Oil for frying
1 medium onion (diced)
1 clove garlic (crushed)
4oz/125g mushrooms (finely sliced)
1 teaspoon chopped fresh basil
Pinch of thyme
Pinch of sage
1 dessertspoon tamari
Sea salt and freshly ground pepper
2 cups cooked rice
1/2 cup breadcrumbs
1 tablespoon chopped fresh parsley
Juice of half a lemon
4 medium peppers (red or green)

FOR THE SAUCE:
1/2oz/10g butter or margarine
1 clove garlic (crushed)
1 small onion (diced)
1 small carrot (grated)
1 stick celery (finely chopped)
Pinch of thyme
1/2oz/10g flour
1 dessertspoon tomato purée
1/2pt/300ml vegetable stock
1 bay leaf
Splash of tamari

_____ 1 _____

Fry the onion and garlic in a little oil for 3 minutes then add the mushrooms, and sprinkle over the basil, thyme, sage and tamari. Cook for 5 minutes and season with a pinch of salt and pepper. Thoroughly mix these vegetables with the rice, bread-crumbs, parsley and lemon juice.

_____ 2 _____

Slice the tops off the peppers and scoop out the seeds and pith. Blanch the peppers by dipping them in a pot of boiling water for 30 seconds. When they are cool enough to handle fill them with the rice mixture and replace their tops.

_____ 3 _____

Stand the peppers in an ovenproof dish with 1/2 inch/1cm of water in the bottom. Cover with foil and bake in a moderately hot oven, 400°F/200°C/Gas Mark 6 for 1 hour.

_____ 4 _____

Melt the butter or margarine in a saucepan and fry the garlic, onion, carrot and celery with the thyme for 5 minutes. Sprinkle over the flour and cook, stirring for 3 minutes. Stir in the tomato purée and cook for 1 more minute then whisk in the stock and add the bay leaf. Bring to the boil, add a splash of tamari and a pinch of salt and pepper and leave on a low simmer until the peppers are cooked. Serve the peppers covered with sauce and garnished with a little parsley.

# Baked Dish Toppings

The topping on a baked dish gives variety to the flavour, texture and appearance of the dish and provides some protection for the vegetables underneath from drying out or developing a skin.

Grated Cheddar cheese is the easiest topping to use and a good covering of melted cheese is always appealing. Try to avoid using too much as it can get quite greasy. A little Parmesan sprinkled over the Cheddar gives it even more zest and goes a lovely golden-brown colour. This is good on pasta, especially with a scattering of ore-gano or marjoram over the top.

A mashed or sliced potato topping turns a bake into a substantial meal on its own. Spread a small amount of grated cheese over cooked, sliced potatoes on top of the bake to get a crisp skin on the potatoes when they're baked. A handful of Cheddar mixed in with mashed potatoes is a nice covering. Make them really creamy by mashing in a good knob of butter or margarine and some fresh or sour cream.

Then mix in one or two eggs and, when cooked, the mashed potato mixture will be light and fluffy.

Breadcrumbs are another standby. Used on their own they tend to go dry and catch on top. They can be mixed with an equal quantity of grated cheese in order to avoid this, or if you don't want a cheesy flavour, mix a dessertspoon of melted butter or margarine through the crumbs. A handful of sesame or sunflower seeds gives a nice crunch to a breadcrumb topping. A small, finely chopped raw onion either mixed through or sprinkled on top of the crumbs should just cook when the bake is finished off in the oven but still leave a tangy onion flavour.

Yogurt, fresh or sour cream and cottage cheese can be used either separately or in combination. Yogurt and/or fresh cream are suitable over curry based dishes and these will moderate the 'bite' of a very spicy dish. If you whisk one or two eggs through the cream or yogurt it will bind and set to a custard-like consistency when cooked. This also reduces the risk of curdling. A mixture of equal quantities of yogurt, sour cream and cottage cheese with 2 eggs mixed through is a delicious topping for a lasagne or moussaka. These dairy toppings must be cooked carefully, it's best to cook them at a lower heat for a longer time (300-350°F/150-180°C/Gas Mark 3-4) as if the temperature is too hot a skin will form on top. If this starts to happen and the bake obviously needs more cooking spread a sheet of greased tinfoil over the dish and finish off the cooking.

Soufflé mixtures are also suitable for topping certain dishes—particularly the heavier ones. See recipe for Leek and Lemon Soufflé on page 107.

# Fresh Vegetable Bakes

These homely bakes are filling and flavoursome. They reflect the seasons with their constituent vegetables, but their nature is best suited to those which grow in the winter—roots in particular.

Rich brown sauces are enlivened with stout, or made piquant with the addition of gherkins or capers. These flavours contrast with and counteract the inherent sweetness of root vegetables. Crumbly oat or cheesy breadcrumb toppings seal in the moisture while cooking.

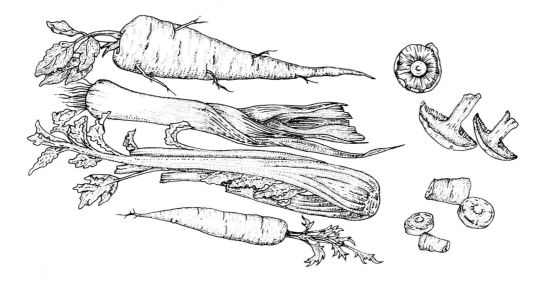

# Savoury Stout Crumble

1oz/25g butter or margarine
1lb/500g onion (diced)
1 teaspoon thyme
1 teaspoon coriander
1 teaspoon cayenne pepper
1oz/25g flour
1 dessertspoon tomato purée
1/2pt/300ml stock
1/2pt/300ml stout
Sea salt and freshly ground pepper
1 teaspoon yeast extract
Oil for frying
1lb/500g parsnips (cut into bite-sized pieces)
8oz/250g leeks (sliced)
8oz/250g carrots (cut into bite-sized)
1 cup rolled oats
1/2 cup mixed sunflower and sesame seeds
1/2 cup flour
1oz/25g butter or margarine

### 1

Melt the butter or margarine in a saucepan and add half of the onion. Fry until lightly browned, about 5 minutes.

### 2

Sprinkle the thyme, coriander, cayenne and flour over the contents of the pan. Cook, stirring, for another 5 minutes then add the tomato purée. Gradually stir in the stock and stout, then add the yeast extract. Bring the sauce to the boil and simmer for 15 minutes.

### 3

Heat 1 tablespoon of oil in a frying pan and toss in the rest of the onion and the parsnips then fry until browned and tender (10-15 minutes). Season with a pinch of salt and pepper and set aside.

### 4

Heat a little more oil in the pan and add the carrots. Fry until tender, seasoning with salt and pepper.

### 5

Cook the leeks in the same way.

### 6

Combine the vegetables and the sauce and taste for seasoning. Place them in an ovenproof dish.

### 7

Mix the oats, seeds and flour together, melt the butter or margarine and mix that in too. Spread the mixture evenly over the vegetables. Bake in the oven at 400°F/200°C/ Gas Mark 6 for 15-20 minutes until hot through.

# Leek and Lemon Soufflé

Oil for frying
1½lbs/750g leeks (thinly sliced)
Pinch of sage
Sea salt and freshly ground pepper
1 large onion (sliced)
8oz/250g mushrooms (thickly sliced)
Pinch of fresh basil
Juice and grated rind of 1 lemon
2oz/50g butter or margarine
2oz/50g flour
1pt/600ml milk
6oz/150g cottage cheese
4oz/125g tofu
3 eggs (separated)
2 tablespoons milk

### 1

Heat a little oil in a large frying pan and fry the leeks with the sage until tender (about 10 minutes). Add a pinch of salt and pepper and put it to one side.

### 2

Heat a little more oil in the pan and fry the onion for about 5 minutes or until transparent. Add the mushrooms and basil and cook for a further 5 minutes or until the mushrooms are just cooked. Season with the lemon juice and a little salt and pepper, then mix with the leeks.

### 3

Melt the butter or margarine in a saucepan and sprinkle the flour over. Cook, stirring for 3 minutes then whisk in the milk. Add the grated lemon rind and gently bring the sauce to the boil. Simmer for 5 minutes, add a pinch of salt and pepper, then combine the sauce with the vegetables and pour into a casserole dish.

### 4

Place the cottage cheese, tofu, egg yolks and 2 tablespoons of milk in a blender and blend for 1 minute.

### 5

Whisk the egg whites until peaks form but are not dry. Gently fold them into the blended mixture and spoon this over the vegetables.

### 6

Bake at 350°F/180°C/Gas Mark 4 for 20 minutes or until lightly browned on top.

107

# Cauliflower and Leeks with Gherkins and Capers

1 dessertspoon butter or margarine
1 medium onion (finely chopped)
1 dessertspoon flour
Pinch of thyme
2 teaspoons mustard powder
2 teaspoons ground coriander
1 teaspoon tomato purée
2 cups stock
2 teaspoons tamari
2 teaspoons sugar or honey
2 teaspoons vinegar
2 teaspoons capers (finely chopped)
1 tablespoon gherkins (finely chopped)
Oil for frying
3 medium carrots (chopped)
3 stalks celery (finely chopped)
1/2 a small head of cauliflower (cut into
bite-sized pieces)
3 medium leeks (chopped)
Squeeze of lemon juice
Sea salt and freshly ground pepper
1/2 cup breadcrumbs mixed with 1/2 cup
grated Cheddar cheese

### 1
In a saucepan fry half of the onion in the butter for a few (3-5) minutes.

### 2
Sprinkle over the flour and thyme and cook at medium heat, stirring occasionally for 5 minutes.

### 3
Sprinkle 1 teaspoon of mustard powder and 1 teaspoon of coriander over the mixture and stir in the tomato purée until well distributed through.

### 4
Whisk in the stock and 1 teaspoon of tamari and heat until simmering then turn heat to low and continue to simmer for 5 minutes

or until it thickens to a good consistency. Whisk in the sugar, vinegar, capers and gherkins and set aside.

### 5
Fry the rest of the onion in a little oil in a hot frying pan for 3-5 minutes then toss in the carrots, turn to a medium heat, cover with a tight fitting lid and cook, stirring once quickly, for 10 minutes.

### 6
Add the celery, 1/2 teaspoon coriander and 1 teaspoon of tamari. Stir well and cook for 5 minutes. Set aside.

### 7
Heat a little oil in the pan and stir the cauliflower around the pan for 3 minutes. Turn heat to medium, sprinkle over a tablespoon of water, cover and cook for 5 minutes before checking. It should be just cooked. Sprinkle over the remaining mustard, coriander and a good pinch of salt and pepper and set aside.

### 8
Heat a little more oil in the frying pan and toss in the leeks and stir them around for a few minutes. Turn heat to medium and cover and cook for 7-8 minutes until cooked. Sprinkle over a squirt of lemon juice and a pinch of salt and pepper.

### 9
Combine the vegetables and sauce in an ovenproof dish. Sprinkle over the cheese and crumbs. Bake at 180°C/350°F/Gas Mark 4 for 30 minutes or until bubbling hot around the edges.

# Stir-Fries and Summer Bakes

These dishes are intended as light meals ideal for the summer, or when appetites are moderate. They are also relatively low in calories, for those who are watching their weight.

Our stir-fried vegetables remains a firm favourite with the dancers and actors when they come to Food For Thought in the afternoon between rehearsals.

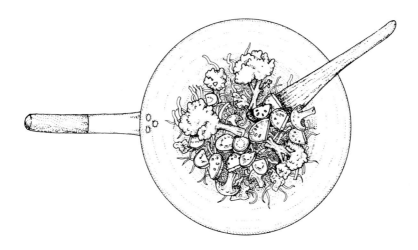

# Siriporn's Savoury Rice

2 tablespoons oil
2 cloves garlic (finely chopped)
1 medium onion (finely sliced)
1 green pepper (seeded and sliced)
1/2 cup fresh or frozen peas
1/2-1 head Chinese leaf (sliced coarsely)
4oz/125g button mushrooms (halved)
2 medium tomatoes (halved and then sliced)
2 carrots (sliced diagonally)
2oz/50g broken cashew nuts or peanuts
Pinch of ground ginger or freshly ground black pepper
Soy sauce to taste
2 1/2 cups cooked brown rice

### 1
Heat the oil in a large, heavy frying pan and sauté the garlic and onion over a medium heat, taking care not to brown the garlic or a bitter taste will result. Add the carrots, green pepper, peas and Chinese leaf and continue cooking over a moderate heat, stirring wtih a wooden spatula.

### 2
After a few minutes add the tomatoes, mushrooms and nuts and cook for a further 3 minutes. The vegetables should retain their fresh colour and crispness, so do not overcook them.

### 3
Season with ground ginger or black pepper and a splash of soy sauce.

### 4
Stir in the cooked rice, combine well and heat right through.

# Stir-Fried Vegetables

VEGETABLES:
2 medium carrots
2 medium courgettes
1 medium head of broccoli
4oz/125g mushrooms (sliced)
1/4 head of green cabbage (finely sliced)
1/2 a small Chinese cabbage (finely sliced)
4oz/125g beanshoots

SAUCE:
1 teaspoon oil
2 cloves garlic (crushed)
1/2 teaspoon ground ginger
2 dessertspoons tamari
2 dessertspoons stock

———————1———————
Cut the carrots in half lengthwise then finely slice them on the diagonal. Prepare the courgettes in the same way but cut them a little thicker.

———————2———————
Break the broccoli into florets and slice through them lengthwise.

———————3———————
To prepare the sauce, heat 1 teaspoon of oil in a small saucepan and add the garlic and ginger. Brown the garlic slightly then add the tamari and stock. Bring to the boil and set aside.

———————4———————
Heat a little oil in a large frying pan or wok and add the carrots. Toss them around for 1 minute then cover tightly and cook for 5 minutes. Add the broccoli and mushrooms and stir them in, cover the pan again and cook them for 5 minutes. Tip the vegetables out of the pan and put them aside.

———————5———————
Heat a little more oil in the pan and add the courgettes. Cover the pan and cook for 3 minutes then stir in the green cabbage and cover the pan again. Stir these vegetables after 2 minutes then cover and cook for a further 2 minutes.

———————6———————
Stir in the Chinese cabbage and bean-shoots, cover the pan and cook for 3 minutes or until hot through. These last 2 vegetables don't have to be 'cooked' at all, just heated. Add the carrots, broccoli and mushrooms and pour over the sauce. Toss the mixture well and serve on a bed of rice.

# Siriporn's Scalloped Vegetables

FOR THE FILLING:
2 tablespoons oil
1 large onion (sliced in rings)
1 clove garlic (finely chopped, optional)
1 medium white cabbage (thinly sliced)
6 sticks celery (thinly sliced)
1 x 8oz/250g tin sweetcorn
1pt/600ml milk
1 tablespoon cornflour
1 teaspoon ground ginger
4oz/125g button mushrooms (halved)
Sea salt and freshly ground black pepper

FOR THE TOPPING:
2 tablespoons oil
2 cups breadcrumbs
5oz/150g grated Cheddar cheese

———————1———————
Heat the oil in a heavy saucepan and sauté the onions and garlic until golden over a medium heat.

———————2———————
Add the cabbage and celery and continue cooking, stirring occasionally, until the vegetables are beginning to soften but still retain much of their crispness and colour.

———————3———————
Strain the sweetcorn and add to the saucepan.

_____ 4 _____

Mix the cornflour with 2 tablespoons of the milk to form a smooth paste. Add the rest of the milk to the vegetables and when it has warmed draw a little off with a ladle and mix with the cornflour paste. Pour the cornflour mixture into the vegetables and stir until the mixture thickens and comes to the boil.

_____ 5 _____

Reduce the heat and continue to stir adding the ginger and mushrooms. Turn out into an ovenproof dish and set aside.

_____ 6 _____

To prepare the topping, heat the oil in a heavy frying pan and add the breadcrumbs, stirring continuously until brown. Turn the breadcrumbs onto a plate and when cool mix in the grated cheese.

_____ 7 _____

Sprinkle the topping over the vegetables and cook in a moderate oven (250°F/ 180°C/Gas Mark 4) for 15-20 minutes.

# Oeufs Florentine

Oil for frying
1 clove garlic (crushed)
1 large onion (diced)
8oz/250g mushrooms (sliced)
1lb/500g spinach (roughly chopped)
Good grating of nutmeg
4 eggs
1oz/25g butter or margarine
1oz/25g flour
Pinch of coriander
Pinch of nutmeg
1/4 teaspoon mustard powder
1/2pt/300ml milk
2oz/50g grated Cheddar cheese
2 tablespoons breadcrumbs
Sea salt and freshly ground pepper

_____ 1 _____

In a large saucepan fry the garlic and onion for 5 minutes, then add the mushrooms and cook for another 5 minutes, season with a pinch of salt and pepper.

_____ 2 _____

Add the spinach and a good pinch of nutmeg and cover the pan for about 5 minutes on a medium heat until the spinach has reduced.

_____ 3 _____

Place the vegetables in a shallow casserole dish and smooth down the surface. With the back of a tablespoon, press 4 imprints into the surface. Break one egg into each of these.

_____ 4 _____

Melt the butter or margarine in a saucepan and sprinkle over the flour. Cook, stirring for 1 minute then sprinkle the rest of the spices over and gradually whisk in the milk. Slowly bring the sauce to the boil and simmer for 5 minutes stirring often.

_____ 5 _____

Take the sauce off the heat and stir in most of the cheese, saving a little for topping. Carefully pour the sauce over the vegetables then sprinkle over the breadcrumbs and cheese.

_____ 6 _____

Bake at 350°F/180°C/Gas Mark 4 for 20 minutes until lightly browned on top.

# Hot Pots Casseroles and Stews

These dishes are all cooked on top of the stove and rely on generous quantities of sauce to keep them moist and tasty. I have divided them into the following categories:

1. 'Exotic', spicy or hot dishes.
2. Winter stews and casseroles.
3. Lighter ragouts and hot pots.

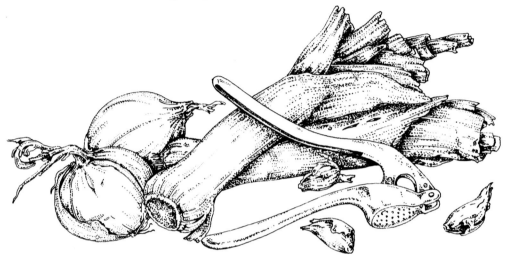

# 'Exotic' or Spicy Hot Pots

These dishes range from the North African inspired Tagine and Indian curries, through to the more subtle Cauliflower and Courgette Gado-Gado which uses a rich peanut butter sauce. Served on a bed of rice and accompanied perhaps with poppadoms or a swirl of natural yogurt in the dish itself, they sell well even in very hot weather.

Use fresh herbs and spices where ever possible. Keep your kitchen well stocked with fresh spices if you are partial to such dishes.

# Spicy Chickpea Saag

1 1/2 cups chickpeas (soaked overnight
will give 3 cups)
1 1/2 tablespoons oil
3 onions (diced)
1 clove garlic (crushed)
1 dessertspoon tomato purée
1 teaspoon cumin
1 teaspoon coriander
1 teaspoon garam masala
1 teaspoon paprika
1/2 teaspoon ground ginger
1 bay leaf
1pt/600ml vegetable stock
1 medium carrot (cut into strips)
1 dessertspoon tamari
1lb/500g spinach
2oz/50g raisins
Sea salt

### 1

Drain and rinse the beans then cover with water and boil for 1 hour or until tender. Set aside reserving the stock.

### 2

Heat the oil in a large saucepan and fry the onion and garlic for 10 minutes. Add the tomato purée, spices and the bay leaf and continue cooking for 5 minutes. Then add the stock, the carrot strips and the tamari, bring to the boil and leave on a low simmer.

### 3

Trim the stalks from the spinach and wash it well. Put about an inch of water in a saucepan and bring to the boil then put the spinach in the pan, pressing it all in. Cover with a tight fitting lid and cook on a high heat for 5 minutes. Rinse the spinach well in lots of cold water and drain. Squeeze out any excess water and chop finely.

### 4

Add the spinach, chickpeas, and raisins to the sauce with a little more stock if necessary. Bring to the boil and simmer for 10 minutes, then taste for seasoning adding more salt if you think it needs it.

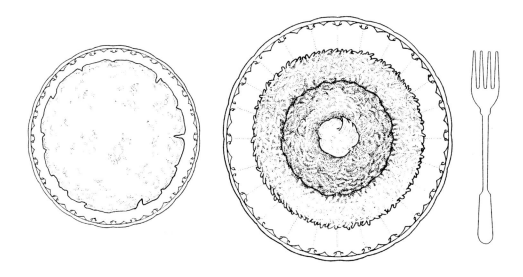

# Chilli

1 cup red kidney beans (soaked
overnight will give 2 cups)
Oil
2 medium onions (chopped)
3 cloves garlic
2 fresh green chillies (seeded)
1 dessertspoon tomato purée
2oz/50g raw ground almonds
1/2pint/300ml vegetable stock
4oz/100g chopped carrots
1/2 teaspoon ground coriander
1/2 teaspoon mustard powder
Splash of tamari
4oz/100g tinned sweetcorn, drained
1 large red pepper (seeded and cut into
strips)
Sea salt and freshly ground pepper
Chopped parsley or fresh coriander for
garnish

###### 1

Drain and rinse the kidney beans then
cover with water, add a splash of oil and boil
for 1 hour or until tender. Drain and rinse
well.

###### 2

In a large saucepan fry the onions in a little
oil until well browned (10-15 minutes).
Meanwhile blend the garlic, chillies, tomatoes and tomato purée to a paste. Pour this
mixture over the onions (it will hiss and
splatter a bit), boil for a few minutes then
add the stock, almonds and kidney beans
and leave on a low heat.

###### 3

Heat a little oil in a frying pan then add the
carrots and stir for a couple of minutes.
Sprinkle over 1 dessertspoon of water,
cover tightly and turn heat to low. Check
after 8-10 minutes; they should be just
tender. Sprinkle over the coriander, mustard and tamari then add the carrots to the
sauce.

###### 4

Check the chilli for seasoning, it may need a

little tamari, salt and pepper. If the dish
stands for 20-30 minutes its flavour will
improve and mellow.

###### 5

Heat the chilli until bubbling then add the
sweetcorn and red pepper. Allow a couple of
minutes for them to heat through then
serve garnished with fresh parsley or
coriander.

# Cauliflower and Mushroom Dahl

1 cup brown lentils (soaked for 1 hour in
hot water)
Oil for frying
2 onions (diced)
3 cloves garlic (crushed)
1 teaspoon curry powder
2 teaspoons garam masala
1 teaspoon coriander
1 teaspoon cumin
1/2 teaspoon ground cardamom
1 dessertspoon tomato purée
1 dessertspoon tamari
1/2pt/300ml vegetable stock
1 small cauliflower (cut into bite-sized
florets)
2 carrots (cut into strips)
2 courgettes (cut into bite-sized pieces)
8oz/250g button mushrooms
Sea salt and freshly ground pepper
Plain yogurt for garnish

###### 1

Drain and rinse the lentils then cover with
water and boil for 20 minutes or until
tender. Drain and rinse and set aside.

###### 2

Heat a little oil in a saucepan and fry the
onion and garlic for 10 minutes. Add the
spices, tomato purée and tamari then stir in
the stock. Bring to the boil and leave on a
low simmer.

###### 3

Heat a little oil in another saucepan and

###### 114

toss in the cauliflower with 1/2 a cup of water. Cover with a tight fitting lid and steam on a high heat for 5 minutes then set aside.

—————————— 4 ——————————

Heat a little more oil in the pan and toss in the carrots. Fry for 3 minutes then add the courgettes. Stir fry these for another 3 minutes then add the mushrooms and continue frying for 5 minutes. Sprinkle over a good pinch of salt and pepper.

—————————— 5 ——————————

Add the vegetables to the sauce, bring the mixture to the boil and simmer for 5 minutes. Taste for seasoning and serve on a bed of rice with a dessertspoon of yogurt over the top.

# Courgette and Chickpea Curry

1 cup chickpeas (soaked overnight will give 2 cups)
1 dessertspoon butter or margarine
1 small onion (finely chopped)
1 dessertspoon flour
2 teaspoons medium curry powder
1 tablespoon tomato purée
1pt/600ml vegetable stock
1 tablespoon peanut butter
1 teaspoon tamari
Oil for frying
1/4 of a medium head of cauliflower (cut into florets)
1 dessertspoon water
3 medium courgettes (cut into bite-sized pieces)
1/2 pint/300ml natural yogurt
Pinch of cayenne pepper

—————————— 1 ——————————

Drain and rinse the chickpeas, cover with water and boil for 1 hour or until cooked. Reserve the stock.

—————————— 2 ——————————

Melt the butter in a saucepan and fry the

onion for a few minutes. Sprinkle over the flour and cook, stirring for 5 minutes. Mix in the curry powder, tomato purée and stock, and simmer for 5 minutes. Stir in the peanut butter and tamari.

—————————— 3 ——————————

Heat a little oil in a pan and stir the cauliflower around in it for 2 minutes. Sprinkle over 1 dessertspoon of water, cover tightly and cook for just 5 minutes on a low heat. Set aside.

—————————— 4 ——————————

Heat a little more oil in the pan and fry the courgettes until just cooked (5 minutes or so).

—————————— 5 ——————————

Combine the vegetables and sauce and place in a ovenproof dish. Whisk the yogurt with a fork and spread over the top. Bake at a moderate heat, 350°F/180 C/ Gas Mark 4 for 40 minutes until hot through. The yogurt may curdle a little bit but this will not affect the flavour.

—————————— 6 ——————————

Garnish with a very light dusting of cayenne pepper and serve.

# Cauliflower and Courgette Gado Gado

2 tablespoons oil
2 medium onions (diced)
3 cloves garlic (crushed)
1 heaped teaspoon grated fresh ginger
1 dessertspoon tomato purée
4oz/125g crunchy peanut butter
1 dessertspoon tamari
1/2pt/300ml vegetable stock
1/2 teaspoon chilli powder
1 x 15oz/420g tin plum tomatoes
1 medium cauliflower (cut into bite-sized florets)
2 carrots (cut into bite-sized pieces)
3 courgettes (cut into bite-sized pieces)
8oz/250g mushrooms (sliced)
Sea salt and freshly ground pepper

### 1

Heat the oil in a large saucepan and fry the onions and garlic in it for 10 minutes. Add the ginger and tomato purée and cook for 3 minutes, then add the peanut butter, tamari, stock and chilli powder. Either blend or roughly chop the tomatoes and stir them in. Bring the mixture to the boil and leave on a low simmer.

### 2

Heat a thin film of oil in a saucepan and toss in the cauliflower. Throw over 1/4pt/150ml of water, cover with a tight fitting lid and let it steam over a medium heat for 5 minutes. The cauliflower should be barely cooked and quite crunchy. Set aside.

### 3

Heat a little more oil in the pan and toss in the carrots and stir them around for 3 minutes. Cover and cook on a medium heat for 7-10 minutes until just cooked then set aside.

### 4

Heat a little more oil in the pan and toss in the courgettes. Stir fry for 3 minutes then add the mushrooms. Continue cooking on a medium heat stirring occasionally for 5 minutes.

### 5

Add the vegetables to the sauce with a good pinch of salt and pepper. Heat through, taste for seasoning and serve on a bed of rice.

# Chickpea and Cashew Tagine

1 cup chickpeas (soaked overnight will give 2 cups)
Oil for frying
1 large onion (finely chopped)
4 cloves garlic (chopped)
2 teaspoons garam masala
1 teaspoon curry powder
1lb/500g tomatoes (chopped)
1/2 cup sultanas
1/2 cup dried apricots or prunes (chopped)
1 dessertspoon peanut butter
1/4pt/150ml apple juice concentrate
1/2 cup broken cashew nuts
Splash of tamari
Juice of half a lemon
Sea salt and freshly ground pepper

### 1

Drain and rinse the chickpeas then cover with water and boil for 1 hour or until cooked. Reserve the stock.

### 2

Fry the onion and garlic in a little oil in a medium saucepan until very soft, at least 10 minutes.

### 3

Sprinkle over the garam masala and curry powder, then add the tomatoes, dried fruit, peanut butter, apple concentrate and a little chickpea stock (or water if they are still cooking) to make a sauce. Simmer for 20 minutes adding more stock if necessary.

_____ 4 _____

Roast the cashewnuts in the oven at a moderate heat until they start to change colour (10 minutes or so), then splash over a little tamari while still hot and set aside.

_____ 5 _____

Combine the chickpeas with the sauce in a pot and sprinkle over a little salt and pepper. Gently bring to the boil then stir in the lemon juice and taste for seasoning. It should be mildly spicy and slightly sweet and sour. Adjust with tamari, sweetener, lemon juice or vinegar as you think fit.

_____ 6 _____

Mix in the cashews just before serving saving a few to sprinkle on the top.

# Christian's Hot Pot

1/2 cup haricot beans (soaked overnight)
2 tablespoons olive oil
2 medium onions (finely chopped)
2 cloves garlic (crushed)
3 tablespoons tomato purée
1lb/500g fresh tomatoes (or 1 large tin)
1 wine glass red wine
4 tablespoons fresh coriander (finely chopped)
1/2 teaspoon chilli powder (to taste)
2 tablespoons parsley (chopped)
1-2 lemons for juice (to taste)
Sea salt and freshly ground pepper
4oz/125g sphagetti
4oz/125g mushrooms (sliced)
1 clove garlic (crushed)
1 small red pepper (finely chopped)
1 small green pepper (finely chopped)
3oz/90g sweetcorn
Parmesan cheese and fresh coriander

_____ 1 _____

Drain and rinse the beans and then cook them in fresh water for 11/2 hours. Drain and rinse with cold water.

_____ 2 _____

Meanwhile, heat the oil in a large saucepan and sauté the onions and garlic until soft but not brown. Stir in the tomato purée, tomatoes (blended), red wine, fresh coriander and chilli powder. Bring to the boil and simmer for an hour or so. Season with parsley, lemon juice and salt and pepper.

_____ 3 _____

Cook the spaghetti in boiling water until just tender, drain and rinse with cold water. Toss with a little olive oil.

_____ 4 _____

Sauté the mushrooms in a little olive oil and crushed garlic for 5 minutes. Toss in the finely chopped peppers and cook for a further 2 minutes. Season with salt and pepper.

_____ 5 _____

Combine the sauce, beans, pasta, mushrooms and peppers and sweetcorn and heat through thoroughly before serving garnished with Parmesan cheese and finely chopped coriander.

# Winter Stews and Casseroles

These are the classic vegetarian main courses. Pulses and fresh vegetables bound by sharp garlic and tomato sauces, rich red wine sauces and piquant mustard sauces. The flavours of such stews may equally be bolstered by the addition of yeast extract, tamari or miso. Although the recipes here assume that cooking will take place on top of the oven it is possible to casserole the dishes in the oven, provided that the casserole is well sealed and the food not over cooked.

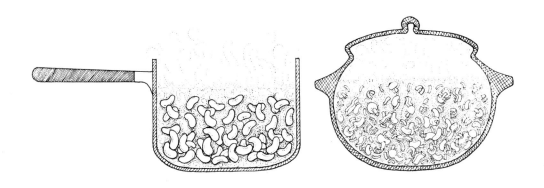

# Haricot Napolitaine

8oz/250g haricot beans (soaked overnight)
1 bay leaf
Oil for frying
4oz/125g mushrooms (sliced)
1 red pepper (seeded and sliced)
1 green pepper (seeded and sliced)
1 teaspoon freshly chopped basil
8oz/250g courgettes (cut into bite-sized slices)
1oz/25g butter or margarine
2 cloves garlic (crushed)
1 small carrot (grated)
1/2 small onion (diced)
1/2 stick celery (finely chopped)
1oz/25g flour
1 teaspoon tomato purée
1pt/600ml vegetable stock
1 bay leaf
1/2 teaspoon oregano
Dash of tamari
Sea salt and freshly ground pepper

―――――――― 1 ――――――――
Drain and rinse the beans then cover them with water, add a bay leaf, bring to the boil and simmer for about 1 hour or until tender. Drain, rinse and set aside.

―――――――― 2 ――――――――
Heat a little oil in a frying pan and fry the mushrooms and peppers with a half teaspoon of basil. When just cooked add a pinch of salt and pepper and put them with the beans.

―――――――― 3 ――――――――
Heat a little more oil in a large saucepan then add the courgettes and fry for 5 minutes or so until just cooked. Season

with a little salt and pepper and set aside.

─────────── 4 ───────────

Melt the butter or margarine in a large saucepan then fry the garlic, carrot, onion and celery until soft (about 5 minutes). Sprinkle over the flour and cook, stirring for 3 minutes then stir in the tomato purée. Whisk in the stock and gradually bring the sauce to the boil. Add 1/2 teaspoon oregano, the bay leaf, the oregano and a splash of tamari. Simmer the sauce for 15 minutes then stir in the vegetables and heat through. Serve on a bed of rice or spaghetti and garnish with a little grated cheese

# Kidney Beans and Mushrooms Bordelaise

1 cup kidney beans (soaked overnight will give 2 cups)
1 dessertspoon butter or margarine
1 small onion (finely chopped)
1 stalk celery (finely chopped)
1 dessertspoon flour
Pinch of thyme
1 teaspoon coriander
1 teaspoon mustard powder
1 teaspoon paprika
1 teaspoon tomato purée
1/2pt/300ml vegetable stock or hot water
1/2pt/300ml red wine
2 cloves garlic (crushed)
1lb/500g button mushrooms
1 dessertspoon tamari
1 small red pepper (seeded and chopped)
3 stalks celery (chopped)
1 teaspoon oregano
1/2 teaspoon fresh chopped basil
Pinch of marjoram
Sea salt and freshly ground pepper
Parsley for garnish

─────────── 1 ───────────

Drain and wash the beans then put them in a pot and cover them with water. Simmer for

1 hour or until tender then tip them into a colander and rinse well.

─────────── 2 ───────────

Meanwhile melt the butter in a saucepan and fry the onion and finely chopped celery in it until soft.

─────────── 3 ───────────

Sprinkle over the flour and thyme and cook, stirring, for 5 minutes then add the coriander, mustard, paprika, tomato purée and stock and whisk well until simmering.

─────────── 4 ───────────

Leave the sauce to simmer slowly while in a separate pan you quickly boil the wine for 2 minutes then stir it into the sauce and leave to simmer.

─────────── 5 ───────────

Heat some oil in a pan, stir in the garlic for a minute, then toss in the mushrooms and cook for 2 minutes. Add the tamari and stir well. Cover and leave to cook for 5 minutes then pour the juices off into the sauce and reserve the mushrooms.

─────────── 6 ───────────

Reheat the pan with a little more oil, toss in the red pepper and remaining celery and cook for 2 minutes. Sprinkle over the rest of the herbs and some salt and pepper and cook for a further minute.

─────────── 7 ───────────

Combine the beans, sauce and vegetables in a large pot and bring to the boil. Add a little more stock if it looks too dry. Simmer for 5 minutes then taste for seasoning, adding salt and pepper if necessary. Serve garnished with parsley.

# Aubergine and Potato Ragout

2 medium aubergines
2 teaspoons sea salt
3 medium potatoes
1 dessertspoon butter or margarine
1 small onion (finely chopped)
1 stalk celery (finely chopped)
1 small carrot (grated)
Pinch of thyme
1 dessertspoon flour
1 teaspoon paprika
1 teaspoon coriander
1 teaspoon mustard powder
1 teaspoon tomato purée
1pt/600ml potato stock
1/2 teaspoon yeast extract
1 teaspoon miso
Olive oil for frying
2 cloves garlic (crushed)
1lb/500g button mushrooms
1 teaspoon tamari
1/2 teaspoon oregano
1/2 teaspoon chopped fresh basil
Freshly ground black pepper

————————— 1 —————————

Trim the stalks from the aubergines, quarter them lengthwise then cut into bite size pieces. Place them in a colander and sprinkle them liberally with salt making sure that it is well mixed through. Leave for 20-30 minutes.

————————— 2 —————————

Cover the potatoes with water and boil until cooked, reserving the stock. When cool cut into bite sized pieces.

————————— 3 —————————

Melt the butter in a saucepan and fry the onion, celery and carrot with a pinch of thyme until very soft (10 minutes). Sprinkle over the flour and cook, stirring for 5 minutes then mix in the paprika, coriander, mustard and tomato purée. Whisk in the stock and stir in the yeast extract and miso. Leave the sauce on a low simmer stirring occasionally.

————————— 4 —————————

Wash the aubergines well under cold running water, shake well and turn onto kitchen paper to dry.

————————— 5 —————————

Heat some oil in a large frying pan and fry the garlic for a minute. Add the mushrooms and stir fry for 3 minutes then add the tamari. When the mushrooms are nearly cooked (about 5 minutes) sprinkle the basil and oregano over and cook for a further 2-3 minutes. Remove from the heat, pour the juices into the sauce and reserve the mushrooms.

————————— 6 —————————

Heat some more oil in the pan, just cover the bottom with some of the aubergines and cook, turning occasionally, until they turn golden brown and soft. Cook all the aubergines in this way (it may take 2 or 3 batches) adding more oil if they become too dry.

————————— 7 —————————

Combine the vegetables and sauce in a large pot and taste for seasoning. It is unlikely to need salt, perhaps just a little pepper.

# Hummus Hot Pot

1/2 cup chickpeas (soaked overnight)
2 tablespoons olive oil
2 medium onions (finely chopped)
2 cloves garlic (crushed)
1 large carrot (grated)
3 tablespoons fresh coriander (finely
chopped)
1/2-1 fresh chilli (finely chopped)
1 teaspoon ginger
2 tablespoons light tahini
1/2pt/300ml vegetable stock
Fresh lemon juice
Olive oil for frying
1 medium cauliflower (cut into florets)
A little ginger
2 carrots (cut into bite-sized pieces)
3 courgettes (cut into bite-sized pieces)
2 tablespoons sesame seeds (roasted)
1 handful finely chopped parsley
2oz/50g natural yogurt (blended to
pour)
Sea salt and freshly ground pepper

———————— 1 ————————

Drain and rinse the chickpeas then cover
with fresh water and boil for 1 1/2 hours or
until they are very soft.

———————— 2 ————————

Heat the oil in a large saucepan and sauté
the onions and garlic until soft (but not
brown). Stir in the grated carrot, coriander,
chilli and ginger, cover and simmer until the
carrots are tender. Remove from the heat
and blend with the tahini, chickpeas and
stock until the mixture is light and smooth.
It should pour like milk. Season with lemon
juice, salt and pepper and set the sauce
aside.

———————— 3 ————————

Heat a dessertspoon of olive oil in a large
saucepan, add a thin film of water and a
squeeze of lemon juice. Add the cauliflower,
cover and cook until the bright white colour
turns slightly milky; the florets should

remain crisp and crunchy. Sprinkle with
salt and a little ginger and set aside.

———————— 4 ————————

Heat a little more oil in the pan and cook the
carrots under cover but stirring frequently.
If the carrots stick to the bottom of the pan
add a little water. Cook until 'al dente',
season with salt, pepper and lemon juice
and set aside.

———————— 5 ————————

Add a little more oil to the pan and a clove of
crushed garlic and lightly cook the courgettes. They should just begin to turn
transparent and lose their colour. Season
with salt and pepper and set aside.

———————— 6 ————————

Combine all the ingredients and taste for
seasoning. Simmer for 5-10 minutes. Garnish with a sprinkle of sesame seeds and
finely chopped parsley and a swirl of
yogurt. Serve in a bowl with a slice of hot
pitta bread.

# Light Ragouts and Hot Pots

These dishes are similar to the stews and casseroles, but tend to be less heavy with lighter, more subtle sauces. Pulses, when used, are generally in smaller proportions and of the lighter type. The recipes range from apple-flavoured West Country Hot Pot to the tangy Sweet and Sour Vegetables. If you have never tried Jerusalem artichokes, the recipe on page 124 provides an excellent introduction to this underrated vegetable.

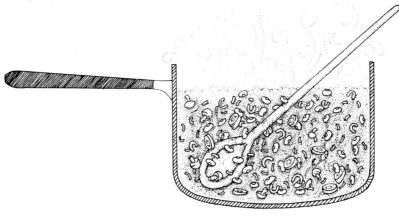

# Sweet and Sour Haricot Beans

1 cup haricot beans (soaked overnight
will give 2 cups)
Oil for frying
2 inch/5cm piece of ginger (grated)
3 cloves garlic (chopped)
1 fresh green chilli (seeded and chopped)
2 medium onions (finely chopped)
1 dessertspoon tomato purée
1/2 pint/300ml orange or pineapple juice
1 dessertspoon tamari
1 tin tomatoes
1 dessertspoon molasses
1 tablespoon vinegar (cider or malt)
1 tablespoon sugar or honey
Sea salt and freshly ground pepper
2 medium carrots (cut into strips)
2 stalks celery (chopped on the diagonal)
1 red pepper (cut into strips)
1 teaspoon ground coriander
1 teaspoon mustard powder
3 medium courgettes (chopped into bite-
sized pieces)
Juice of half a lemon

_____ 1 _____

Drain and rinse the beans then cover with water and simmer for 1 hour or until cooked. Reserve a cupful of stock.

_____ 2 _____

Heat a little oil in a medium-sized sauce-pan, fry the ginger, garlic and chilli for a few minutes then add the onions and cook, stirring often, until well done (at least 10 minutes).

_____ 3 _____

Add the tomato purée, orange or pineapple juice and tamari. Drain the juice from the tomatoes into the sauce, roughly chop the tomatoes then add them also. Heat the mixture to a low simmer then add the molasses, vinegar, sugar and a good pinch of salt. Leave on a low heat while you cook the vegetables.

_____ 4 _____

Heat a little oil in a frying pan and cook the carrots for 5 minutes. Stir in the celery, red pepper, coriander, mustard and a pinch of salt and pepper and cook for a further 3 minutes then set aside.

###### 5

Heat a little more oil in the frying pan and fry the courgettes for about 5 minutes or until just cooked. Sprinkle over a pinch of salt and pepper.

###### 6

Combine the beans, sauce and vegetables in a large pot. Heat gently to a simmer then test for seasoning. Add a little bean stock if it looks too dry. If it is too watery you can thicken it by stirring in 1 heaped teaspoon of cornflour dissolved in 3 fl oz/75ml of stock.

###### 7

Just before serving squeeze over the juice of half a lemon. Serve on brown rice.

# West Country Hot Pot

Serves 4-6
11/2 cups of butterbeans soaked overnight
1 teaspoon of English mustard powder
1 teaspoon of paprika
1/4 teaspoon of ground ginger
1 teaspoon of ground coriander
1 rounded dessertspoon of butter or margarine
1 small onion, finely chopped
2 cloves of garlic, crushed
1 rounded dessertspoon of wholewheat flour
A pinch of thyme
1pt/600ml medium sweet cider
3 medium courgettes, cut into bite-sized pieces
8oz/250g button mushrooms
4 sticks of celery, chopped
1 red pepper, chopped
1 green pepper, chopped
1/2 teaspoon fresh chopped basil
1/4pt/150ml apple juice concentrate
Sea salt and freshly ground pepper

###### 1

Rinse beans and cover with water, boil for 45 minutes or until nearly soft.

###### 2

Stir in mustard, paprika, coriander and ginger and continue simmering until beans are cooked. Drain and reserve the stock.

###### 3

Fry onion and garlic gently for 3 minutes in the butter, then add flour and thyme and cook for 3 more minutes over a low heat.

###### 4

Gradually stir in some of the bean stock until the sauce is thick, then add the cider and simmer for 5 minutes.

###### 5

Lightly fry the courgettes in oil and set aside. Fry mushrooms until they release their juices, then add celery. After a few minutes add pepper and heat through.

###### 6

Check and adjust seasoning, add a little basil.

###### 7

Combine all the ingredients and enhance flavour if necessary with apple juice concentrate. Simmer for 5-10 minutes and serve.

# Cauliflower Mornay

1 large cauliflower (broken into bite-sized florets)
1 medium onion (diced)
2 green peppers (thinly sliced)
4oz/125g mushrooms (sliced)
Sea salt and freshly ground pepper
1 teaspoon lemon juice
1oz/25g butter or margarine
1oz/25g flour
1/2 teaspoon mustard powder
Pinch of ground coriander
Pinch of nutmeg
Pinch of ground cloves
1pt/600ml milk
3oz/90g grated Cheddar cheese
1 x 12oz/340g tin sweetcorn
Pinch of paprika

––––––––––––– 1 –––––––––––––
Cook the cauliflower in salted boiling water until almost tender but still a little crunchy to bite (3-5 minutes). Drain and rinse in cold water and set aside.

––––––––––––– 2 –––––––––––––
In a little oil fry the onion, peppers and mushrooms for a few minutes until the onion is just cooked (about 5 minutes). Season with a pinch of salt and pepper and the lemon juice and set aside.

––––––––––––– 3 –––––––––––––
Melt the butter or margarine in a small saucepan and sprinkle the flour over. Cook, stirring for 3 minutes then add the spices and gradually whisk in the milk. Gently bring the mixture to the boil and simmer for 10 minutes stirring frequently.

––––––––––––– 4 –––––––––––––
Stir in the cheese and then add the sweetcorn. After 1 minute add the other vegetables. Heat through for about 3 minutes and taste for seasoning. Serve on a bed of rice garnished with a light dusting of paprika.

# Jerusalem Artichoke, Mushroom and Tahini Casserole

1oz/25g butter or margarine
1 small onion (diced)
1oz/25g flour
1 teaspoon garam masala
1 teaspoon coriander
1 teaspoon marjoram
1/2pt/300ml water or vegetable stock
1/2pt/300ml milk
1 bay leaf
2 tablespoons oil
1lb/500g Jerusalem artichokes (cut into bite-sized pieces)
1 medium carrot (cut into bite-sized pieces)
1 medium courgette (cut into bite-sized pieces)
8oz/250g mushrooms (sliced)
1 dessertspoon tamari
2 tablespoons tahini
Sea salt and freshly ground pepper

––––––––––––– 1 –––––––––––––
Melt the butter or margarine in a saucepan and fry the onion in it for 3 minutes. Sprinkle the flour, garam masala, coriander and marjoram in and cook, stirring for 3 minutes. Whisk in the stock or water and milk, add the bay leaf and gently bring to the boil and simmer for 10-15 minutes.

––––––––––––– 2 –––––––––––––
Heat the oil in a large frying pan and add the artichokes and carrot. Cover with a lid and cook on a medium heat for 10 minutes then add the courgette and mushrooms with a pinch of salt and pepper and cook, stirring for a further 3 minutes.

––––––––––––– 3 –––––––––––––
Whisk the tamari and tahini into the sauce then add the vegetables. Simmer for 5 minutes and taste for seasoning and serve.

# Courgette and Mushroom Chasseur

1oz/25g butter or margarine
1 small onion (finely chopped)
1 small carrot (grated)
Pinch of thyme
1 bay leaf
1oz/25g flour
1 teaspoon tomato purée
1/2pt/300ml stock
1 teaspoon tamari
Knob of butter or margarine
1 small onion (finely chopped)
3 or 4 mushrooms (finely sliced)
2 fresh tomatoes (chopped)
8 fl oz/250ml dry white wine
1/2 teaspoon tarragon
Sea salt and freshly ground pepper
Oil for frying
2 cloves garlic, crushed
3 courgettes (cut into bite-sized pieces)
8oz/250g button mushrooms
1/2 teaspoon basil
2 carrots (cut into bite-sized pieces)
2 sticks of celery (chopped)
1 red pepper (diced)
Chopped parsley for garnish

### 1

Melt 1oz/25g butter or margarine in a saucepan and add the first onion, carrot, thyme and bay leaf and fry for 5 minutes. Sprinkle over the flour and cook, stirring for a further 5 minutes then stir in the tomato purée and whisk in the stock and tamari. Bring to the boil and leave on a low simmer. The sauce should be quite thick.

### 2

In another saucepan melt the knob of butter or margarine and add the other onion and fry for 3 minutes. Add the finely sliced mushrooms and tomatoes, cover with a lid and cook gently for 5 minutes. Pour in the wine and boil rapidly with the lid off for 5 minutes then sprinkle over the tarragon and a pinch of salt and pepper and stir this mixture in with the other sauce.

### 3

Heat a little oil in a large saucepan and add the garlic and courgettes. Cover and cook for 3 minutes then add the mushrooms and cook for a further 5 minutes or until the vegetables are done. Season with the basil and a pinch of salt and pepper and set aside.

### 4

Heat a little more oil in the pan and add the carrots, then cover and cook for 7 or 8 minutes. Add the celery and continue cooking until the carrots are just cooked (3 or 4 minutes) then stir in the red pepper and a pinch of salt and pepper and cook for 1 minute.

### 5

Combine the vegetables and sauce in the pot and test for seasoning and consistency.

# Haricot Bean Ragout

1 cup haricot beans (soaked overnight
will give 2 cups)
1oz/25g butter or margarine
1 small onion (finely chopped)
1 small carrot (grated)
1 stick of celery (finely chopped)
Pinch of thyme
1oz/25g flour
1 teaspoon tomato purée
1pt/600ml stock
1 teaspoon yeast extract
1 teaspoon tamari
Oil for frying
2 leeks (finely sliced)
1/2 teaspoon sage
3 carrots (chopped into bite-sized
pieces)
1/2 teaspoon mustard powder
Splash of tamari
2 sticks of celery (chopped into bite-
sized pieces)
8oz/250g button mushrooms
Sea salt and freshly ground pepper
Chopped parsley for garnish

—————————— 1 ——————————
Drain and rinse the beans then cover them
with fresh water, bring to the boil and
simmer for 40-60 minutes until tender.
Drain and rinse and set aside.

—————————— 2 ——————————
Melt the butter or margarine in a saucepan
and add the onion, grated carrot and finely
chopped celery. Sprinkle over a pinch of
thyme and fry for 5 minutes. Sprinkle over
the flour and cook, stirring for 5 minutes
until lightly browned. Stir in the tomato
purée then gradually whisk in the stock and
stir in the tamari and yeast extract. Bring
the sauce to the boil then leave on a low
simmer, whisking occasionally.

—————————— 3 ——————————
Heat a little oil in a large saucepan and add
the leeks. Cover and cook for 7-10 minutes
stirring occasionally until just cooked.

Season with the sage and a pinch of salt and
pepper and set aside.

—————————— 4 ——————————
Heat a little more oil in the pan and add the
carrots. Cook as for the leeks for 10 minutes
or until cooked, season with a pinch of salt
and pepper, the mustard powder and a
splash of tamari and set aside.

—————————— 5 ——————————
Heat a little more oil in the pan and add the
celery and mushrooms. Cover and cook for
5 minutes or until the mushrooms are just
done, then season with a pinch of salt and
pepper.

—————————— 6 ——————————
Combine the beans, vegetables and sauce
in the pot. Bring the stew to a simmer and
taste for seasoning. The sauce should be a
rich brown colour, if it is a little pale stir in a
little more tamari to darken it. Garnish with
a little chopped parsley.

# Ratatouille Provençal

2 tablespoons oil
1 large onion (diced)
2 cloves garlic (crushed)
1 medium aubergine (cut into bite-sized pieces and sprinkled with salt)
1 medium carrot (cut into bite-sized pieces)
1 red and 1 green pepper (cut into strips)
3 courgettes (cut into bite-sized pieces)
1/2 teaspoon oregano
1/2 teaspoon marjoram
1/2 teaspoon cumin
1/2 teaspoon cayenne pepper
1 tablespoon tomato purée
1 x 15oz/420g tin plum tomatoes
1/2pt/300ml vegetable stock
1 tablespoon tamari
2 teaspoons cornflour
Sea salt and freshly ground pepper

### 1

Heat the oil in a large saucepan and fry the onion and garlic for 3 minutes.

### 2

Rinse the aubergines and add to the pan along with the carrot and peppers, cover with a lid and cook on a medium heat for 5 minutes.

### 3

Add the courgettes and the herbs and spices and cook, stirring occasionally for 3 minutes, then add the tomato purée, tomatoes, tamari and stock. Bring to the boil and simmer for 3 minutes then add a good pinch of salt and pepper.

### 4

Mix the cornflour to a paste with 2 tablespoons of cold water and gradually stir into the ratatouille. Simmer for a further 5 minutes then check for seasoning and serve.

# Chapter 6
# Quiches

Quiches form a vital part of our daily menus between the busy lunch time period and the evening rush. Quiche is perceived as being the ideal accompaniment to mixed salad almost to the point of monotony. This is unfortunate because, properly prepared and freshly consumed, quiche need never be the bland and rather tasteless offering that is all too common.

Quiche as its name suggests has its origins in France, although now just about every western country has its own version of the dish. The recipes that follow are designed to be eaten hot and fresh. In this state it is a delicious dish; light, fluffy and golden-brown. It should bear no resemblance to the old, cold and pale variety so often masquerading as quiche.

Quiches are easy to make and can include a wide variety of ingredients. The main points to remember are to use the best quality vegetables available, fresh herbs and that vegetable quiches should be eaten while hot. This is because vegetables are high in water content and tend to make the quiche soggy when cold.

# Wholewheat Shortcrust Pastry

This recipe is suitable for all the following quiches and makes enough to cover a 7 inch (18cm) round tin or fluted flan dish.

6oz/150g wholewheat flour
3oz/90g cold margarine
1/4 teaspoon salt
3 tablespoons cold water

### 1
Place flour and salt into a large mixing bowl and dice the margarine onto the flour.

### 2
Rub the margarine and flour between the fingers and thumb until a consistency of breadcrumbs is achieved. This should be done as quickly as possible to avoid warming the fat too much.

### 3
Add the water and mix in with a palette knife. Forming the pastry into a ball.

### 4
Transfer to a cool, floured surface and knead lightly for a few seconds.

### 5
Using a rolling pin, roll the pastry to a thickness of between 1/4 and 1/2 inch (6-12mm).

### 6
Grease the flan dish and line it with the pastry. Press the pastry to the edge of the flan dish between finger and thumb and trim off the excess pastry with a wet knife. The base is now ready for filling.

Note: In its raw state, pastry does not like heat. To this end avoid unnecessary handling of the pastry, use the coolest surfaces and receptacles and store in a container in the fridge. Pastry will keep in the fridge for up to 3 days.

129

# Basic Egg Mix for Quiche

2 eggs
1/2pt/300ml milk
1/2 teaspoon sea salt
1/2 teaspoon cayenne pepper

##### 1
Whisk the eggs, salt and pepper until slightly foamy. Add the milk and whisk for a further minute.

##### 2
The mixture may now be poured over the vegetables and cheese in the pastry case prior to baking.

Note: For a very light, fluffy quiche whisk for an extra 3 minutes.

# Some Quiche Fillings

## Courgette and Basil Quiche

3 medium courgettes
1 pastry case (see page 129)
4 leaves fresh basil (chopped)
2oz/50g grated Cheddar cheese
1/2pt/300ml egg mix (see above)

##### 1
Wash the courgettes, trim the ends and dice very finely and scatter in the pastry case.

##### 2
Sprinkle the basil and cheese over the courgettes.

##### 3
Cover with egg mix, being careful not to overfill the case because the filling will rise as it cooks.

##### 4
Cook in an oven preheated to 400°F/ 200°C/Gas Mark 6 for 30-35 minutes. The quiche should appear fluffy but firm and should not wobble when removed from the oven.

## Provençal Quiche

1 red pepper (sliced length-ways)
1 small onion (thinly sliced)
3oz/90g mushrooms (thinly sliced)
1 courgette (thinly sliced)
1 pastry case (see page 129)
1 teaspoon oregano
2oz/50g grated Cheddar cheese
1/2pt/300ml egg mix (see above)
2 tomatoes for decoration (sliced)

##### 1
Wash and prepare the vegetables, discarding the pips from the pepper.

##### 2
Place the vegetables in the pastry case, sprinkle over half the oregano and the grated cheese and then pour over the egg mix.

##### 3
Place the sliced tomatoes and the rest of the oregano on top. Bake in oven preheated to 400°F/200°C/Gas Mark 6 for 30-35 minutes.

# Mushroom and Onion Quiche

8oz/250g button mushrooms
1 medium onion
1oz/25g margarine
Pinch of black pepper
4 leaves fresh basil (chopped)
1 pastry case (see page 129)
2oz/50g grated Cheddar cheese
1/2pt/300ml egg mix (see page 130)

_____ 1 _____

Wash and dry mushrooms, cutting into quarters or halving depending on size. Chop onion finely.

_____ 2 _____

Melt the margarine in a saucepan and add the onions, cooking until transparent and soft.

_____ 3 _____

Add mushrooms to the saucepan and cover. When they have released their juices add the pepper and cook for a further minute.

_____ 4 _____

Remove saucepan from the heat, drain and reserve the juice as this is useful in soup or stock making.

_____ 5 _____

Put the cooked vegetables into the pastry case and sprinkle with basil. Cover the whole with grated cheese and egg mix.

_____ 6 _____

Bake in oven preheated to 400°F/200°C/ Gas Mark 6 for 30-35 minutes.

# Red and Green Pepper Quiche

2 red peppers
2 green peppers
1 pastry case (see page 129)
2oz/50g grated Cheddar cheese
1/2pt/300ml egg mix (see page 130)

_____ 1 _____

Cut 3 rings from one of the red peppers and 3 from one of the green and set aside for decoration.

_____ 2 _____

Chop the remaining peppers discarding the pips.

_____ 3 _____

Place the peppers into pastry case and cover with cheese and egg mix. Arrange the 6 rings on top.

_____ 4 _____

Bake in oven preheated to 400°F/200°C/ Gas Mark 6 for 30-35 minutes.

# Celery, Walnut and Sweetcorn Quiche

4 sticks celery
1 dessertspoon oil
1 teaspoon thyme
1 8oz/250g can sweetcorn
1oz/25g broken walnuts
1 pastry case (see page 129)
2oz/50g grated Cheddar cheese
1/2pt/300ml egg mix (see page 130)

———————— 1 ————————
Wash and chop celery into 1/2 inch/1.5cm pieces.

———————— 2 ————————
Heat the oil in a saucepan and gently cook the celery until tender, adding the thyme after 5 minutes of cooking.

———————— 3 ————————
Drain the sweetcorn thoroughly and combine with the celery and walnuts in the pastry case.

———————— 4 ————————
Cover with cheese and egg mix and bake in an oven preheated to 400°F/200°C/Gas Mark 6 for 30-35 minutes.

# Spinach Quiche

1 lb/500g fresh young spinach leaves
Sea salt
1 pastry case (see page 129)
1/2 teaspoon nutmeg
2oz/50g grated Cheddar cheese
1/2pt/300ml egg mix (see page 130)

———————— 1 ————————
Wash the spinach two or more times in plenty of running cold water or until there is no trace of grit.

———————— 2 ————————
Chop the spinach roughly and place in a saucepan to which has been added 1 tablespoon of water. Sprinkle a little salt over the spinach, cover and cook gently stirring occasionally.

———————— 3 ————————
When the spinach is tender drain and remove excess water by pressing down on the spinach with a potato masher. This method ensures maximum flavour from the spinach and prevents a soggy quiche.

———————— 4 ————————
Place cooked spinach in pastry case, sprinkle with nutmeg and cover with the cheese and the egg mix.

———————— 5 ————————
Bake in an oven preheated to 400°F/200°C/Gas Mark 6 for 30-35 minutes.

# Leek Quiche

2 medium-sized leeks
1 tablespoon oil
1 teaspoon sage
Pinch of sea salt
1/2 teaspoon English mustard powder
1 pastry case (see page 129)
2oz/50g grated Cheddar cheese
1/2pt/300ml egg mix (see page 130)

————————— 1 —————————
Top and tail the leeks, cut length ways and chop into 1 inch pieces. Place in a colander and wash thoroughly under running water.

————————— 2 —————————
Heat the oil in a saucepan and add the leeks, sage and mustard and cook gently until tender, add salt to taste.

————————— 3 —————————
Strain and reserve the juice (it is useful for sauce making) transferring the leeks to the pastry case.

————————— 4 —————————
Cover with cheese and egg mix, and bake in an oven preheated to 400°F/200°C/Gas Mark 6 for 30-35 minutes.

# Watercress Quiche

2 bunches watercress
1 pastry case (see page 129)
2oz/50g grated Cheddar cheese
1/2pt/300ml egg mix (see page 130)

————————— 1 —————————
Wash and thoroughly dry the watercress, discarding any discoloured leaves or roots. Chop roughly and place in pastry case.

————————— 2 —————————
Cover with cheese and egg mix.

————————— 3 —————————
Bake in oven preheated to 400°F/200 C/ Gas Mark 6 for 30-35 minutes.

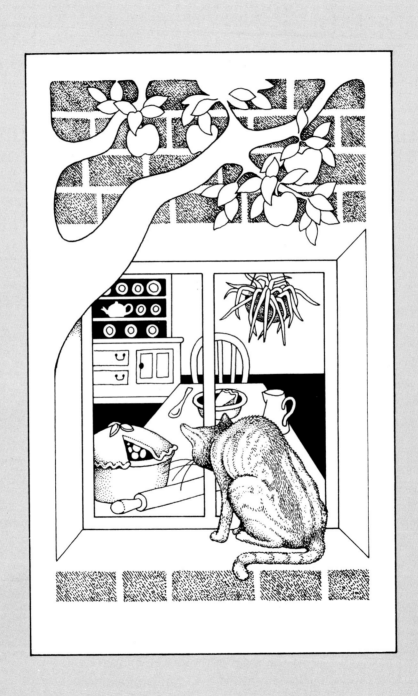

# Chapter 7
# Fresh Fruit and Fruit Desserts

## Choosing and Using Fresh Fruit

As with fresh vegetables it is as well to be aware of the seasonal nature of fruit. While it is true that much fruit is available for six or seven months of the year, it is wise, however, to take advantage of a particular fruit when it is naturally in season. This is when fruit is at its best in terms of quality and value. No matter the time of year there are always delicious fruits to choose from; in winter for example alongside the more normal apples and bananas, there are juicy mandarins, tangerines, clementines and a whole host of new crop nuts available (Brazil nuts, walnuts, hazelnuts, cobnuts to name but a few).

In late spring and early summer the first of the soft fruits arrive; peaches, nectarines, strawberries and various melons. These are followed in high summer and autumn by a myriad of berries; raspberries, blackcurrants, redcurrants, bilberries and loganberries. At this time of year the hedgerows are full of delicious wild blackberries—so much better than the commercial varieties. The best grapes, apples, eating pears and plums are also available at this time. If you are lucky enough to have a good greengrocer then this is also a good time to buy imported tropical fruit.

I have never understood the desire to merge one season with another and in the process produce expensive and tasteless fruit. Strawberries, for example, are available very early in the year but such fruit rarely has the flavour of those grown in the season. At Food For Thought we tend to buy home grown produce whenever possible. This is not because British produce is inherently better than that of any other country, rather it is because it travels a shorter distance and as a result is picked in a riper state without such a risk of damage in transit. This is particularly true of soft fruit, which is prone to bruising.

When choosing fresh fruit you should look for a healthy gloss to the skin and, where applicable, the skin itself should be taut and unblemished. Organically grown produce may well have a less attractive appearance but such blemishes as do exist should only be superficial. The flavour of such produce is often a revelation but it is no guarantee of superiority. Certain fruits—grapes, bilberries and plums for example—have a natural 'bloom' on them which does not necessarily indicate the presence of some sinister agricultural spray. It is, however, wise to wash all fruit before use, in view of the intensive methods of agriculture employed today.

In the following pages, I have attempted to give a rough idea of the seasons and their fruits, with a few (completely partial!) comments where necessary.

# Fruits Available all Year Round

## Apples

The staple fruit of Food For Thought is apples. We use them extensively in our crumbles, sponges and tarts, where the sharp and robust flavour of the Bramley cooking apple is incomparable. This variety is widely available, keeps well and is generally of good quality. There is a wider choice of eating apples available, though sadly much diminished in comparison with Victorian times. The reason is familiar; the desire to standardize crops and maximize output. This results in the varieties which are tricky to grow or low yielders, even though they may taste delicious, disappearing without trace. The best varieties of eating apples currently available are Cox's Orange Pippins, Granny Smiths, Sturmers, Red Worcesters and Russets. Acceptable alternatives are Golden Delicious—rather watery in flavour—or Star Kings, which are woolly and prone to bruising. It is worth noting that these eating apples may be used in preference to Bramleys in recipes for tarts where their natural sweetness reduces the need to sweeten the dessert with honey or sugar.

Most sliced apples will brown unless a little lemon juice is squeezed over them.

## Bananas

Quality is pretty even and there is little variation in flavour all year round. They are ripe when their skins are lightly speckled with brown spots and do not keep for more than a few days in this condition. Essential in fruit salads where their natural sweetness is vital, they also make an excellent alternative to apples as winter dessert 'bases'.

## Grapes

Sadly, the grapes available in this country are almost always disappointing. They tend to have been picked under-ripe and often possess a sour flavour and a tough skin. They do have their uses however, in particular for decoration and for adding colour and shape to fruit salads. In reality they bear no resemblance to the luscious and heady flavour of, for example, the French Muscat grape which, predictably, the French keep to themselves!

## Oranges and Lemons

Citrus fruits are remarkably consistent in quality, although they are best in winter. Oranges are an essential ingredient in fruit salads and, sliced finely, they are excellent for decorating trifles and cakes. Lemon juice is vital in fruit salads both for the sharpness it imparts and for its quality of preventing apples and bananas from browning. Lemon juice is also a useful ingredient in toppings and sponges where its sharpness counteracts any sweetness to produce another dimension of flavour.

# Seasonal Fruits

## _____ Winter Fruits _____

Winter is often seen as a lean time for fruit. True, it lacks the variety and sheer lusciousness of autumn, but the citrus fruits are particularly good. Tangerines, mandarins, clementines, mandoras (a cross between mandarins and oranges) and topaz—they are all variations on a theme and are wonderful used as decoration on cream—and yogurt—topped desserts. Pears are also available at this time of year, though they often have to be cooked before they are palatable. Try Poires Belle Kerreagh (see page 162) or Pears Poached in Port (see page 193).

There is a multitude of nuts freely available in winter. For example, Brazils, walnuts, hazelnuts and almonds can all be used to enrich our traditional puddings and fruit cakes. It is always possible to supplement fresh fruits with dried fruits, the use of which is often neglected.

## _____ Spring Fruits _____

In addition to the winter fruits above, we have to rely on imported fruits for variation in spring. Such fruit is often expensive and relatively flavourless, although exceptions include Kiwi fruits—a delicious and decorative addition to any dessert—Galia melons and some varieties of strawberries. It is therefore a good time of year to use dried fruits such as peaches, apricots, pears, prunes, dates, figs and bananas. The important point to note when using dried fruit is that their flavour suffers as a result of the drying process and that, weight for weight, dried fruit is much sweeter than its fresh counterpart. This sweetness can cause the dessert to be sickly; dryness and relative lack of flavour are also problems where dried fruit is concerned. For further guidance on the cooking of dried fruit, see page 138.

## _____ Summer Fruit _____

This is a marvellous time of year for British and imported soft fruit. Strawberries are in abundance and there are now many excellent varieties available. English and Scottish strawberries generally have the best flavour although this will depend largely on whether or not the sun shines!

Cherries are also widely available; the dark red imported varieties tend to have a sweeter fuller flavour, the paler English varieties being sharper and harder.

Peaches and nectarines are superb from southern France and Italy; make sure that the ones you buy are reasonably ripe or they will lack flavour.

Later in the season raspberries and loganberries will appear although somehow they always lack the flavour of home-grown fruit. Bilberries, blackcurrants and redcurrants are also in season but their quality is variable and their applications limited.

Gooseberries are much neglected, which is a shame because they make excellent tarts and fools, though it should be remembered that plenty of sweetening will be required in the cooking.

Melons abound; water melons, Galia melons, rock or Charantais melons (small, intensely-flavoured, orange-fleshed), this refreshing fruit is suitable for breakfast or starters. It tends to be too watery to use successfully in desserts except fruit salads.

The variety of tropical fruits is becoming wider and wider; along with kiwi fruits and pineapples there are now guavas, passion fruit, mangoes, star fruit and paw-paws. These are more easily available at large supermarkets although many high street green-grocers are now selling them. Tropical fruit is often expensive and thus is best reserved for special occasions when it should be eaten ripe and uncooked.

## _____ Autumn Fruit _____

The clichéd season of 'mellow fruitfulness' saying is certainly true for this time of year when the most luscious sun-ripened fruit is available.

Late apricots, peaches, and nectarines, sweeter and juicier than earlier in the year, are available at the beginning of this season. Blackberries, grapes and bilberries—marvellous at this time of year—are good for decorating desserts with creamy toppings. Damsons and plums provide welcome relief from the ubiquitous apple or rhubarb in crumbles. Another treat at this time of year are eating-pears, which when perfectly ripe should smell fragrant and sweet and yield slightly to the touch.

## Dried Fruit

Dried fruit suffers an unfortunate reputation for making dull desserts and being a ferocious laxative. Try as we might at Food For Thought, we cannot persuade customers to eat it unless heavily disguised.

Served by itself, dried fruit tends to be both over-sweet and over-rich. This is the result of the drying process itself.

In order to avoid this, it is recommended that you mix dried fruit with fresh. For example, the tartness of fresh apple will counteract the sweetness of the dried fruit. A good combination is that given in the recipe on page 161.

The most commonly available dried fruits are peaches, apricots, bananas, dates, figs and pears. These should be cooked by poaching for 1/2 an hour in a mixture of water and fruit juices, such as apple or orange. Allow twice the volume of liquid to fruit. Spices such as nutmeg, cloves, ginger or cinnamon enhance the flavour enormously. You may reduce the cooking time by pre-soaking the fruit, either overnight or for at least two hours in water, fruit juice or a little brandy.

It is wise not to mix too many dried fruits together as this will result in a confusion of flavours. In order to make a compote mix an equal amount of figs, apricots and prunes (or your particular favourites) and poach in brandy, cinnamon and apple juice. Serve with natural yogurt.

# Choosing Soft Fruit

An expert will tell you that each fruit has its own specific signs indicating ripeness. While this is true it is none the less possible to discern a few general characteristics.

- It has already been mentioned that soft fruits are susceptible to manhandling en route and, for this reason, it is usually best to buy the locally grown produce.
- Soft fruits are far more aromatic than harder fruits and this is often the best guide to their ripeness. The intensity of the fragrance of any soft fruit is in direct proportion to its ripeness; many more enlightened greengrocers will allow you to check exactly this—do not be afraid to pick up the fruit and smell it. Resist the temptation to press the fruit as this will bruise it and not endear you to the greengrocer!
- Once ripe, soft fruit will not keep for long.

It is, however, possible to keep most soft fruits in the refrigerator for up to two days provided they are covered, but it will do nothing to improve their flavour. Avoid over chilling as this will destroy their delicate cell structure and result in mushy fruit. To preserve the appearance of soft fruit in desserts it is possible to use lemon juice or fruit glaze—recipes for such glazes follow later.

Most of the fresh fruit recipes in this book are very simple to make. This is the best way to serve fruit of high quality; its flavour should be allowed to come through without being smothered by sugars and cream. Having said this, judicious use of a combination of freshly whipped cream, natural yogurt and honey makes a wonderful contrast, both in terms of colour and flavour, to the fruit. The following recipes will, I hope, give an insight to the best use of the wide range of fruits available.

# Sauces, Toppings and Custards

All too often the sauces used in sweets are tasteless and thin, the custards floury and gelatinous and the toppings of artificial cream would be better suited to a shaving kit in a bathroom, rather than the decorating accoutrements of the kitchen. Familiar also is the use of sauces to cover up bland and uninteresting bases: the excuses are economy and convenience. I hope the following recipes will show how easy it is to make really effective sauces and toppings without great effort, complexity or expense. They should enhance, enrich, provide the contrast and enliven the appearance of the dish they are used in. These recipes, though few in number, may be varied to form a good range: for example, substitution of various fruit yogurts in place of natural yogurt to suit the base fruit in the Cream and Yogurt Topping recipe. Or the substitution of instant coffee powder or essence for cocoa to make a coffee sauce.

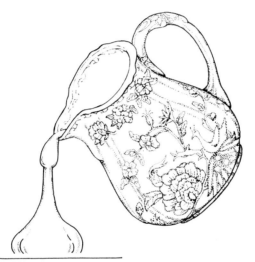

## Cream and Yogurt Topping

This is our most often used and most versatile summer dessert topping. In appearance it has a stark whiteness and a pearl-like sheen while its texture is creamy, smooth and light. Its flavour is a delicate balance of the sweetness of honey and the sharpness of natural yogurt.

Once again, the quantities used in this recipe are suitable for the subsequent recipes, unless otherwise indicated.

1/4pt/150ml natural yogurt
1/2pt/300ml whipped cream
1 dessertspoon clear honey

_____ 1 _____
Using a hand whisk, mix the honey and yogurt thoroughly.

_____ 2 _____
Fold in the whipped cream with a palette knife. The consistency should be light, fluffy and spreadable. It is now ready for use.

Note: If desired, a few drops of vanilla essence may be added for extra flavour or a little lemon juice can be used for greater sharpness.

The topping may be kept in the fridge for two days but remember to whisk it again before use.

139

# Chocolate Sauce

This is a rich, dark chocolate sauce ideal for decorating creamy desserts and for inclusion in banana sponges.

2oz/50g margarine
1 tablespoon clear honey
2oz/50g sifted cocoa powder
3fl oz/100ml milk
1 tablespoon whipped cream
1 tablespoon dark rum (optional—this enriches the flavour and has a preserving effect)

_____ 1 _____

Place the ingredients, except the cream, into a small saucepan and heat gently stirring all the time. Once the ingredients have blended, allow to boil then remove from the heat.

_____ 2 _____

The cream is then added to counteract the rather bitter taste of the cocoa, and if desired a little rum or coffee essence may be added at this stage.

The sauce is now ready to be used. If it is to be used for decoration allow it to cool until it becomes more viscous, then trickle it onto the well-cooked dessert.

# Real Custard

1/2pt/300ml milk
1 tablespoon raw brown sugar
1 vanilla pod, split
2 whole eggs
1 level dessertspoon arrowroot
1 dessertspoon brandy (optional)

_____ 1 _____

Heat the milk, sugar and vanilla pod gently in a saucepan and bring to the boil.

_____ 2 _____

Meanwhile, beat the eggs and arrowroot together in a mixing bowl with a wooden spoon until a smooth paste has been formed.

_____ 3 _____

Add the boiled milk gradually to the paste stirring all the time.

_____ 4 _____

Return the mixture to the saucepan and reheat, stirring all the time. When the custard begins to coat the back of the spoon it is ready—be careful not to boil the custard or it will curdle.

# Fruit Desserts

Dessert-making at Food For Thought is of necessity simple. Fresh fruit desserts are usually on a base which acts as a sweetener and also provides substance so that the dessert may be cut. The fruit is generally covered in a topping or glaze to enrich it.

# Sweet Pastry Base

6oz/150g wholewheat flour
2oz/50g cold margarine
1oz/25g soft raw cane sugar
1 egg yolk
1 tablespoon cold water
Greaseproof paper to line flan dish
1/2 cup dried haricot (or similar) beans

_____ 1 _____

Make sure your hands are clean and dry. Sift the flour into a large mixing bowl and dice in the margarine. Rub the mixture between finger and thumb until a consistency of 'breadcrumbs' is achieved.

_____ 2 _____

Cream the egg yolk and sugar until the mixture begins to lighten in colour.

_____ 3 _____

Add the egg and sugar to the flour mixture and mix in with a palette knife.

_____ 4 _____

Add water until the mixture has binded; it should be soft and malleable in texture, but not sticky or 'pasty'.

_____ 5 _____

When the correct consistency has been reached, turn the dough onto a cool, floured surface and knead lightly. Do not over knead or the dough will become over-warm and rubbery.

_____ 6 _____

Roll out the pastry with a floured rolling-pin to the required size using a firm and positive pressure. Then roll the dough around the pin and spread over a greased 8 inch (20cm) flan dish, pressing the pastry firmly into the dish and on the sides and then trimming off any excess.

_____ 7 _____

Prick the base of the pastry all over with a fork and place the greaseproof paper in the pastry case and cover with the dried beans. This is to prevent the pastry rising too much when it is being baked 'blind'.

_____ 8 _____

Bake the pastry for 10 minutes in an oven preheated to 400°F/200°C/Gas Mark 6 or until the pastry has a dry rather than oily look. The case is now ready to be filled but remember that the pastry will need at least a further 20 minutes cooking. If you are using soft fruit for the filling (which will not need any cooking) you must completely cook the pastry before filling it i.e. for 25-30 minutes.

141

# Sweet Pastry Based Desserts

The following desserts are sweet pastry based and as such require moister fillings to counteract the relative dryness of the pastry base. These pastries tend to make better winter desserts.

# Apple and Raisin Lattice Tart

3 Bramley cooking apples
2oz/50g raisins
1 teaspoon mixed spice
1 tablespoon Demerara sugar
8oz/250g sweet pastry case and scraps
for lattice decoration
A little milk for brushing
16 whole walnuts

### 1

Wash the apples, core and slice them. Place in a heavy saucepan with the sugar, spice and 2 tablespoons water. Cover with a tightly fitting lid and cook gently until the apples are soft and pulpy. Purée the apples with a wooden spoon.

### 2

Add the raisins to the puréed apple and leave them to absorb the juice.

### 3

Bake 'blind' for 10 minutes then remove the paper and pulses and return the pastry to the oven for a few minutes to dry it out.

### 4

With remaining scraps of pastry, knead together and roll out in a rectangular shape approximately 8 x 4 inches (20 x 10cm) and 1/4 inch (5mm) thick. Brush with milk and cut lengthways into 8 thin strips.

### 5

Fill the pastry case with the apple and raisin mixture and lay four of the pastry strips across the fruit. Lay the remaining strips at right angles across these to form a lattice. Press the strips down to the edge of the pastry case, trim and decorate each intersection with a walnut.

### 6

Bake at 375°F/190°C/Gas Mark 5 until the pastry is golden—about 20 minutes. This dessert may be eaten hot or cold served with cream or fruit yogurt.

# Rhubarb Meringue

2lb/1kg rhubarb
4oz/125g Demerara sugar or clear honey
1 tablespoon soured cream
2 egg whites
3oz/90g soft light raw cane sugar
1oz/25g flaked almonds
Sweet pastry case (see page 141)

_____ 1 _____

Wash rhubarb and cut into one inch pieces, discarding any that are coarse or discoloured.

_____ 2 _____

Place the rhubarb in a heavy saucepan, add the sugar or honey and 1 tablespoon of water. Cover with a tight fighting lid and cook over a low heat until soft. Rhubarb contains a lot of water, so plenty of juice should be given out during the cooking. Once cooked leave the rhubarb to stand in its own juice for a while.

_____ 3 _____

Preheat oven to 375° F/190° C/Gas Mark 5.

_____ 4 _____

Roll out pastry and line a 7 inch (18cm) round cake tin which has been well greased. Pinch the edge of the pastry onto the cake tin, prick the base with a fork all over and place a piece of greaseproof paper over the pastry weighed down with two cupfuls of haricot beans or uncooked macaroni.

_____ 5 _____

Meanwhile bake the pastry case blind. (See previous recipe.)

_____ 6 _____

Separate the whites from two eggs thoroughly—or the meringue will not stiffen properly.

_____ 7 _____

Whisk egg whites until they form 'peaks', then fold in the soft brown sugar, a spoonful at a time, whisking to maintain the texture.

_____ 8 _____

Drain the juice from the rhubarb (this may be kept if you wish and used in crumble making) and add the soured cream. Whisk the mixture until the cream is well incorporated and the rhubarb breaks into strands.

_____ 9 _____

Pour the rhubarb into the pastry case, smoothing it down with a palette knife.

_____ 10 _____

Spoon the meringue mixture over the rhubarb making sure that the fruit is completely covered but leave the top uneven. This will help the meringue to remain light—it does not like being handled—and gives a pleasantly 'peaked' effect.

_____ 11 _____

Sprinkle flaked almonds over the meringue and cook for 20 minutes at 325° F/170° C/Gas Mark 3 until golden. Cut when cool.

# Bakewell Tart

1 x 8 inch (20cm) sweet pastry case
(see page 141)
2 tablespoons fruit 'extra' jam
(blackcherry, strawberry or
blackcurrant)

FOR SPONGE MIX:
3oz/90g soft margarine
3oz/90g soft raw can sugar
2 eggs
2oz/50g wholewheat flour
1 level teaspoon baking powder
2oz/50g ground almonds
1/2 teaspoon almond essence
1 tablespoon milk
1oz/25g flaked almonds

———————— 1 ————————
Preheat the oven to 350°F/180°C/Gas
Mark 4.

———————— 2 ————————
Spread the jam evenly over the sweet pastry
case.

———————— 3 ————————
Make up the sponge mix following the
recipe on page 151. Spread the sponge mix
over the jam and sprinkle with flaked
almonds.

———————— 4 ————————
Bake until golden and well risen—about
35-40 minutes.

# Pineapple and Almond Slice

6oz/150g shortcrust pastry
(see page 141)
4oz/125g butter or margarine
5oz/140g soft brown sugar
1 egg
4oz/125g flour
3/4 cup ground almonds
1 level teaspoon baking powder
1/3 of a medium fresh pineapple for
decoration

———————— 1 ————————
Roll out the pastry and line a greased,
shallow baking tin.

———————— 2 ————————
Beat the sugar and butter or margarine until
light and fluffy, add the beaten egg and fold
in the flour, ground almonds and baking
powder.

———————— 3 ————————
Spread the mixture over the pastry case.

———————— 4 ————————
Cut the pineapple across in 1/2 inch/1cm
slices, trim off the skin and cut out the hard
centre. Place the rings on top of the
mixture. (Tinned pineapple may be used.)

———————— 5 ————————
Bake in an oven preheated to 325°F/
170°C/Gas Mark 3 until the mixture has
risen and is slightly brown. A good way of
testing whether a sponge mixture like this
is cooked is to lightly press it with the
finger. If it leaves a dent, it needs a few more
minutes in the oven.

———————— 6 ————————
Leave to cool and serve with cream.

# Trifles

This most traditional of English desserts has, unfortunately, earned itself an unpleasant reputation at the hands of unsympathetic chefs and mean proprieters. However, when properly made they are delicious and easy to prepare. The use of fresh fruit is essential, real sherry or brandy (the essences are artifical and unpleasant in flavour) and home made custards are desirable though not essential.

Trifles should be rich, light and refreshing. Here are four variations on a theme.

# Tutti Frutti Trifle

1 cereal bowl full of fresh fruit salad (such as orange, grapefruit, apple, banana, pineapple, peach, strawberries and grapes)
12oz/340g vanilla sponge (see page 151)
1/4pt/150ml sweet or medium-sweet sherry
1pt/600ml vanilla custard (see page 140)
1 tablespoon whipped cream (to lighten custard)
1/4pt/150ml whipping cream (for decoration)
1 tablespoon roasted chopped hazelnuts

### 1

Crumble the sponge into an 8 inch (20cm) clear serving bowl.

### 2

Cover the sponge with the fruit and pour over the sherry.

### 3

Make the vanilla custard and leave to cool for 15 minutes, then fold in the whipped cream for a lighter, creamier texture.

### 4

Pour the custard over the fruit and leave to cool completely. At this point the trifle may be put in the fridge for a day or so to allow the fruit and sponge to mingle with the flavour of the sherry.

### 5

To decorate, pipe twirls of whipped cream and top with chopped hazelnuts.

145

# Banana Rumba

2 tablespoons dark rum
3/4 cup raisins
1 chocolate sponge (see page 152)
3 bananas
Juice of half a lemon
1/4 fresh pineapple (tinned is acceptable
out of season)
Cream and yogurt topping
(see page 139)
1 tablespoon toasted desiccated coconut

―――――― 1 ――――――
Pour the rum over the raisins and allow to
soak, turning once or twice, for at least 1
hour.

―――――― 2 ――――――
Make up the sponge following the recipe on
page 00. Crumble the sponge into an 8 inch
(20cm) serving dish and sprinkle the rum
soaked raisins over them.

―――――― 3 ――――――
Peel and slice the bananas, squeezing the
lemon juice over them to prevent them
browning.

―――――― 4 ――――――
Place the bananas over the raisins and then
cover with the cream and yogurt topping.

―――――― 5 ――――――
Decorate the dessert with slices of pineapple and orange and scatter with the
coconut. Chill and serve.

# Chocolate, Banana and Walnut Trifle

1 walnut sponge (see page 152)

FOR THE CHOCOLATE CUSTARD:
1pt/600ml milk
2 level tablespoons cornflour
1 level tablespoon cocoa powder
1 level tablespoon sugar
3 bananas
Juice of half a lemon
1/4pt/150ml whipping cream
2 tablespoons coffee essence
8 roast walnuts

―――――― 1 ――――――
Make up the walnut sponge as in the recipe
on page 152. Crumble into a clear glass bowl
measuring 8 inches (20cm) across.

―――――― 2 ――――――
Heat the milk and sugar in a saucepan until
hot but not boiling.

―――――― 3 ――――――
Sift the cocoa powder into the milk and
whisk.

―――――― 4 ――――――
Cream the cornflour with a little water to
produce a smooth runny paste, add this to
the milk and cocoa.

―――――― 5 ――――――
Return the pan to the heat and whisk
thoroughly. Boil for 2-3 minutes to ensure
proper cooking and thickening. (If the
cocoa and cornflour are not properly cooked
the custard will have a powdery texture.)

―――――― 6 ――――――
Allow the custard to cool a little before
pouring over the fruit.

―――――― 7 ――――――
Meanwhile, slice up the bananas, squeeze
the lemon juice over them and place over
the sponge crumbs. Cover the bananas with
the slightly cooled chocolate custard.

―――――― 8 ――――――
Whip the cream and fold in the coffee
essence with a metal spoon.

―――――― 9 ――――――
When the custard has cooled completely,
pipe coffee cream twirls and top with whole
walnuts.

# Summer Trifle

12oz/340g vanilla sponge (see page 151)
2 tablespoons brandy
2 bananas
1pt/600ml vanilla custard
(see page 140)
8oz/250g black grapes
1 punnet strawberries
1oz/25g roasted hazelnuts
1/4pt/150ml single cream

_____ 1 _____
Crumble the sponge into a serving bowl and sprinkle with the brandy.

_____ 2 _____
Thinly slice the bananas and scatter over the sponge.

_____ 3 _____
Prepare the custard and pour over the bananas.

_____ 4 _____
Remove the stalks from the fruit and halve the larger strawberries. Halve and de-pip the grapes.

_____ 5 _____
Scatter the strawberries and grapes over the cold, set custard and top with a few nuts. Serve with single cream.

# Shortbread Based Desserts

These recipes are shortbread based and are good winter desserts using fruit which is readily available at that time of year.

They are more substantial than the previous recipes, but need not be heavy.

# Cheesecake Shortbread Base

This recipe is used primarily for cheese-cakes, but may also be used for any of the recipes using a scrunch or sweet pastry base. It has a crumbly, melt-in-the-mouth texture that is a little more luxurious than the other bases.

2oz/50g butter or margarine
2oz/50g wholewheat flour
2oz/50g small rolled oats
1oz/25g soft raw cane sugar

#### 1
Gently heat the butter in a small saucepan until it is clear but not brown.

#### 2
Add the remaining ingredients to the pan and mix thoroughly with a wooden spoon.

#### 3
Transfer the mixture to greased 8 inch (20cm) cake tin and press down with the finger tips.

#### 4
Bake for 10-15 minutes at 375°F/190°C/Gas Mark 5 until golden. Take care not to over cook as when the base is used for cheesecake it will have to cook for a further 25-30 minutes.
If the base is to be used for fresh fruit which requires no cooking, bake for a full 30-35 minutes.

TROUBLESHOOTING:
Shortbread bases have a habit of sticking to whatever they are cooked in. If you use a cake tin with a removeable base and line it with grease proof paper before filling you should avoid any trouble.

# Pear and Blackcurrant Shortbread

FOR THE BASE:
4oz/125g soft margarine
2oz/50g soft raw cane sugar
6oz/150g wholewheat flour

FOR THE TOP:
2 pears (ripe Conference are best)
2 tablespoons blackcurrant 'extra' jam
2 tablespoons apple juice
1/2 teaspoon cornflour

FOR THE SHORTBREAD:
#### 1
Cream the margarine and sugar in a mixing bowl with a wooden spoon until light and fluffy. The longer the mixture is creamed, the lighter the texture of the shortbread.

#### 2
Add the flour gradually to the mixture using finger tips to rub it in when the mixture becomes too stiff to use a spoon.

#### 3
When the flour has been incorporated, turn the mixture onto a floured surface and knead very gently before rolling the dough into a ball.

#### 4
Grease an 8 inch (20cm) baking tin generously and press the shortbread into it forming an even surface. Prick the short-bread several times with a fork.

#### 5
Bake for 30 minutes at 350°F/180°C/Gas Mark 4 until golden brown.

#### 6
When completely cool, remove the short-bread from the tin by inverting the tin and giving the based a sharp tap. The shortbread should then be ready to ease out with a

palette knife. Place the shortbread on a flat plate or a cake board.

## FOR THE TOPPING:

_____ 1 _____

Wash the pears and remove the stalks. Cut in half length-ways and cut out the pips. Slice the pears length-ways as thinly as possible.

_____ 2 _____

Layer the pear slices, overlapping each other, over the shortbread.

_____ 3 _____

In a small saucepan, mix the jam and apple juice and heat gently.

_____ 4 _____

Meanwhile mix the cornflour with a little cold water to form a smooth paste and add to the jam when the mixture begins to bubble. Stir in well. When any cloudiness has disappeared spoon the sauce over the fruit.

_____ 5 _____

Leave the dessert to cool and set before serving.

# Peach Brandy Surprise

FOR THE BASE:
4oz/125g soft margarine
2oz/50g soft raw cane sugar
6oz/150g wholewheat flour

FOR THE TOP:
2-3 ripe peaches
3 tablespoons brandy
1 tablespoon strawberry 'extra' jam
1 tablespoon apple juice
1/2 teaspoon cornflour

FOR DECORATION:
1/4pt/150ml whipping cream
6 fresh strawberries

_____ 1 _____

Make the shortbread base as for Pear and Blackcurrant Shortbread on page 148.

_____ 3 _____

Wash and dry the peaches, halve and remove the stones. Slice the peaches finely, placing them in a shallow dish. Sprinkle the peaches with 1 tablespoon of the brandy and leave to marinade for at least 10 minutes.

_____ 3 _____

Meanwhile, place the jam, apple juice and the remaining 2 tablespoons of brandy in a saucepan and heat gently, stirring with a wooden spoon, until the mixture is smooth.

_____ 4 _____

Mix the cornflour with a little water to form a paste, add to the saucepan and stir in well. The initial cloudiness will disappear as the cornflour cooks.

_____ 5 _____

Arrange the peach slices on the shortbread, overlapping the slices for an attractive effect.

_____ 6 _____

Spoon the glaze over the peaches, but leave the peaches just uncovered. (Any remaining glaze may be stored in the refrigerator for up to 2 days and served with ice cream or yogurt).

_____ 7 _____

When the glaze is cool and has set, whip the cream and pipe 6 whirls of cream on top of the dessert. Finally decorate the cream with strawberries.

149

# St Clements Cheesecake

SHORTBREAD BASE:
2oz/50g butter or margarine
2oz/50g wholewheat flour
2oz/50g small rolled oats
1oz/25g soft raw cane sugar

FOR THE TOPPING:
Juice and zest of 1 lemon
Zest of 1 orange
2oz/50g clear honey
1 egg
12oz/340g cottage cheese
1 tablespoon soured cream

FOR DECORATION:
1 orange
1 lemon

### 1

Follow method on page 148 for Cheesecake Shortbread.

### 2

Zest the orange and lemon using a zester or a fine grater, collect the zest on a saucer. Squeeze the lemon over the zest.

### 3

Place the cottage cheese in a blender and blend on a medium speed until it has the texture of thick yogurt.

### 4

Add the contents of the saucer and the honey to the cheese.

### 5

Whisk the egg until fluffy.

### 6

Stir the sour cream into the cottage cheese mix and fold in the whisked egg.

### 7

Pour this mixture over the shortbread base.

### 8

Cook at 325°F/170°C/Gas Mark 3 for 25 minutes or until the cheesecake is slightly firm. Don't overcook or the flavour will be drab and eggy.

### 9

Leave to cool, then refrigerate. Decorate with thinly sliced oranges and lemons, strawberries or black and white grapes, depending on the season.

# Sponges

These recipes are strictly for summer: the abundance of attractive soft fruit and lighter appetites of that time of year are most appropriate.

Fresh fruit is generously laid across a light sponge base, glazed if necessary and then attractively decorated with piped, whipped cream. The permutations are endless using different fruits and sauces, varying sponge flavourings and toppings.

The effect is to allow the beauty of the fruit to show through, decorating should be kept to a minimum.

In the following pages you will find hints and information to help stimulate your imagination—and so too your taste buds!

# Basic Vanilla Sponge

This is suitable for all subsequent recipes using sponge bases.

4oz/125g soft margarine
4oz/125g soft brown sugar
2 whole eggs
1 teaspoon real vanilla essence
4oz/125g wholewheat flour
1 teaspoon baking powder
2 tablespoons milk (if necessary)

———————— 1 ————————
Preheat oven to 350°F/180°C/Gas Mark 4.

———————— 2 ————————
Cream the margarine and sugar together in a large mixing bowl with a wooden spoon until light and fluffy. The longer the mixture is creamed the lighter the sponge will be. If you have a mixer, use it!

———————— 3 ————————
Add the lightly whisked eggs and vanilla essence and mix briefly.

———————— 4 ————————
Using a metal spoon, add the flour, a third at a time, using a cutting and 'scraping-round-the-bowl' motion. This is known as 'folding in' and helps to prevent the forcing out of air incorporated in the mixture at stage 2.

———————— 5 ————————
Next thoroughly incorporate the baking powder. If the mixture is too stiff some milk may be added at this stage.

———————— 6 ————————
Spoon the sponge mix into a greased 8 inch (20cm) cake tin and cook in the preheated oven on the middle shelf for 30 minutes.

———————— 7 ————————
The sponge will be cooked when it has risen, has shrunk slightly from the sides of the tin and has a springy texture. Insert a skewer into the sponge—if it emerges clean the sponge is cooked.
When ready carefully turn out the sponge and place on a cooling rack to cool.

# Some Variations Based on the Vanilla Sponge

## CHOCOLATE SPONGE:
In place of the vanilla essence and 1 tablespoon of flour, add 1 tablespoon of cocoa powder and 1 extra tablespoon of milk.

## ALMOND SPONGE:
In place of 3oz/75g flour and vanilla essence, add 2oz/50g ground almonds (expensive but worth it), 1 teaspoon almond essence and 1 extra tablespoon milk.

## WALNUT SPONGE:
Replace the vanilla with almond essence and add 2oz/50g finely chopped walnuts.

# Hints on Sponge Making

- Wholewheat flour gives a richer flavour and better texture to sponges. However, it is important to use a finely milled brand of flour if you are to avoid a rather heavy sponge. If the flour is coarse, sift it before weighing. Be sure you know whether or not the flour you use contains a rising agent. If not, the addition of baking powder is essential.
- The sugar used should be 'soft raw cane' or 'muscovado' (unrefined) as these are fine and therefore dissolve more completely when creamed. Demerara sugar crystals are too large and can remain undissolved during the cooking process.
- The margarine should be of good quality and soft. This aids the creaming process.
- The eggs are size 3 or 4—this helps in the consistency of proportions.
- The oven should always be preheated.
- Baking powder: although sodium bicarbonate is a chemical rather than a living organism, it is like yeast in its effect on sponge. Because it starts working as soon as it is mixed in, it is important to transfer the mixture to the oven without delay. Remember, too, that baking powder does not keep for ever!
- If it is necessary to add milk to alter the consistency of the mix, it should be done so by the spoonful.
- Cooking tins should be greased before being used.
- Finally, resist the temptation to open the oven door—especially during the early stages of baking—as this will cause the sponge to collapse.

# Sponge Desserts

The following desserts are sponge based, using a variation of the basic sponge recipe on page 151.

They are all excellent summer desserts making full use of the abundant soft fruit available at that time of year.

These desserts should be served lightly chilled, but remember that over-exposure to fridge temperatures will dry out and damage the appearance of the fruit.

## Strawberry and Blackcurrant Flan

1 punnet (8oz/250g) of strawberries

FOR THE GLAZE:
5oz/140g blackcurrant 'extra' jam
1/4pt/150ml apple juice
1 level teaspoon cornflour
1/4pt/150ml whipping cream

———————— 1 ————————
Wash and hull the strawberries leaving three with their stalks on—set these aside for decoration.

———————— 2 ————————
Prepare the vanilla sponge as described on page 151. Allow sponge to cool and remove from flan case. Place all but 3 strawberries onto the sponge.

———————— 3 ————————
Mix the cornflour with 1 tablespoon of the apple juice to form a smooth paste.

———————— 4 ————————
In a small, heavy saucepan heat the jam and the remainder of the apple juice gently. When the jam begins to bubble, add the cornflour and stir in well with a wooden spoon. The cloudiness in the mixture will disappear when it has boiled and the cornflour is cooked.

———————— 5 ————————
When the glaze has cooled slightly, but before it has thickened too much, pour it evenly over the strawberries and leave to cool completely.

———————— 6 ————————
While the glaze sets, whip the cream until it is light and fluffy. Using a 'star' nozzle on a piping bag, pipe the cream around the walls of the flan case and then pipe six 'twirls' of cream onto the strawberries at regular intervals.

———————— 7 ————————
Cut the reserved strawberries into quarters and place them on top of the cream twirls and around the edge of the flan.

153

# Chocolate Blackberry Excess

1 chocolate sponge (see page 152)
made with: 4oz/125g soft margarine
4oz/125g soft raw cane sugar
2 whole eggs
3oz/90g wholewheat flour
1 tablespoon cocoa powder
1 teaspoon baking powder
2-3 tablespoons milk

Chocolate sauce (see page 140)
Cream and yogurt topping (see page 139)

1 punnet (8oz/200g) blackberries
1/4 cup chopped roasted hazelnuts

———————— 1 ————————
Make the chocolate sponge, chocolate sauce and cream and yogurt topping as directed.

———————— 2 ————————
When cool, break the sponge into pieces and place in the serving dish. Spoon over two-thirds of the warmed chocolate sauce.

———————— 3 ————————
Wash and dry the blackberries and sprinkle half of them onto the sponge and sauce. Then spread the yogurt topping over the fruit with a palette knife.

———————— 4 ————————
Sprinkle the remaining blackberries and the hazelnuts over the yogurt topping.

———————— 5 ————————
Dribble the rest of the chocolate sauce, in large zig-zags, across the fruit and yogurt using a jug with a fine spout. This helps to give an authentic sundae effect.

Note: Various combinations of berries may be used in this dessert—try strawberries and raspberries.

# Strawberry and Kiwi Delight

1 vanilla sponge (see page 151)
Cream and yogurt topping (see page 139)
1 punnet (8oz/250g) of strawberries
1 kiwi fruit
1 dessertspoon toasted coconut

———————— 1 ————————
Make up the vanilla sponge as on page 151
Allow to cool and break into a 8-inch (20cm) serving dish.

———————— 12 ————————
Spread the cream and yogurt topping over the cake crumbs.

———————— 3 ————————
Wash and hull the strawberries, halving them. Peel the kiwi fruit and slice it finely with a sharp knife.
The kiwi slices and strawberries may be arranged neatly on the cream and yogurt topping or scattered over—it will still look nice.

———————— 4 ————————
Sprinkle the toasted coconut over the fruit.

# Tangerine Dream

1 chocolate sponge (page 152)
Cream and yogurt topping (see page 139)
Zest of 1 orange
3 tangerines
Chocolate sauce (see page 140)
1oz/25g chopped toasted hazelnuts

———————— 1 ————————
Make up chocolate sponge as on page 152. Allow to cool and crumble the sponge into an 8 x 3 inch (20 x 8cm) pyrex serving dish.

———————— 2 ————————

With a zester or fine grater, zest the orange and add to the cream and yogurt mixture. Spread the topping over the cake crumbs.

———————— 3 ————————

Peel the tangerines carefully, ensuring that they remain intact, then with a very sharp knife cut thin slices across the fruit. Arrange the slices over the cream and yogurt, in neat patterns but do not cover the cream and yogurt completely.

———————— 4 ————————

Pour over the warm (but not too hot) chocolate sauce in the spaces around the fruit. Sprinkle the chopped hazelnuts over the tangerines.

Note: Orange peel is more suitable for zesting than tangerine peel as the latter is extremely bitter.

# Peach Melba Supreme

1 vanilla sponge (see page 151)
Cream and yogurt topping (see page 139)
2 ripe peaches
1/2 punnet raspberries

FOR THE MELBA SAUCE:
1 tablespoon raspberry 'extra' jam
1 tablespoon apple juice

———————— 1 ————————

Crumble the vanilla sponge into an 8 inch (20cm) serving dish.

———————— 2 ————————

Cover the cake crumbs with cream and yogurt topping, smoothing it with a palette knife.

———————— 3 ————————

Wash and dry the peaches, then cut through to the stone and separate the halves by gentle twisting in opposite directions. If the peach is ripe this should be easy. Slice the peach halves thinly and arrange them over the topping.

———————— 4 ————————

Wash the raspberries and scatter them among the peach slices.

———————— 5 ————————

Put the raspberry jam and the apple juice into a blender and blend until smooth. It is optional whether or not you strain the sauce to remove the raspberry pips which will be unaffected by the blending. The sauce will be smoother if it is strained but the dessert will look more interesting if it is left unstrained.

———————— 6 ————————

Using a jug with a fine spout, trickle the sauce over the peaches—this should be a delightful colour combination.

Note: If you have any sauce left over it will keep for 2 days in the fridge and is delicious mixed with natural yogurt.

Four Winter Sponges:

# Danish Apple Cake

1 almond sponge (see page 152)
2lb/1kg Bramley cooking apples
4oz/125g raw cane sugar
4 cloves
2 tablespoons apple juice
1 teaspoon mixed spice
2oz/50g raisins
Cream and yogurt topping (see page 139)
3oz/90g chopped almonds or hazelnuts
1 tablespoon clear honey

——————— 1 ———————
Crumble the sponge into an 8 inch (20cm) serving dish.

——————— 2 ———————
Wash, core and slice the apples. Cook them in a tightly lidded saucepan with the apple juice, sugar and cloves until soft and pulpy.

——————— 3 ———————
Add the mixed spice and the raisins, allow to cool and then spread over the sponge. The sponge should absorb any excess moisture.

——————— 4 ———————
Spread the cream and yogurt topping over the fruit.

——————— 5 ———————
Combine the honey and the chopped nuts, warm slightly and pour randomly over the dessert.

# Apple and Almond Sponge

2lb/1kg Bramley cooking apples
1 teaspoon mixed spice—optional
1 teaspoon cinnamon—optional
Almond sponge mix (see page 152)
1 tablespoon flaked or chopped almonds
1/4pt/150ml whipping cream
1 small green eating apple
Juice of 1 lemon

——————— 1 ———————
Preheat oven to 375°F/190°C/Gas Mark 5.

——————— 2 ———————
Lightly grease a 7-8 inch (18-20cm) pyrex dish.

——————— 3 ———————
Spoon cooked apple (see crumble recipe on page 161) into dish.

——————— 4 ———————
Prepare the almond sponge mix and spoon it over the apple smoothing it with a palette knife.

——————— 5 ———————
Sprinkle the almonds on top and bake for 30-35 minutes or until golden.

——————— 6 ———————
Wash and quarter the eating apple, removing the core. Slice thinly and squeeze the lemon juice over to prevent the apple browning.

——————— 7 ———————
To serve this dessert hot, arrange the sliced apple on the cooked sponge and serve with whipped cream. The sponge will be lighter if it is served hot but is deliciously moist served cold decorated with twirls of whipped cream topped with the sliced apple.

# Pear and Brandy Sponge

3 soft pears
1 tablespoon brandy
Vanilla sponge mix (see page 151)
1 orange—for decoration

———————— 1 ————————
Preheat oven to 375°F/190°C/Gas Mark 5.

———————— 3 ————————
Wash pears, halve and remove stalks and pips. Slice thinly.

———————— 3 ————————
Arrange the pears in a shallow 8 inch (20cm) greased pyrex dish and sprinkle most of the brandy over.

———————— 4 ————————
Prepare the vanilla sponge mix and smooth it over the pears with a palette knife.

———————— 5 ————————
Bake for 30-35 minutes or until golden brown.

———————— 6 ————————
When the sponge is cooked sprinkle the rest of the brandy over the sponge and serve, decorated with slices of orange, while still hot and before the brandy evaporates!

# Bananas in Bed

4 bananas
2oz/50g cashew nuts or walnuts
Chocolate sauce (see page 140)
1 quantity vanilla sponge mixture (see page 151)
A few nuts for decoration

———————— 1 ————————
Preheat oven to 375°F/190°C/Gas Mark 5.

———————— 2 ————————
Peel and cut the bananas in half, then cut the halves lengthways. Arrange the bananas in a well-greased pyrex dish (8 inch/20cm) and sprinkle with the nuts.

———————— 3 ————————
Make up the chocolate sauce and pour evenly over the bananas.

———————— 4 ————————
Prepare the sponge mixture and spoon it over the bananas, smoothing it with a palette knife. Sprinkle a few nuts over the mixture.

———————— 5 ————————
Bake in the preheated oven for 25-30 minutes until golden and serve immediately with cream or vanilla custard.

157

# Scrunches

Many of our desserts are termed 'scrunch' and these prove to be our most popular sweets. Scrunch refers to the sweet, oaty base which, when baked and broken up, readily absorbs the juice of the fruit covering it. It is chewy and substantial and makes an excellent backdrop to soft fruit such as strawberries and raspberries. Scrunch can be made up an hour or so before serving and will then be a moist dessert which should melt in the mouth. Alternatively, scrunch may be used while still hot in which case it will be crunchy and like a toasted cereal.

# Basic Scrunch Recipe

This is suitable for all subsequent recipes demanding a scrunch-type base.

3oz/75g margarine
3oz/75g raw cane sugar
2oz/50g jumbo rolled oats
2oz/50g medium rolled oats
2oz/50g wholewheat flour

### 1

Place all the ingredients into a large mixing bowl, dicing the margarine and rubbing it between finger and thumb until thoroughly mixed in.

### 2

Grease a shallow baking tray and press the mixture onto the tray with the palm of your hand to a depth of approximately 1/2 inch (1cm).

### 3

Bake in an oven preheated to 375°F/190°C/Gas Mark 5 for 15-20 minutes until golden.

### 4

When cooked leave to cool, then cut it into sections and lift these out with a palette knife. Break the scrunch into nugget-sized pieces before covering with fruit.

Note: For variety, some of the following may be substituted before baking: Replace 2oz/50g jumbo oats with 2oz/50g chopped almonds or 2oz/50g chopped hazelnuts or 2oz/50g desiccated coconut.
Raisins may be added to the scrunch base after it has been cooked and broken up.

# Raspberry or Blackberry Scrunch

1 punnet (8oz/250g) of raspberries or blackberries
Scrunch base (see page 158)
Cream and yogurt topping (see page 139)

### 1
Wash and dry the fruit.

### 2
Cover the bottom of a shallow dessert dish with broken scrunch base to the depth of approximately 3/4 inch (2 cm).

### 3
Spread the cream and yogurt topping evenly over the scrunch base to the depth of approximately 1/2 inch (1cm).

### 4
Scatter the raspberries or blackberries over the cream and yogurt. Serve lightly chilled.

# Strawberry and Coconut Scrunch

1 punnet (8oz/250g) of strawberries
Scrunch base (see page 158), but made by substituting 2oz/50g desiccated coconut for 2oz/50g jumbo oats)
Cream and yogurt topping (see page 139)
2oz/50g desiccated coconut (lightly toasted) for decoration

### 1
Wash, halve and hull the strawberries.

### 2
Cover the bottom of a shallow dessert dish with broken scrunch base to a depth of 3/4 inch (2cm).

### 3
Spread the cream and yogurt topping evenly over the scrunch to a depth of 1/2 inch (1cm).

### 4
Arrange the strawberries, cut side down, on top of the topping and sprinkle the toasted coconut over the top. Refrigerate before serving.

# Banana and Raisin Scrunch

2-3 thinly sliced bananas
Juice of 1 lemon
2oz/50g raisins
3 halved slices of orange for decoration
(6 halves)
Scrunch base (see page 158)
Cream and yogurt topping (see page 139)

———————— 1 ————————
Squeeze the lemon juice over the sliced bananas to prevent them browning.

———————— 2 ————————
Cover the bottom of a shallow dessert dish with broken scrunch to the depth of 3/4 inch (2cm), scatter the raisins over the scrunch and then arrange the sliced banana on top.

———————— 3 ————————
Spread the cream and yogurt topping over the fruit with a palette knife and arrange the orange halves decoratively on top.

# Banana and Lemon Scrunch

3 lemons
Scrunch base (see page 158)
2-3 thinly sliced bananas
Cream and yogurt topping (see page 139)

———————— 1 ————————
Wash and dry the lemons.

———————— 2 ————————
Thinly slice one of the lemons and set aside for decoration.

———————— 3 ————————
Using a zester or the finest holes on a grater. zest the two remaining lemons and add the zest to the cream and yogurt mixture.

———————— 4 ————————
Squeeze the juice of the two zested lemons over the sliced bananas.

———————— 5 ————————
Cover the bottom of a shallow dessert dish with broken scrunch base to a depth of about 3/4 inch (2cm). Arrange the bananas over the scrunch.

———————— 6 ————————
Spread the topping over the bananas with a palette knife and decorate with lemon slices.
This sharp and refreshing dessert should be well chilled before serving.

# Crumbles

Fruit crumbles remain the most enduringly popular pudding we make at Food For Thought. There are numerous variations on the crumble theme, but it is worth saying a few words of general guidance.

First, always use good quality cooking apples, Bramleys are best, or any fruit that is naturally sharp in flavour, such as plums, rhubarb or blackberries. This counteracts the sweetness of the topping and gives a more robust flavour.

Second, use Demerara sugar in the topping as this results in an agreeable crunchy texture.

# Apple Crumble

1½lbs/750g large Bramley apples
1 level tablespoon Demerara sugar
1 tablespoon apple juice
4 cloves

### FOR THE TOPPING:
3oz/90g butter or margarine
2oz/50g Demerara sugar
2oz/50g medium rolled oats
2oz/50g large rolled oats
2oz/50g wholewheat flour

---
### 1
---
Preheat oven to 375°F/190°C/Gas Mark 5.

---
### 2
---
Wash, core and cut apples into bite-sized pieces. Place the apples in a large saucepan with the sugar, apple juice and cloves. Cover and cook gently until the apples are soft but not pulpy, stirring occasionally to prevent sticking. When cooked, transfer into an ovenproof dish and set aside.

---
### 3
---
To prepare the topping, place the oats and flour into a large mixing bowl and run in the butter until the texture of breadcrumbs is achieved. Mix in the sugar.

---
### 4
---
Spoon the crumble topping over the apples and smooth over lightly with the finger tips.

---
### 5
---
Cook for 25 minutes or until golden. Serve with whipped cream or blackcurrant yogurt.

Note: As a variation on crumble toppings, replace the large oats with desiccated coconut or replace 1oz/25g of the large oats with 1oz/25g chopped hazelnuts, almonds or walnuts.

## APPLE AND RHUBARB

12oz/340g apples
12oz/340g rhubarb
4oz/125g Demerara sugar

Cook the apple as in recipe for apple crumble.
Wash the rhubarb and cut into 2 inch (5cm) pieces. Place in an ovenproof dish and sprinkle with the sugar. Cover with foil and cook in the oven at 425°F/220°C/Gas Mark 7 for 25 minutes or until soft.
Leave the rhubarb to stand in its own juices for 10 minutes before draining and adding to the cooked apple.
Then proceed as for apple crumble.

## 'HEDGE ROW'

8oz/250g apples
1 punnet blackberries
1 punnet raspberries

Add the soft fruit to the cooked apple and proceed as for the original recipe.

## TURKISH FRUIT

8oz/250g apples
1lb/450g cooked dried fruit—figs, dates, apricots, prunes, etc. (see page 138)
1 lemon

Combine the cooked dried fruit with the cooked apple and add the lemon juice. Proceed as for original recipe.

## APPLE AND PEAR

12oz/340g apples
12oz/340g soft pears

Wash, halve and core the pears then slice them thinly. Add to the cooked apple and proceed as for original recipe.

And finally, a creamy, pear-based custard:

# Poires Belle Kerreagh

6 pears (peeled, cored and halved)
8oz/250g plain chocolate
3/4 cup mixed roasted chopped nuts
3 large eggs
2 tablespoons honey
1pt/600ml milk
Pinch of cinnamon

—————————— 1 ——————————
Cover the bottom of a 9 inch/23cm soufflé or ovenproof dish with the prepared pears.

—————————— 2 ——————————
Melt the chocolate in a bowl placed over hot, but not boiling, water and pour over the pear halves.

—————————— 3 ——————————
Sprinkle over the chopped nuts. Don't be too generous with the nuts and chocolate as this is rather a rich dessert.

—————————— 4 ——————————
Whisk the eggs, honey and milk, add a pinch of cinnamon and pour the mixture over the pears.

—————————— 5 ——————————
Bake in a slow oven—325 F/170°C/Gas Mark 3 until the custard is set and firm, about 45 minutes.

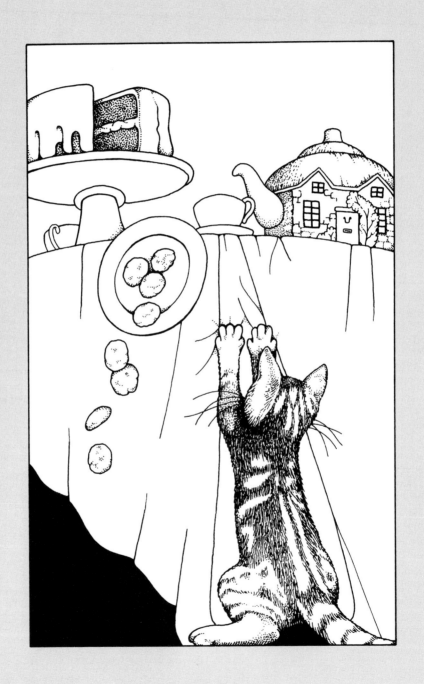

# Chapter 8
# Breads, Cakes and Flapjacks

## Bread Baking

We have always baked our own bread at Food For Thought and, although it is hardly cost effective to do so, the benefits in terms of customer satisfaction are considerable. People often comment on its quality, asking if there is some special ingredient. The answer is no, but the fact that it is fresh and made traditionally probably explains why it tastes so much better than commercially produced loaves which are often soggy, over light and none too fresh.

Bread making has earned itself an undeserved reputation as being fraught with pitfalls. The process itself has an almost mystical status to some. Without wishing to reduce this fascinating process to one of chemical formulae, a little explanation is necessary to throw light on the subject.

Bread itself is a simple enough product, but the interactions of its ingredients are relatively complex and variable.

The basic process is as follows:
Flour and warm water are mixed together to form an elastic dough. Yeast, which responds to moist warmth by producing a gas, $CO_2$, is used to cause the dough to rise. The gas given off by the yeast is trapped in the dough and forms bubbles thus swelling the dough. Incidentally, a byproduct of this reaction is alcohol, which you can smell before the dough goes into the oven.

When the dough has been allowed to rise for some time, it is placed in a hot oven where the shock of sudden heat causes the yeast to react more vigorously and thus the dough to rise relatively swiftly. After only a few minutes the yeast will become inactive, killed by the heat, and a crust will form and the dough will cook.

From this brief summary, it can be seen how the variables interact. The yeast needs warmth and moisture to perform, but it should be remembered that yeast is a living organism and is therefore sensitive to its environment. Too little heat and moisture and it will react very slowly resulting in a dense, sour tasting bread, too much and the yeast will react far too rapidly and shortly be killed by the heat. Yeast also reacts to sugars; modern fresh yeasts generally do not need sugar to work well, but their reaction can be speeded up by the presence of sugar.

It is perhaps the apparent complexity of these interactions that has given bread making this air of mystery. In truth, once mastered, the technique is both enjoyable and straightforward. It is even claimed by some to be therapeutic, but I would favour the consumption of the final product as being more so!

Here then is a summary of the main ingredients in bread making:

## The Flour

Wholewheat flour is used in the following recipes because it is nutritionally more complete than refined white flours, has more flavour and has the added bonus of being a little easier to work. It is more absorbent than refined flours and has a heavier texture but, provided it is well mixed and kneaded, a surprisingly light loaf can be achieved.

The fresher the flour, the better is the result. 'Stoneground' varieties are usually the best. 'Granary' flours too are excellent and produce a loaf with a crunchy, nutty flavour.

# The Yeast

The best yeast is fresh baker's yeast generally available from good bakeries. It is a living organism and as such must be treated with respect. It should be used with hand-warm water (blood temperature) as too much heat will kill it and too little will inhibit its activity. It is therefore essential in bread baking to maintain a constant and warm environment, preferably draught free, in order to promote yeast activity. Ensure that the mixing bowl is warm, that the kneading surface is a warm, preferably wooden, surface and that you use a warm, draught free place to allow rising to take place.

It is possible to store fresh yeast in a sealed container in the fridge at a temperature between 3-6°C for up to two weeks. Good yeast will have a velvety, crumbly texture and should have a rich and appetizing smell. If it is slimy, runny or foul-smelling discard it and buy fresh. Modern yeasts are so good that it is no longer the unpredictable raising agent it once was.

# The Water

Water should be used at what is called 'blood temperature'. That is to say it should feel warm to an already warm hand and not hot. If in doubt, err on the cool side as the yeast can always be activated later during the rising stage. Water that is too hot, however, will kill the yeast and a fresh brew will then be needed.

The use of filtered water is beneficial but not essential to the end result.

# Salt

Salt is vital in enhancing the flavour of bread, but care is needed in its use. Too little and a bland, sweet loaf will result; too much and the salt will have an adverse effect on the yeast, resulting in a heavy, sour tasting loaf.

Unrefined, pure salt is best, but make sure that it is well sifted.

# Oil

Oil is not an essential ingredient in baking when wholewheat flour is used, but it does have certain benefits. Its inclusion in these recipes is entirely a matter of taste. Added at the mixing stage, 2-3 tablespoons will result in a more elastic dough which is easier to knead. It will also produce a loaf with a finer texture and help it to keep better. Disadvantages can be a soggier crust and some feel that it imparts an unpleasant flavour to the bread, though this depends on personal preference and the oil used. Sunflower seed oil is recommended.

# Sugar

Once sugar was necessary in order to ensure an active yeast. These days this is no longer so, although it may be used to speed up the response of the yeast. Use with great care—too much sugar will spoil the flavour of the bread and, worse still, kill the yeast. For the recipes given here, add up to one tablespoonful to the crumbled fresh yeast before adding the water. Muscovado or soft raw cane sugar or even honey are all suitable.

# Storing Bread

It is possible to bake a batch of bread in order to save time: set aside the loaf or loaves you need for your immediate consumption and place the rest in sealed polythene bags. Store in the deep freeze and allow up to 3 hours to defrost. The bread is then perfectly usable but never as good as when fresh baked.

An alternative to freezing the bread is to freeze the dough itself, sealed in a suitable plastic container, before it has been allowed to rise. The frozen dough should then be thawed slowly in the fridge for up to 6 hours and can then be treated as fresh dough. It must be remembered, however, that this technique demands the use of very fresh yeast in order to avoid problems with leavening.

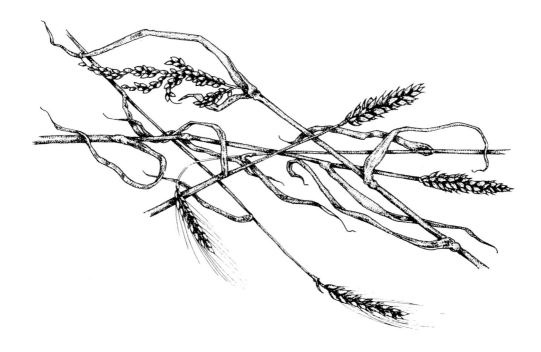

# Basic Wholewheat Loaf

## METHOD 1: Without Sugar or Oil

2 tablespoons fresh crumbled yeast
13fl oz/350ml water (at blood temperature)
20oz/600g wholewheat flour
1-2 tablespoons salt

### 1

Measure the flour and salt into a large mixing bowl, mix well with a wooden spoon, then crumble in the fresh yeast and make sure that it is well incorporated.

### 2

Make a small well in the centre of the mixture and pour a third of the water into it. Stir the mixture adding more water as the flour absorbs it.

### 3

Continue adding the water and mixing until the flour binds forming a workable dough. The ideal consistency is one of elasticity without too much stickiness. If it is too sticky sprinkle on a little more flour. If the dough is too heavy, add a little water by the tablespoonful until the correct consistency is achieved.

### 4

Turn the dough out of the bowl, and onto a floured, wooden surface. Knead the dough as follows: form the dough into a ball and using the heel of one hand press the dough firmly away from you, with the other hand fold the dough over and onto itself at the end of each 'push'. You will develop your own technique, but the point to remember is that kneading should both mix the ingredients and introduce air into the dough. The longer you knead the bread, the better the texture of the final loaf, but at this stage 2-5 minutes kneading is usually adequate.

### 5

Transfer the kneaded dough back to the floured mixing bowl and cover with a clean tea towel. Place the mixing bowl in a warm, draught free place to allow the dough to rise—an airing cupboard or above a warm oven are both suitable places. It will take between 3/4 and 1 hour, depending on the conditions, but the dough should have doubled in size and have a more oozy, bubbly appearance.

### 6

Sprinkle a little flour onto the risen dough and firmly press the centre of the dough with your fist 2 or 3 times before transferring it to the floured board. This process is called 'knocking back'. Knead as before for a further 5 minutes, sprinkling flour onto the board as necessary.

### 7

Form the dough into a loaf shape and place in a 2lb or 1kg or oiled loaf tin. Make a shallow incision across the length of the loaf to promote even rising.

### 8

Cover with a tea towel and put in a warm place to 'prove' for a further half hour.

### 9

When the dough has an elastic texture that springs back to shape when lightly pressed with your finger tip, place in an oven preheated to 425°F/220°C/Gas Mark 7 on the middle shelf and bake for 20 minutes. Then turn the loaf around and bake for a further 15 minutes to ensure even browning.

### 10

The loaf may now be removed from its tin—a light tap on the base should release it—and baked upside down for 5-10 minutes. It will be ready when it has a rich brown appearance and produces a hollow sound when tapped on the base.

### 11

Allow to cool on a cake rack if you can resist eating it immediately.

# Basic Wholewheat Loaf

## METHOD 2: For a Quicker Result Using Oil and Sugar

2 tablespoons fresh yeast
1 level tablespoon soft raw cane sugar
13fl oz/350ml water (at blood
temperature)
20oz/600g wholewheat flour
1-2 tablespoons salt
2-3 tablespoons oil

### 1

Crumble the yeast into a measuring jug and sprinkle the sugar on top.

### 2

Add a little warm water and cream the yeast and sugar together, adding the rest of the water when smooth. Set aside in a warm place.

### 3

In a large mixing bowl, place the flour, sifted salt and oil and mix thoroughly with a wooden spoon.

### 4

After 5-10 minutes, when the yeast and water mixture has started to look bubbly, pour it, a little at a time, into the flour, stirring with a wooden spoon. The flour will not necessarily need all the water, so add only what is needed is form an elastic ball.

### 5

Transfer the dough to a floured board and knead for 5 minutes.

### 6

Transfer to a fresh bowl which has been oiled and put in a warm place covered with a tea towel. Allow to rise for 20 minutes.

### 7

Return the risen dough to the board and knead it for a further 5 minutes, then form it into a loaf shape and place in an oiled loaf tin. Make three diagonal incisions across the loaf and cover with a tea towel.

### 8

Place in a warm place and leave to prove for 20 minutes.

### 9

Bake in an oven preheated to 425°F/ 220°C/Gas Mark 7 on the middle shelf for 35-40 minutes until dark brown.

### 10

Invert the loaf tin and tap sharply on the base to release the loaf. Cool on a cake rack before eating or storing.

# Trouble Shooting

1. The dough is sticky and difficult to handle.
   Remedy: add flour by sprinkling a little at a time and kneading into the dough until the correct consistency is achieved.
2. The dough is heavy and difficult to knead.
   Remedy: add water, a tablespoon at a time, by making a small well in the centre of the dough and folding over. Oil may be added, but in smaller quantities.
3. The dough fails to rise.
   Remedy: this is the difficult one! Assuming that the yeast is good and the quantities are correct, the problem is probably with the warmth. Make sure that the dough is blood temperature or slighly above. If it is rather cool, allow extra time for proving—it will eventually rise. If the dough has been allowed to get too hot the yeast will have been killed. At this stage it is better to go to the shop and buy your day's supply of bread!
4. If the finished loaf is:
   - pale in colour and rather dry, the temperature of the oven was too low.
   - blackened on the outside and raw and sticky inside, the temperature is too high.
     Is your oven thermostat working properly? This can be checked by the Gas or Electricity Board.
   - If the texture of the loaf is open and crumbly it could be that it has over risen. Use less yeast and don't over prove. A dense and rather hard texture will result from over use of oil, but it will keep well.

# Breakfast Loaf

This loaf provides a delicious morning toast that is complete without marmalade or jam. The raisins also provide an additional early morning boost of iron.

To the original basic loaf, method 1 or 2, add:
2oz/50g crushed sesame seeds
2oz/50g sunflower seeds
2¹/₂oz/60g raisins
2 tablespoons honey

_____ 1 _____

Follow the original recipe, method 1, and incorporate the above ingredients at stage 6 during the second kneading. Fold the ingredients into the dough while kneading, then follow the recipe as normal.

# Cheese and Herb Bread

This is an excellent savoury bread to eat as an accompaniment to minestrone soup or sliced thinly served with olive pâté and crudités.

To the orginal basic loaf, method 1 or 2, add:
4oz/125g grated mild Cheddar cheese
2 tablespoons chopped parsley
1 heaped tablespoon of mixed chopped basil, oregano and thyme

Incorporate the above ingredients at stage 6 of recipe 1 for the basic wholewheat loaf.

# Mushroom Cheese Bread

This loaf was enormously popular during our 'Gourmet Evenings' when it was served still warm and cut finely as an appetizer while customers deliberated over the menu. It sounds more fiddly and difficult to make than it actually is, so don't be put off by the long, involved description.

You may vary the filling according to choice, but remember to sauté the vegetables before including them in the loaf: this ensures that they will be thoroughly cooked and reduces their water content.

### FOR THE DOUGH:
Follow original bread recipe method 1

### FOR THE FILLING:
8oz/250g button mushrooms (sliced)
3 cloves garlic (finely chopped)
2 tablespoons olive oil
1 tablespoon chopped parsley
1 level teaspoon mixed dried oregano and basil
Pinch of paprika
Sea salt and freshly ground pepper to taste
4oz/125g Cheddar cheese (grated)

##### 1
Follow wholewheat bread method 1 up to and including stage 5.

##### 2
While the dough rises, sauté the mushrooms and garlic in olive oil, adding the herbs, paprika and seasoning after 2 minutes.

##### 3
When the mushrooms have released their juices, drain and cool. (The juice may be reserved and used in other cooking.)

##### 4
When the dough has risen nicely, turn out onto a floured board and roll out with a rolling pin to as near perfect a rectangle as possible and to a thickness of 1cm or 1/3 inch.

##### 5
Spread the cooled mushrooms along the centre of the rolled dough, leaving enough space at the ends and sides to allow the dough to be folded over the filling. The filling should cover one third of the entire area of the rolled dough. Sprinkle the Cheddar cheese over the filling.

##### 6
Fold one 'side flap' over the filling and seal it to the dough immediately adjacent to the filling with a little olive oil. Fold the other side flap over the first, tucking it under the roll and sealing it with oil. Seal the ends by pinching together.

##### 7
Lift the loaf carefully, with the aid of two spatulas, and transfer it to a lightly oiled baking tray. Cover with a tea towel and leave the loaf to prove for 20 minutes.

##### 8
When the loaf has proved (its rising will be minimal) transfer it to an oven preheated to 400°F/200°C/Gas Mark 6 and bake for 25-30 minutes until a rich brown.
Serve thinly sliced, hot or cold as an appetizer or as an accompaniment to crudités.

# Thick Crust Pizza

The following recipe makes two 9 inch/ 23cm pizzas.

**FOR THE BASE:**
Bread dough—see recipe for original loaf
**1 on page 168**
**1 egg (beaten)**
A little cayenne pepper

**FOR THE FILLING:**
1 medium onion (finely chopped)
1 clove garlic (crushed)
1-2 tablespoons olive oil
4oz/125g mushrooms (roughly chopped)
1 large tin plum tomatoes
1 tablespoon tomato purée
1 level teaspoon basil and oregano (mixed)
1 teaspoon Tabasco and 1 teaspoon cayenne pepper
Sea salt and freshly ground pepper to taste
1/2 a small courgette (thinly sliced)
1/2 a red or a green pepper (seeded and sliced)

**FOR THE TOPPING:**
4oz/125g Mozzarella cheese (grated)
12 black or green olives

—————————— 1 ——————————
Prepare the dough according to original recipe 1 on page 168, incorporating the beaten egg and cayenne pepper at stage 3, and set aside to rise as in stage 5.

—————————— 2 ——————————
Meanwhile prepare the filling; fry the onion and garlic gently in a heavy frying pan in olive oil until soft and lightly golden. Add the mushrooms and continue to cook until they release their juices.

—————————— 3 ——————————
Add the tomatoes, tomato purée, basil, oregano, Tabasco, cayenne, salt and pepper and simmer, stirring well for 5 minutes.

Add extra tomato juice if necessary (the mixture should not be too dry).

—————————— 4 ——————————
Add the courgette and pepper and continue to simmer for a further 2 minutes. Set aside and allow to cool slightly.

—————————— 5 ——————————
Preheat the oven to 375°F/190°C/Gas Mark 5.

—————————— 6 ——————————
Take the risen dough and knead for a few minutes on a floured board. Divide into two pieces—one for each pizza.

—————————— 7 ——————————
Grease two 9 inch/23cm cake tins, or pie dishes of similar proportions will do.

—————————— 8 ——————————
Roll out the two pieces of dough to a depth of about 1.5cm/3/4 inch and lay them in the cake tins ensuring that both the base and the sides are covered. Set aside and leave to 'prove' in a warm place, covered with a tea towel for 10 minutes.

—————————— 9 ——————————
Pour the cooled pizza filling onto the risen bases and top with grated cheese and olives.

—————————— 10 ——————————
Bake for 15-20 minutes or until the cheese is golden brown.

Note: A useful hint is to make a little extra dough when bread making and set this aside for Pizzas. Adjust quantities accordingly!

(The quantities given here are large due to the difficulties involved in making anything less than enough dough for a 2lb/500g loaf.)

# Cakes and Flapjacks

Our rather limited selection of cakes and flapjacks reflects their limited importance in terms of trade. True, they have their own particular devotees, but in general Food For Thought is not identified as being one of Covent Garden's outstanding teashops. However, there are always a few who make the journey to our basement in search of tea and solace and we hope to provide something to rejuvenate their energy.

Flapjacks are excellent sources of energy and keep well in an air-tight container. Our cakes are generally simple to prepare and people often remark with surprise how light and moist they are even made as they are with wholewheat flour.

# Basic Flapjack Recipe

8oz/250g margarine
1lb/500g mixed large and small rolled oats
2oz/50g Demerara sugar
2oz/50g thin honey

### 1

Melt the margarine in a saucepan.

### 2

Add all the ingredients and mix together heating gently. The mixture should be moist and hold together loosely.

### 3

Brush a suitable sized baking tray with a little margarine or oil. Pour in the the mixture and smooth it by pressing down firmly with a palette knife.

### 4

Bake in a moderate oven, 350°F/180°C/ Gas Mark 4 for 40 minutes or until lightly browned.

### 5

When cooked, remove from the oven and allow to cool for a few minutes until just warm—this makes cutting easier. When cut leave till the next day before turning out with a palette knife, being careful not to break them.

Note: To this basic flapjack mixture various ingredients may be added in a quantity of 1/2-1 cupful. Try sesame seeds, currants, sultanas, apricots, dates, peanuts, walnuts, etc.

The addition of a little orange or lemon juice also adds interest.

# Cakes

## Basic Sponge Cake

8oz/250g margarine
8oz/250g Demerara sugar
4 eggs
8oz/250g wholewheat flour
1 teaspoon baking powder
2 tablespoons milk

———————— 1 ————————
Grease and line an 8 inch (20cm) cake tin.

———————— 2 ————————
Cream the margarine and sugar together until pale and creamy.

———————— 3 ————————
Gradually add the eggs one at a time, beating very well after each addition. At this point the chosen flavouring may be added.

———————— 4 ————————
Sift the flour and baking powder together and carefully fold in half of the flour. Then add the milk followed by the rest of the flour, folding gradually all the time.

———————— 5 ————————
Spoon the mixture into the prepared tin and bake in a moderate oven, 350°F/180°C/. Gas Mark 4 for 25-35 minutes. Test the cake with a skewer or the point of a sharp knife—when withdrawn, the skewer should be clean with no trace of cake mix on it. If this is not the case, bake for another 5 minutes and test again.

———————— 6 ————————
Turn onto a wire rack to cool.

# Variations on the Basic Sponge

### APPLE UPSIDE-DOWN-CAKE
Spoon 3 tablespoons of apricot jam into the tin and spread evenly over the base. Core and quarter a large green dessert apple. Slice thinly and arrange over the jam. Spoon the cake mixture over the apple and bake as for the basic sponge. Do take extra care turning the cake out.

### LEMON CAKE
Add the grated rind of 1 lemon to the cake mixture at stage 3. Meanwhile dissolve 2 tablespoons Demerara sugar in the juice of 2 lemons over gentle heat. As soon as the cake is cooked, brush the syrup over it.

### RUM AND RAISIN CAKE
Soak 12oz/340g raisins in 1 small cup of rum for 1 hour.
Drain the raisins and reserve the liquid. Mix the raisins into the cake mix at stage 4 and bake as for the basic sponge.

Once the cake is cooked, brush it with the reserved rum.

### DATE AND WALNUT CAKE
Add 2oz/50g chopped walnuts and 4oz/125g chopped dates to the basic sponge at stage 4.

### CHOCOLATE AND ORANGE CAKE
Replace 1½oz/37g flour with 1½oz/37g cocoa powder and replace the milk with the grated rind and juice of 1 orange.

### BANANA AND COFFEE CAKE
Mash 4 bananas and dissolve 1 teaspoon instant coffee in 2 tablespoons hot water. Mix into the basic sponge but omit the milk from this recipe.

### CARROT AND ORANGE CAKE
Grate 2 carrots and add this with the grated rind and juice of 1 orange to the basic sponge. Omit the milk from this recipe.

# Banana Breadcake

This recipe is an interesting cross between bread and cake—hence the name.

9fl oz/250ml of oil or margarine
1lb 11oz/770g Demerara sugar
9fl oz/250ml milk
6 ripe bananas, mashed
A few drops of vanilla essence
1lb/500g wholewheat flour
2 teaspoons Bicarbonate of Soda
2 teaspoons ground ginger
Pinch of ground cardamom
1 cup of chopped walnuts

_____ 1 _____

Cream the oil/margarine and sugar together, and then beat in the milk, mashed bananas and vanilla essence.

_____ 2 _____

Mix the dry ingredients together and combine with the liquid mixture.

_____ 3 _____

Beat thoroughly and pour into a lightly greased and floured bread tin.

_____ 4 _____

Bake in a pre-heated oven on 325°F/170°C/Gas Mark 3, for 40-60 minutes. It takes a surprisingly long time to cook. When the bread has browned nicely and risen, cover with foil to prevent burning, as it will probably take another 20 minutes to cook through thoroughly.

_____ 5 _____

Remove from the oven and allow to cool thoroughly, before turning out. If required, decorate with fresh whipped cream and sliced bananas, previously sprinkled with lemon juice to prevent browning.

# Rich Fruit Cake

1 cup water
1 1/2 lbs/750g mixed dried fruit
4oz/125g butter
1 cup soft raw cane sugar
1 tablespoon golden syrup
1/2 teaspoon nutmeg
1 teaspoon mixed spice
1/2 teaspoon allspice
1 teaspoon baking soda
2 eggs
2 tablespoons sherry or brandy
2 cups self-raising wholemeal flour
1/2 teaspoon almond essence

_____ 1 _____

Place the water, fruit, butter, sugar, golden syrup, nutmeg, spices and baking soda in a saucepan. Bring to the boil and simmer for 10 minutes. Leave to cool.

_____ 2 _____

When completely cool beat in the eggs.

_____ 3 _____

Add the sherry, flour and almond essence and stir in well.

_____ 4 _____

Bake in a lined cake tin in a moderate oven, 350°F/180°C/Gas Mark 4 for 45 minutes-1 hour. Test the cake with a skewer to make sure that it is cooked right through.

_____ 5 _____

Turn onto a cooling rack and allow to cool.

Note: In this recipe a 'cup' is a 1/3pt/200ml cup.

# Chapter 9
# Gourmet Evenings

In this chapter I have collected a number of rather different recipes, which might be suitable for entertaining. They are designed to use a few unusual ingredients and are, in general, a little more demanding to prepare. The recipes themselves actually came about as an 'experiment' in 1985, when we decided for a limited period to run a series of 'Gourmet Evenings'.

What we hoped to do was to expand our own repertoire and widen the boundaries of our hitherto rather basic cooking. The format we eventually settled on ran something like this:

We would open one Saturday per month, having, hopefully, pre-booked the Restaurant with would-be diners. The menus would have been discussed, designed and tested two weeks previously and posted on the notice board for customers perusal: the bookings that followed, in theory, would allow us to gauge quantities.

As to the contents of the menu, as our samples show, we tried to keep the choices simple so that everything could be prepared fresh. Influences from all over the world were used: Japan with our Vegetable Kebabs in Teriaki Sauce and our Eggplant Oriental, Mexico with our Smoked Tofu and Red Bean Enchiladas and there were many other dishes with European influences.

To our great relief the public response was massive and we soon found our Gourmet Evenings to be fully booked up, often a week in advance. We learnt a great deal from the experience, both of the limitations and advantages inherent in vegetarian cooking.

On the debit side, in order to produce an extensive and interesting set menu it is extremely important not to 'over-face' the customer. Vegetarian food is by nature bulky and the temptation is simply to place too much food on the plate. The answer we found, apart from reducing quantities, was to create as much variety between each course as possible, alternating 'light' and 'heavy' dishes.

On the credit side we found that vegetables, by their subtle nature, will accept an enormous range of accompanying sauces and flavours. The sheer variety of such ingredients which are now easily available is a great help here.

Not all of our dishes were unqualified successes; it was understood by those who took part in these evenings that a certain amount of experimentation was in progress. In fact, probably the most gratifying aspect of the whole venture was the way our customers entered into the experimental spirit, telling us with very un-English frankness if something had not worked as well as complimenting our successes.

The most interesting point to emerge, however, was just how interested people were in 'expanding' their palates. Each day a group of people would form around our Gourmet menu, intrigued by the concept.

We were also helped enormously by our friends at the Dairy in Neal's Yard who provided us with a magnificent array of unusual English, Welsh and Irish cheeses for our cheese board. Such was the quality of their produce that one French Gourmet diner was moved to express his feelings that English cheeses were kept secret in order to protect the French market. His wine bottle was well empty, it should be pointed out!

There were many hilarious moments during our Gourmet Evenings: Food For Thought is hardly the ideal environment for such food. No amount of soft music, mellow light, candles, table cloths and shaky waiter service can really disguise the fact that you are sitting on stools, in a rustic basement with crockery that is straight out of a Brueghel scene. And yet we never received one complaint on account of this. Quite the contrary: we were told that it took the stuffiness out of eating out. Could this be a new form of masochism, we ask ourselves?

In any case, here are the best of our Gourmet recipes with a couple of sample menus which may prove useful when planning your own home entertainment. You may, if you wish, go the whole way and make your guests sit in impossibly cramped circumstances on hard little stools with Vivaldi's Four Seasons blasting away interminably, but this is entirely optional.

# The Fourth Gourmet Evening

## The Gourmet Menu @ 12·50

Cream of Pimento Soup & Homemade
Mushroom Bread.
or
Crudités - Fresh Vegetables & a selection
of Dips.

Tofu Kebabs - Marinated Tofu Peppers,
& Baby Sweetcorn in a Teriaki Sauce.
or
Felafel - Chickpea Croquettes served in
a Chutney & Cummin Sauce.
or
Stuffed Mushrooms Forrestiere - Field
Mushrooms filled with Breadcrumbs,
Celery & Bulghur in a light Chive Sauce

All served with Fresh Asparagus Spears,
Scalloped Potatoes & Sauté Courgettes
& Green Salad.

A selection of French & English Cheeses
served with Biscuits.

Chocolate Roulade - Light Sponge &
Cream Melba
or
Pineapple Soufflé
or
Strawberries Parisienne

Coffee - Served with Mints.

# The Seventh Gourmet Evening

## Full Menu @ 12:50

Midsummer Salad - Quail Eggs,
Redichio, Endive, Mâche, Peppers,
Olive Pâté, in Walnut Dressing.
*or*
Consommé Oriental - Clear Miso Soup,
Garnished with Oriental Vegetables
& Wontons.

Pâté aux Légumes de Campagne -
A Mousseline of Tofu & Celeriac layered
with
Vegetables & Saffron in Sauce Verte
*or*
Buckwheat Crêpe - Aurore - Light
Pancake filled with Ricotta & Spinach
in White Wine & Tomato Sauce.
*or*
Croquette Pois Chiche - Chickpea &
Mushroom Croquettes grilled with
Gouda Cheese in a Burgundy Sauce.

All served with - Potato Marquis,
Broccoli & Almonds, & Petits Pois Flamande.

A selection of French & English Cheeses
served with Homemade Bread or Biscuits.

Gâteau Kahlua - Sponge, Cream,
Kahlua & Walnuts
*or*
Crêpes aux Cerises - Sweet Pancakes
filled with Cherries & Kirsch.
*or*
Salade des Fruits Panachées - Seasonal
Fruits served on Creamed Greek Yoghurt.

Coffee or Herb Tea served with Mints.

# Gourmet Soups

We have a limited selection here, as many of the lighter soups in Chapter 4 will serve perfectly well as starters. As an alternative to the various soups already described, one may use crudités such as speared carrots, peppers and radishes served, for example, with a selection of savoury dips as described in Chapter 3.

Alternatively, an attractive salad with a touch of the exotic always works well; our Midsummer Salad consisted of quail's eggs served on a bed of colourful chicory, mache, radicchio, spring onions, accompanied with various dressings: Avocado, Blue Cheese, and Chilli.

Simple starters, such as globe artichokes or asparagus, when in season, are both effective and easy. Always bear in mind the fact that 'Starters' should be just that: they should stimulate the gastric juices, leaving plenty of room for what is to follow.

# Chilled Avocado Soup

3 soft, ripe avocados
1/2 a lemon
1 clove garlic (crushed)
1/2 teaspoon chopped fresh coriander
1 dessertspoon chopped fresh parsley
1/2pt/300ml plain yogurt
Sea salt and freshly ground pepper
1 tablespoon dry white wine (optional)

—————— 1 ——————
Cut the avocados in half, remove the stone and scoop out the flesh with a spoon. Squeeze over the juice of half a lemon. Mash the avocado and press through a sieve.

—————— 2 ——————
Combine all of the ingredients in a bowl and whisk until thoroughly mixed. Taste for seasoning and chill well before serving.

# Crème Harlequin

6oz/150g cottage cheese
1 clove garlic (crushed)
2 tablespoons dry white wine (optional)
1pt/600ml plain yogurt
2 medium green peppers
2 medium red peppers
4oz/125g tomatoes
1 tablespoon chopped fresh chives
1/4pt/150ml single cream
2 teaspoons sea salt
Freshly ground pepper

———————— 1 ————————
Briefly liquidize the cottage cheese, garlic and wine, then whisk in the yogurt.

———————— 2 ————————
Remove the seeds and pith from the peppers and slice them crosswise. Blanch them in boiling water for 2 minutes, then drain and rinse under cold water.

———————— 3 ————————
Cut out the eyes of the tomatoes and make a small cross on the bottom of them. Plunge them into boiling water for 10 seconds then rinse in cold water. Remove the skins, quarter them and scoop out the seeds. Finely slice the remaining flesh lengthwise.

———————— 4 ————————
Combine all of the ingredients adding pepper to taste. Chill before serving.

# Pimento Soup with White Wine and Cheese

A little oil
1 medium onion, chopped
2 sticks celery, chopped
4 red peppers (seeded and chopped)
1 green pepper (seeded and chopped)
1/2pt/300ml dry white wine
1 pint/600ml vegetable stock or hot water
A pinch of basil and marjoram
1/4 teaspoon of whole cumin seeds
4oz/125g very mature Cheddar cheese, grated
Sea salt and freshly ground pepper
Fresh chives for garnish

———————— 1 ————————
Fry the onion in a little oil for a few minutes then add celery and peppers and cook until soft.

———————— 2 ————————
Add wine and simmer for a further 5 minutes.

———————— 3 ————————
Add stock, cumin seeds and season sparingly with herbs, salt and pepper.

———————— 4 ————————
Take from heat, liquidize, return to heat until just below boiling point.

———————— 5 ————————
Gradually stir in grated cheese until completely melted.

———————— 6 ————————
Check the seasoning and garnish with plenty of chopped chives.

Note: If you do not have a blender simply chop finely and neatly all the vegetables before cooking.

# Gourmet Entrées

We have selected a range of dishes here, which, it is hoped expresses some of the variety possible in vegetarian cuisine. The use of relatively unusual ingredients such as smoked Tofu, Madeira wine, Pistachio kernels, Gruyère cheese and Enchiladas add a touch of the exotic to what are, for the most part, straight-forward recipes. Others are more time-consuming, but worth trying for all that.

These dishes are designed to be light enough in terms of bulk, but with flavours assertive enough to be served with conventionally cooked vegetables, or an imaginative salad. During our Gourmet Evenings we tended to serve such dishes with two or three other seasonal vegetables. For example, fresh runner or broad beans, asparagus, courgettes or green peas. Potatoes were served 'A la Lyonnaise' cooked, then sautéed with shallots. Also mashed with a little sour cream, black pepper and nutmeg. Tomatoes were used for their marvellous colour stuffed with garlic, basil, breadcrumbs and grilled.

· The basic rule, as always, is to give colour combinations plenty of thought in order to avoid a bland and unappetizing appearance.

Bon Appetit!

# Roulade of Spinach and Pistachio Kernels with Dijon Mustard Sauce

4 large egg whites
2oz/50g shelled pistachio nuts, (finely chopped)
4oz/125g fresh spinach, (cooked, drained and squeezed of ALL excess water)
1oz/25g butter
Sea salt and freshly milled black pepper

_____ 1 _____

Sauté the spinach in butter for a few minutes, season with salt and pepper, add pistachios and set aside.

_____ 2 _____

Whisk egg whites with salt and pepper until stiff, then fold into the spinach mixture carefully.

_____ 3 _____

Spread the mixture onto a Swiss-roll tub which has been lined with greaseproof paper. Bake in a preheated oven for 15 minutes at 375°F/190°C/Gas Mark 5.

_____ 4 _____

As soon as sponge is cooked roll it up and cut into 12 thin slices

FOR THE SAUCE:
1 heaped teaspoon of Dijon mustard
1 clove of garlic, (finely chopped)
1oz/25g butter
2 fl oz/60ml single cream
4 shallots, (thinly sliced)
Sea salt and freshly milled black pepper

_____ 1 _____

Sauté garlic and shallots gently in butter until soft.

_____ 2 _____

Add mustard, cook for 1 minute longer.

_____ 3 _____

Remove from heat, liquidize, return to heat and bring to the boil, after adding the cream.

_____ 4 _____

Season with salt and pepper.

Note: The quantity of mustard may be doubled if desired.

# Stuffed Gruyère Pastry

FOR THE PASTRY:
1oz/25g Gruyère cheese (grated)
2oz/50g butter (cut into small pieces)
2 eggs (well beaten)
2oz/50g strong white flour
1/4pt/150ml cold water
A pinch of paprika

_____ 1 _____

Preheat oven to 400°F/200°C/Gas Mark 6.

_____ 2 _____

Put water and butter into a saucepan over medium heat.

_____ 3 _____

When butter has melted and just before mixture boils, remove from heat and stir in all the flour beating vigorously with a wooden spoon.

_____ 4 _____

Beat until mixture forms a smooth paste. Add the beaten eggs a little at a time beating continuously until a glossy paste has formed.

_____ 5 _____

Mix in the Gruyère.

184

_____ 6 _____

Lightly grease a baking tray, run it under cold water and give it a sharp tap to get rid of excess water. (A little moisture helps the pastry to rise.)

_____ 7 _____

Put the mixture into a piping bag with a plain 1/2 inch/1cm nozzle attached. Squeeze onto the baking tray one circle approximately 7 inches (18cm) in diameter, then another inside the first just touching it. Pipe a third circle on top of the first two. While the pastry is cooking the circles should merge to become one ring.

_____ 8 _____

Bake on top shelf for 20 minutes or until golden brown.

_____ 9 _____

When cooked use a sharp knife to cut the pastry in two, horizontally.

### FOR THE FILLING:
8oz/250g broccoli (washed, trimmed and cut into small pieces)
4oz/125g French beans (trimmed, and broken into 1/2 inch/1cm pieces)
4oz/125g button mushrooms (cut into thick slices)
2 carrots (scraped and cut into strips)
A little sunflower oil, sea salt and freshly ground pepper

_____ 1 _____

Sauté the vegetables in oil fairly briskly for 4 minutes keeping them covered. Season with salt and pepper.

_____ 2 _____

Remove from heat. The vegetables should be only very lightly cooked and to prevent them cooking further remove the lid.

### FOR THE SAUCE:
1 small stick of celery (finely sliced)
1 clove of garlic (finely chopped)
1 small onion (diced)
2 tomatoes (skinned and sliced)
2oz/50g butter
A little vegetable stock or milk
English mustard
1 teaspoon strong white flour, sea salt and freshly ground pepper

_____ 1 _____

Melt butter, add onion, garlic and celery, cover and cook gently, stirring from time to time.

_____ 2 _____

When soft, add the tomatoes and cook for a further 5 minutes.

_____ 3 _____

Add a pinch of mustard, salt and pepper and flour. Stir well and add up to a cup of vegetable stock or milk.

_____ 4 _____

Remove from heat, liquidize, return to heat and bring to the boil, gently. The sauce should be thick, Add the pre-cooked vegetables, heat through and adjust the seasoning.

To Serve: Fill the pastry ring with the vegetables and decorate with sauté julienne of carrots and florets of broccoli.

# Aduki Bean Rissoles with Madeira Sauce

**FOR THE RISSOLES:**
1 cup aduki beans (soaked overnight)
1 bay leaf
1oz/25g margarine
1 small onion (finely chopped)
1oz/25g flour
1 teaspoon cumin
1/2 teaspoon marjoram
1 teaspoon celery salt
2 teaspoons tamari
1/2 pint/300ml stock or water
Pinch of sea salt and freshly ground pepper

**FOR THE SAUCE:**
1 small onion (finely chopped)
1oz/25g margarine
1 clove garlic (crushed)
1 small carrot (grated)
1/2 stick celery (finely chopped)
1 bay leaf
1oz/25g flour
1/2 teaspoon thyme
1/2 teaspoon coriander
2 teaspoons tomato purée
1 tablespoon tamari
1pt/600ml stock
1 teaspoon yeast extract
1 1/2 tablespoons Madeira or cream sherry
3 tablespoons oil
3oz/90g Emmenthal cheese

**1**
Drain and rinse the beans then cover with water and boil for 1 hour with the bay leaf or until they are quite soft. Drain well.

**2**
Melt 1oz/25g margarine in a saucepan and toss in the finely chopped onion. Fry for 3 minutes then sprinkle over 1oz/25g flour, the cumin, marjoram and celery salt. Cook, stirring on a low heat for 3 minutes.

**3**
Add the tamari and gradually whisk in the stock. Cook on a low heat for a further 5 minutes. Remove from heat and mix in the beans and a pinch of salt and pepper. Cool well.

**4**
Melt the remaining margarine in a saucepan and add the onion, garlic, carrot, celery and bay leaf. Fry until lightly browned then sprinkle over the flour, thyme and coriander. Cook, stirring for a few minutes then stir in the tomato purée. Whisk in the stock and tamari and stir in the yeast extract. Simmer for 20 minutes.

**5**
Put the sauce in a liquidizer with the Madeira or sherry. Blend until smooth then pass through a sieve. Return the sauce to the stove on a low heat and test for seasoning and consistency.

**6**
Form 4-6 rissoles from the cooled bean mixture and roll them in a little flour until lightly coated.

**7**
Heat the oil in a frying pan and fry the rissoles on both sides until golden brown. Place them on a baking tray. Thinly slice the cheese and place on top of the rissoles. Grill them on a medium heat until the cheese is well melted. Serve covered with Madeira sauce.

# Ricotta and Spinach Crêpes with Onion Sauce

SAUCE:
1oz/25g margarine
1 large onion (finely chopped)
1oz/25g flour
1 teaspoon mustard powder
1/4 teaspoon nutmeg
1/2 teaspoon paprika
1/2pt/300ml milk
1/2pt/300ml stock
Pinch of sea salt and freshly ground pepper

CRÊPES:
5 tablespoons flour
1/3pt/200ml milk
1 egg
1/2 teaspoon sea salt
3 tablespoons oil

FILLING:
8oz/250g spinach
1 teaspoon sea salt
1 clove garlic (crushed)
8oz/250g Ricotta cheese
Pinch of fresh ground pepper

——————— 1 ———————
Melt the margarine in a saucepan and fry the onion lightly for 5 minutes. Sprinkle over the flour, mustard, nutmeg and paprika. Cook, stirring for 3 minutes then whisk in the milk and stock. Add a pinch of salt and pepper and simmer 15-20 minutes.

——————— 2 ———————
Whisk together the flour, milk, egg and salt until smooth.

——————— 3 ———————
Thinly coat a crêpe pan or flat-bottomed frying pan with a little oil and heat. Pour enough of the crêpe mixture in to just cover the bottom of the pan. Brown lightly on one side then shake the pan and/or ease the crêpe away from the pan with a spatula so it moves freely. Then toss or turn it and cook the other side. Cook the remainder of the batter in the same way. It is important to have a hot pan and a lightly oiled surface.

——————— 4 ———————
Trim and wash the spinach and blanch in boiling water with 1 teaspoon of salt. Rinse well in cold water then squeeze dry and chop finely.

——————— 5 ———————
Combine the spinach, garlic, Ricotta and pepper then fill and roll the crêpes with the mixture. Reheat the crêpes in a medium oven, 350°F/180°C/Gas Mark 4, for 10-15 minutes and serve with the onion sauce.

**187**

# Vegetable Kebabs with Teriaki Sauce

1 large red pepper
1 large green pepper
1 large onion
4oz/125g button mushrooms
1 small tin whole baby sweetcorn
8oz/250g firm tofu
4-6 skewers
2 1/2 tablespoons oil
1 clove garlic (crushed)
1 teaspoon ground ginger
1/4pt/150ml tamari
1 cup apple juice
2 tablespoons water
1 tablespoon arrowroot

———————— 1 ————————
Cut the peppers in half lengthwise, remove the seeds and pith and cut into squares about 1 1/2 inches/3cm in size.

———————— 2 ————————
Peel the onion and cut in half lengthwise. Remove the outer layers and separate them and cut into squares the same size as the peppers.

———————— 3 ————————
Trim the stems from the mushrooms.

———————— 4 ————————
Cut the baby corn cobs in half widthwise.

———————— 5 ————————
Carefully cut the tofu into 1 1/2 inch/3cm cubes.

———————— 6 ————————
Arrange the vegetables and tofu on the skewers. Place them in a baking tray and sprinkle 2 tablespoons of oil over them. Bake in a medium oven, 350°F/180°C/ Gas Mark 4 for 15-20 minutes turning occasionally.

———————— 7 ————————
Heat the remaining 1/2 teaspoon of oil in a small saucepan. Add the garlic and ginger and fry for a few minutes until the garlic is lightly browned. Add the tamari and apple juice, bring to the boil and simmer. Mix the water and arrowroot together and whisk in the sauce. Simmer for 2-3 minutes.

———————— 8 ————————
Serve the kebabs on rice with a light coating of sauce.

# Eggplant Oriental

FOR THE SAUCE:
Oil
2 cloves garlic (crushed)
1 heaped teaspoon grated ginger
1/4 pint/150ml tamari
1/2 pint/300ml stock
1 dessertspoon sherry
1 dessertspoon apple concentrate
A little cornflour if necessary
2 large aubergines
Sea salt
2 eggs (beaten)
1/2 cup wheatgerm mixed with 1/2 cup flour
1 medium onion (finely chopped)
2 tablespoons light miso
Juice of half a lemon
2 teaspoons honey

———————— 1 ————————
Heat a little oil in a saucepan and fry the garlic and ginger for 3 minutes, then add the tamari, stock, sherry and apple concentrate. Leave on a low simmer and, just before serving, test for seasoning and thicken with a little cornflour. It should be quite strong tasting and fairly thin.

———————— 2 ————————
Trim the tops off the aubergines and slice them into 3 lengthwise allowing one slice per portion. Trim away the skin on the two outside slices of each aubergine. Sprinkle the slices generously with salt and leave in

a colander for 20 minutes, then rinse and dry well.

_____ 3 _____

Dip the slices in the beaten eggs then coat them with the wheatgerm and flour mixture. Heat 1/4 pint/150ml of oil in a frying pan and fry them on both sides, one or two at a time until the batter is lightly browned. Place the slices in a shallow ovenproof dish and bake in a medium oven (350°F/ 180°C/Gas Mark 4) until the aubergines are tender (about 30 minutes).

_____ 4 _____

Meanwhile fry the onion in a little oil until soft then stir in the miso, lemon juice and honey. Either blend or mash the mixture.

_____ 5 _____

When the aubergines are cooked spread the miso mixture over the top and serve with a thin covering of sauce.

# Smoked Tofu and Red Bean Enchiladas

1 cup kidney beans (soaked overnight)
1 tablespoon butter or margarine
1 medium onion (chopped)
3 cloves garlic (crushed)
1 fresh chilli (finely chopped)
1 dessertspoon tomato purée
8oz/250g smoked tofu
1 small tin whole kernel sweetcorn
8-12 enchilada shells
1 cup grated strong Cheddar cheese

FOR THE SAUCE:
1 dessertspoon butter or margarine
1 large onion (finely chopped)
3 fresh chillies (finely sliced)
1lb/500g tomatoes (roughly chopped)
1/2pt/300ml stock
Pinch of cloves
1/2 teaspoon cinnamon
1 dessertspoon grated dark chocolate
Sea salt to taste

_____ 1 _____

Boil the beans in plenty of water for 1-1 1/2 hours until slightly over cooked so that they can be mashed, then drain and rinse well.

_____ 2 _____

To make the sauce, heat a dessertspoon of butter or margarine in a saucepan and add the onion and chillies. Fry for 10-15 minutes until browned. Add the tomatoes and stock and leave to simmer for as long as possible. Just before using stir in the cloves, cinnamon, chocolate and a pinch of salt to taste for seasoning.

_____ 3 _____

Heat a tablespoon of butter or margarine in a large frying pan and fry the onion, garlic and chilli until soft. Stir in the tomato purée and keeping the heat high roughly mash in a couple of spoonfuls of beans mixing them in well. Mash in the rest of the beans a spoonful at a time then take off the heat.

_____ 4 _____

Coarsely crumble the tofu into the bean mixture and add the drained sweetcorn. Mix them well then taste for seasoning.

_____ 5 _____

In a frying pan heat enough oil to cover an enchilada. When the oil is hot deepfry an enchilada for 20-30 seconds until it is pliable. Don't overcook it as it will turn crisp. Immediately fill and roll it with about 2 dessertspoons of the mixture before frying the next one as they harden within a couple of minutes. Proceed with the rest of the enchiladas and place them in an ovenproof dish, leaving a little space between each one for the sauce to run down.

_____ 6 _____

Pour half of the sauce over the enchiladas and bake in a hot oven (400°F/200°C/Gas Mark 6) for 20 minutes. Spoon a little more sauce over them if they start to dry out.

_____ 7 _____

Serve with the rest of the sauce and grated Cheddar over the top.

# Stuffed Field Mushrooms

FOR THE SAUCE:
1 dessertspoon butter or margarine
1 dessertspoon flour
1/2 pint/300ml milk
1/4 pint/150ml white wine
Sea salt and freshly ground pepper
1/4 pint/150ml sour cream
4-6 large field mushrooms (1 per portion)
1 medium onion (finely chopped)
3 cloves garlic (crushed)
Butter or margarine for frying
2 sticks celery (finely chopped)
Sea salt and freshly ground pepper
2 cups breadcrumbs
1 teaspoon mustard powder
1 teaspoon paprika
Pinch of nutmeg
1 tablespoon chopped fresh parsley
1 teaspoon grated Parmesan cheese
1 bunch chives (chopped)

———————— 1 ————————

To make the sauce, melt a dessertspoon of butter or margarine in a saucepan and sprinkle over the flour. Cook, stirring for a few minutes then whisk in the milk. Bring to the boil and simmer for 5 minutes, then whisk in the wine and simmer for a further 5 minutes. Add a pinch of salt and pepper and taste for seasoning. If the wine has left any bitter flavour correct with a little sweetener—apple concentrate or sugar. Otherwise the flavour should be quite mild. Just before serving stir in the sour cream.

———————— 2 ————————

Trim and reserve the stalks off the mushrooms. Bring a large pot of salted water to the boil and blanch the mushrooms a couple at a time for 2-3 minutes until they are just cooked but before they go limp. Rinse them in cold water and leave on kitchen paper to dry.

———————— 3 ————————

Fry the onion and garlic in a knob of butter

or margarine for 10 minutes or until browned. Add the celery and chopped mushroom stalks and cook for a further 5 minutes. Season with a pinch of salt and pepper, drain any juices off into the sauce and set aside.

———————— 4 ————————

Melt a dessertspoon of butter or margarine in a frying pan and add the breadcrumbs. Fry until lightly browned and toasted (about 5-10 minutes) then sprinkle over the mustard, paprika and nutmeg.

———————— 5 ————————

Mix the breadcrumbs, onion mixture and parsley together and taste for seasoning. Press a tablespoon or more of the mixture on to the grilled side of each mushroom and sprinkle them with Parmesan cheese. Place them in a greased baking tray and bake in a medium oven (350°F/180°C/Gas Mark 4) for 20 minutes or until hot through. Watch that the breadcrumbs don't start to catch in the oven—if they do cover with tin foil. Serve with the cream sauce and a generous sprinkling of chives.

# Mushroom Brioches with Stilton Sauce

8oz/250g wholemeal flour
8oz/250g unbleached white flour
1oz/25g sugar
1oz/25g sea salt
8oz/250g butter
4 eggs
1oz/25g fresh yeast
Knob of butter
1lb/500g button mushrooms
1/4pt/150ml port or red vermouth
Sea salt and freshly ground pepper
1/4 pint/150ml sour cream
Egg for eggwash
1 dessertspoon poppy seeds
2-3 cloves garlic (finely chopped)

FOR THE SAUCE:
1 dessertspoon butter or margarine
1 small onion (finely chopped)
1 stick celery (finely chopped)
Pinch of marjoram
1 dessertspoon flour
3/4pt/400ml milk
Sea salt and freshly gound pepper
4oz/25g Stilton cheese

### 1

Combine the flours, sugar and salt. Cut in the butter, lightly beat the eggs and mix them in too. Dissolve the yeast in a little hand hot water and mix it in, then make a dough adding as much warm water as you need to get it smooth and pliable. Knead for 5 minutes then wrap in clingfilm and place in the fridge until needed.

### 2

To make the sauce, melt the butter or margarine in a saucepan and fry the onion, celery and marjoram in it for 3 minutes. Sprinkle over the flour and cook for a further 3 minutes. Whisk in the milk and bring to the boil and leave on a low simmer. Just before serving add a pinch of salt and pepper and crumble half of the Stilton in. Taste the sauce and add more cheese if you like.

### 3

Melt a knob of butter in a frying pan and add the garlic. Cook for a minute until just starting to brown then toss in the mushrooms. Cook, turning for 3 minutes then splash over the port or vermouth. Cook for 5 minutes then sprinkle over a pinch of salt and pepper, remove from the heat and drain well. Mix the mushrooms with the sour cream.

### 4

Roll out the dough and cut 6 saucer sized circles and eggwash the edges. Place a heaped tablespoon of mushrooms in the centre of each one then gather up the edges and crimp them well. Place them on a greased oventray, brush with eggwash and sprinkle over the poppy seeds. Cover with a damp teatowel and leave to rise in a warm place for 20 minutes or until doubled in size. Bake in a hot oven (400°F/200°C/Gas Mark 6) for 15 minutes until golden brown and hollow sounding when tapped.
Serve with the Stilton sauce.

# Gourmet Desserts

191

# Praline Pears with Fresh Plum Sauce

1lb/500g plums
Sugar
Cornflour
2oz/50g hazelnuts
2oz/50g almonds
4oz/125g Demerara sugar
4-6 firm, large pears (1 per portion)

————— 1 —————

Boil the plums in a minimum of water until mushy. Press the mixture through a sieve discarding the stones and skins. Return to a saucepan and taste for sweetness and flavour, adding a little sugar if necessary and reducing by boiling if the flavour is too thin. Thicken with a little cornflour so the sauce will coat the pears—not run off them.

————— 2 —————

Toast the hazelnuts and almonds in a moderate oven for 10-15 minutes until lightly browned. Melt the sugar, either in a double boiler or in a saucepan on low heat—it will need constant watching and stirring and could take up to 20 minutes. When syrupy, quickly add the nuts and stir around and then turn out onto a bench to cool. The sugar will set almost instantly. When cool (10 minutes or so) cover with a clean tea-towel and bash with a rolling pin. It can be ground as fine as you like but, if left a little bit coarse, it will have a pleasant crunchy texture.

————— 3 —————

Quarter the pears lengthwise and scoop out the cores. Poach the pears in water until just tender then drain, rinse and pat dry. If possible, serve the pears standing upright in a dessert bowl or large wineglass with a spoonful of sauce and a good scattering of praline.

# Chocolate Coffee Trifle

(Serves 6)
6oz/150g margarine
4oz/125g Demerara sugar
3 eggs
6oz/150g wholewheat flour
1 rounded teaspoon of baking powder
3 drops of vanilla essence
1 dessertspoon of coffee and chicory essence
A little milk (optional)
1 cup mixed sultanas and raisins, combined with 1 tablespoon of rum
3 bananas, sliced
1pt/600ml prepared custard (see Real Custard recipe on page 140)
2oz/50g dark chocolate, grated
1 dessertspoon Demerara sugar
Grated chocolate for garnish

————— 1 —————

Cream margarine and sugar until fluffy, beat the eggs in one at a time, and stir in sifted flour and baking powder.

————— 2 —————

Add vanilla and coffee essences and if necessary a little milk to achieve a smooth mixture.

————— 3 —————

Spread mixture into a greased sandwich tin and bake at 300°F/150°C/Gas Mark 2 for 25-30 minutes. Cool and cut into bite-sized squares.

————— 4 —————

Cover sponge with raisins, sultanas and sliced bananas.

————— 5 —————

Make up the custard and before removing from the heat add chocolate and sugar.

————— 6 —————

Allow to cool a little then pour custard over trifle. When set sprinkle with grated chocolate and serve with freshly whipped cream.

# Gooseberry Fool

1lb/500g gooseberries
4oz/125g Demerara sugar
1/4pt/150ml water
1/4pt/150ml double cream
1/4pt/150ml custard (see Real Custard
recipe on page 140)

_____ 1 _____

Wash and top and tail the fruit. Place in a saucepan with the sugar to sweeten and the water. Cover with a lid and cook gently until the fruit becomes very soft and pulpy. Rub through a sieve or beat until smooth.

_____ 2 _____

Whip the cream lightly and mix it with the purée and the custard.

_____ 3 _____

Pour into a glass dish or 6 individual glasses. Decorate with a little whipped cream.

# Poached Pears in Port with Blackberry Sauce and Brandy-Snaps

2 ripe pears
2fl oz/60ml port
1lb/500g blackberries
2oz/50g caster sugar

_____ 1 _____

Peel the pears and place in a heavy saucepan with the port.

_____ 2 _____

Cover and poach very gently for 15 minutes turning pears once.

_____ 3 _____

When tender, chill and then cut pears in two lengthways discarding pips. Then cut halves into 5-6 thin slices.

_____ 4 _____

To make the sauce place the blackberries and the sugar into a heavy saucepan, cover, and cook gently until tender. Rub blackberries through a sieve and chill the resulting purée.

FOR THE BRANDY-SNAPS:
1oz/25g butter
1oz/25g Demerara sugar
1oz/25g golden syrup
1oz/25g plain flour (warmed)
1 teaspoon lemon juice
Whipped cream flavoured with brandy

_____ 1 _____

Melt sugar, butter and syrup, add the warmed flour and lemon juice.

_____ 2 _____

Stir well and put a teaspoonful of the mixture on a well greased baking tray 6 inches/15cm apart.

_____ 3 _____

Bake in a moderate oven until golden brown, leave for a few moments to cool, then roll up over the thick handle of a wooden spoon and fill with the whipped cream.

# Chapter 10
# Menu Planning

Over the years an awful lot has been written about how one should balance one's eating habits, the relative merits of this or that food and the benefits of wholefood over processed foods. I do not intend to enter these arguments in any depth as I am not qualified to do so. There are a few general points, however, which cannot be over-emphasized.

First, achieving a balanced, nutritious and interesting diet for the vegetarian definitely requires more effort and planning. This is due to a number of reasons ranging from the need to 'process' wholefood yourself, to the difficulties in achieving the correct combination of proteins and vitamins.

Second, it goes without saying that where possible the produce used must be of the best quality. This is especially true of fresh fruit and vegetables which tend to lose many of their nutritious trace elements and vitamins soon after they become ripe.

Third, it is important to include variety in your eating habits. This extends, not simply to vegetables and sauces, but bases as well; rice, pasta, egg, cheese, nut or pulse bases can be varied on a daily basis to stimulate the palate with their varied textures and flavours. This variety is an essential element in our cooking at Food For Thought and a considerable amount of time is spent planning menus.

Fourth, try and organize your meals intelligently. This can be done by the inclusion of summer dishes, such as chilled soup starters or quiches and salads, when the weather allows. Similarly, winter dishes should be warming, filling and give you plenty of energy to combat the cold.

Include seasonal vegetables and fruit as part of your menu. This can give a pleasant feeling of keeping in touch with the seasons and one which your body will probably respond to.

What I have tried to do with the following menu 'planners' is to provide an idea of how we organize and plan our menus at Food For Thought. The idea is that we have our customers' health and interest to sustain and the results of our efforts in this direction may well be useful to the reader.

Without wishing to appear pompous, all-knowing or dictatorial, here then are sample summer and winter menu rotas. Many of the combinations are taken from sample menus from Food For Thought. You will notice that I have attempted to balance the meals in texture and food value; appearance I leave up to you!

These tables cover four hypothetical weeks of the year, two in winter and two in summer. Monday to Saturday are represented by 'ordinary' recipes, for Sundays I have suggested a 'Gourmet' menu.

## Notes on the Menu Planner

1. For the sake of simplicity I have adopted a standard soup—main course—dessert format; this is by no means to be seen as inflexible, it simply reflects the way we form our menus at Food For Thought.

2. At home you will, of course, have greater freedom in your choice. The starters, for example, in summer could be fresh asparagus, globe artichokes and mayonnaise, crudités and dips or perhaps hummus and home made bread. The

choices are virtually limitless and, as always, it is better to take advantage of the delicate summer vegetables available. If, however, you have a family to feed and costs to keep down, the selection of soups suggested should be more economical to make.

3. The main savouries are also geared towards providing for a family; some will take a little time to prepare, but they should all prove to be tasty and nutritious. If you want something more simple and quick to prepare try Stir Fried Vegetables (page 110) or Savoury Rice (page 109). You may also substitute the main courses with quiches or pizzas. If you do this, remember to eat at least two really substantial hot evening meals a week.

4. The menu planner is intended to be used only as a guide to your main daily meal; naturally your two other meals should also consist of a similarly balanced combination of foodstuffs. Your meals, wherever possible, should be taken at regular intervals.

And, of course, be a paragon of moderation in all things except variety!

# Winter Menu Planner

| | | Monday | Tuesday | Wednesday | Thursday | Friday | Saturday | Sunday |
|---|---|---|---|---|---|---|---|---|
| **WEEK ONE** | Soup or Starter | Minestrone & Bread | Carrot & Cashew Nut & Bread | Leek & Potato & Bread | Cream of Mushroom & Bread | Sweetcorn & Celery Chowder & Bread | Split Pea & Garlic & Bread | Potage de Champignon au Porto & Herb & Cheese Bread |
| | Main Course | Kidney Bean Bordelaise | Spicy Chickpea Curry & Rice | Tagliatelle | Leek & Cauliflower au Gratin | Ratatouille Provençal | Oeufs Florentines | Smoked Tofu & Red Bean Enchiladas & Broccoli & Garlic Tomatoes |
| | Dessert or Fruit | Apple & Rhubarb Crumble & Cream | Tutti Frutti Trifle | Blackberry Scrunch | Tangerine Dream | Pear & Blackcurrant Shortbread | Apple & Raisin Lattice Tart | Chocolate & Ginger Mousse |
| **WEEK TWO** | Soup or Starter | Cream of Spinach & Bread | Nutty Parsnip & Bread | Potato & Chive & Bread | Miso & Nori & Bread | Buckwheat & Potato & Bread | Onion Soup & Bread | Cream of Chestnut & Homemade Bread |
| | Main Course | Nut Roast & Tomato Sauce | Shepherdess Pie | Sweet & Sour Hot Pot & Rice | Butter Bean Dijonnaise | Cauliflower Mornay | Savoury Stout Crumble | Eggplant Oriental & Sauté Potatoes & French Beans |
| | Dessert or Fruit | Rhubarb Meringue | Banana Rhumba | St Clement's Cheesecake | Pear & Brandy Sponge & Custard | Bakewell Tart & Custard | Bananas in Bed | Praline Pears with Fresh Plum Sauce |

# Summer Menu Planner

| | | Monday | Tuesday | Wednesday | Thursday | Friday | Saturday | Sunday |
|---|---|---|---|---|---|---|---|---|
| **WEEK ONE** | Soup or Starter | Gazpacho | Fresh Pea | Siriporn's Lemony Soup | Mushroom & Sherry Consomme | Courgette & Coriander | Vegetable Vermicelle | Vegetable Crudités with Various Dips |
| | Main Course | West Country Casserole | Leek Quiche & Salad | Lentil & Mushroom Dahl & Rice | Courgette & Basil Quiche & Salad | Leek & Lemon Soufflé | Pinto Bean Carbonnade | Stuffed Field Mushrooms, Croquette Potatoes & French Beans |
| | Dessert or Fruit | Fresh Fruit Salad | Strawberry & Kiwi Fruit Delight | Peach Melba Supreme | Danish Apple Cake | Fresh Fruit Salad | Banana & Walnut Trifle | Pavlova Aotearoa |
| **WEEK TWO** | Soup or Starter | Chilled Avocado | Borscht | Carrot & Almond Purée | Tomato Soup | Mulligatawny | Mushroom Soup | Fresh Asparagus or Cream of Pimento Soup |
| | Main Course | Tagine | Lentil, Fennel & Celery a l'Espagnol | Provençal Quiche & Salad | Leek & Cauliflower au Gratin or Lyonnaise | Stroganoff | Haricot Napolitaine | Spinach & Ricotta Crêpes |
| | Dessert or Fruit | Raspberry Scrunch | Chocolate Blackberry Excess | Fresh Fruit Salad | Strawberry & Blackcurrant Flan | Summer Trifle | Hedge Row Crumble | Selection of Cheeses or Lemon Soufflé |

# About the Authors

## Guy Garrett (General Editor & Restaurant Manager)

A degree in philosophy set me right on course for a vocational career. A vocation that I was not quick to take up, for the course of events and my own irrationality conspired against me. I cannot honestly say I regret this.

I enjoy my work enormously at Food For Thought, and in writing this book, I have received nothing but support from my friends at the Restaurant.

The fact that this book has finally appeared, after years of requests from our customers, is, however, largely due to the efforts of Fay Franklin, Senior Commissioning Editor at Thorsons. Over a period of four years she fired off letters to my sister and me, at regular intervals, suggesting that we compile such a book. Her sheer determination finally stirred us from our torpor, and set the ball rolling. My sincere thanks to her for her advice and encouragement; it has been a memorable experience.

My gratitude also to those who contributed to the book so willingly with their recipes, and to Kit Norman for his expertise and confidence. I hope Rachel Mendes' beautiful illustrations bring the reader as much pleasure as they do me. I must also thank the late Simpkins the cat, who posed for the drawings; we miss him dearly.

Finally, I wish the readers all the best in their cooking, whatever form it may take and hope this book inspires just a little.

## Kit Norman (Soups, Main Savouries, Gourmet Recipes and Technical Editor)

His story: Kit arrived in London from New Zealand in 1983. An enthusiastic cook at home, he had no restaurant experience when he started work at Food For Thought as a salad hand.

Eventually, he settled into preparing the evening food, learning the popular 'standard' Food For Thought dishes, then developing his own ideas and recipes. Initially, he was inspired by Indian and Asian cuisine but, as time went on, also absorbing many ideas from the wealth of commentary about cooking in the media.

Having just spent the last year at the Victoria café in Wellington, New Zealand, Kit has now returned to Food For Thought.

# David Biddulph (Soups, Savouries & Gourmet Recipes)

Having come from the kitchens of high class French Restaurants, I arrived at Food For Thought a broken man—ready to throw in my chef's hat!

I was soon to be inspired to wield the wooden spoon once again, learning a new cuisine, executed with reverence and love.

Cooking for the Gourmet Evening made me realize some of the potential of meatless cooking—I hope that these recipes reflect this.

Although my interests are still firmly rooted in the wholefood vegetarian scene, I am currently pursuing another interest in holistic medicine—often too far from my favourite restaurant for comfort.

# Steve Wilcox (Soups and Main Savouries)

In 1976 I began working at 'Manna' vegetarian restaurant in Chalk Farm, London. I had found my vocation!

I soon embarked on a three year, day release City and Guilds course in practical cookery. On successfully completing this, I joined Food For Thought as Evening Cook.

Since that time I have worked in every department of the kitchen and have accumulated a large repertoire of vegetarian dishes as well as a great deal of practical experience.

I am happy still to be working at Food For Thought after six years, and proud to be part of this innovative and successful restaurant.

# Josephine Miller (Main Savouries)

Her story: Josephine Miller is a happily married American who learned how to cook by watching her mother cook for so many people.

One day, after a year honeymooning with her husband, she walked into Food For Thought. She wanted to be a cook: the kind of cook who makes large pots of steaming stew and warming winter soups. Not a professional cook, just a motherly cook. Food For Thought had the perfect kitchen atmosphere for feeding extremely large families. Sometimes up to 1,000 children a day!

# Douglas Huggins (Breads and Baking)

His story: Born in Des Moines, Iowa, USA, to parents popularly referred to as 'Rocket Ron' and 'The Big Beave', Douglas was a rather maladjusted child!

In spite of many efforts by his family to help him overcome these slight problems, including membership with his father as an Indian Guide, Douglas still sought the green pastures and quiet lifestyle of his Grandparents' farm. Unlike his Mother, who loathed kitchen tasks, Grandma Daisy was a genius in the art of bread-baking and doughnut-frying.

It is, therefore, to his Grandmother that he owes any natural ability he may possess in the art of bread production.

# Katie Garrett (Salads, Dressings and Dips)

I have always been interested in cookery and found my time at Food For Thought an excellent introduction to the world of vegetables—I refer not to the other members of staff!

I was most surprised at the variety of tastes and textures it is possible to create with vegetables and pulses; I had always thought that meat was the only texture-providing substance in savoury cooking.

Eating a well-balanced vegetarian diet, I have found, leads to a healthier mind and body, as the digestive system no longer has the heavy-duty task of breaking down meat.

I hope you enjoy the salad recipes, many of which, if you are a regular customer, may well be familiar. If you are a meat lover, I hope you will not find it too difficult giving up the odd steak with the aid of this book. If you are a vegetarian I hope you will find something new to tempt you.

# Clarice Ashdown (Main Savouries and Cakes)

I came to Food For Thought three years after I first started cooking. While I was there I gained valuable experience due largely to the fact that I was given freedom, and encouraged to experiment with new ideas while cooking at the restaurant. It was this, in turn, that prevented any feelings of boredom or unrest on my part—feelings that can all too easily reflect badly on the food.

I am now learning Cordon Bleu cookery, but my affinity with and love for vegetarian food will never leave me. I hope once again to work within such a positive atmosphere as that which I found at Food For Thought.

# Angela Gamble (All Desserts and Quiches)

Her story: Having embarked upon a career in banking on leaving school, Angela soon found that there was little scope for her artistic temperament, imagination or pronounced sense of fun!

Contemplating this over a meal in a London restaurant, she casually browsed through a leaflet on the table. Impulsively answering an advertisement for staff, she found fulfilment in joining a team of young people preparing vegetarian food.

Later, seeking employment after returning from an Israeli Kibbutz, a friend recommended that she apply to Food For Thought where she was offered a job, initially washing dishes and cleaning ovens.

Her dessert recipes collected in this book are the result of the flowering of her natural talents. She is currently travelling in India.

# Indexes

## Index of Recipes

# Index of Ingredients

# Vegan Dishes

These dishes contain no eggs, cheese or other dairy products.

# Wheat-free Dishes

These dishes contain no wheat or wheat-flour. However, you should check the contents of your ingredients. We use wheat-free soy sauce (tamari) and a wheat-free miso. Many brands of these products contain wheat.